TARIKH-I-SORATH

TÂRIKH-I-SORATH

A HISTORY

OF THE

PROVINCES OF SORATH AND HÂLÂR IN KÂṬHIÂWÂḌ.

BY RANCHODJI AMARJI,

DIVÂN OF JUNÂGADH.

Translated from the Persian.

BOMBAY:

EDUC. SOC. PRESS, & THACKER & CO., LD.

LONDON: TRÜBNER & CO.

1882.

PREFACE.

THE TÂRIKH-I-SORAṬH, or History of Soraṭh and Hâlâr, forming the western portion of Kâṭhiâwâḍ, was compiled by Ranchoḍji Amarji, Divân or prime minister of Junâgaḍh, about 1825, and gives a pretty circumstantial account of the factions and broils that disturbed these provinces during the lifetime of the author and his father. As a genuine native history, written by a man who took a leading part in most of the events he describes, and who was quite independent of English influence, it ought to possess some interest for all classes of readers.

The Persian MS. of the work was brought to my notice by the late Mr. Gokalji Jhâlâ, then Divân of Junâgaḍh, on my visit to that place in May 1869. Mr. Manilâl Govindrâm, now of the Bhâvanagar High School, also obtained for me a loan of a translation of it into Gujarâti, and made a careful version from it into English. When this was about complete I got a second Persian MS., and submitted both MSS. and the translation of the Gujarâti version to Mr. E. Rehatsek, who very kindly produced another translation, more in accordance with the Persian original than Mr. Manilâl's founded on the Gujarâti only. This lay past for some time, but a few years ago I began to print it, and Colonel J. W. Watson, of the Râjasthânik Court, Râjkot, whose knowledge of the country and its history as well as of the language of the original, eminently qualified him for doing so—very kindly agreed to revise the MS. and look over the proofs as the book passed through the press. The alterations he has made to bring it into accordance with the better copies of the original work in his possession, have been numerous and important.

It was intended to add a considerable amount of additional collateral information to the work as it passed through the press, but frequent—almost constant—absence from the vicinity of any library, and the pressure of work which has frequently interrupted even the printing for long periods of time, have limited the additional matter to a brief introduction and a few notes scattered throughout the book, and amounting in all to about 57 pages.

I have only to add that it is to the offers of patronage of the work on the part of the Chiefs of Junâgaḍh and Bhâvanagar, that the publication of it is due.

J. BURGESS.

Amarâvati, Kṛishṇâ District,
31*st December* 1881.

CONTENTS.

PAGE

Introduction, by the Editor.............. 1

Târikh-i-Soraṭh 23

Description of the Sirkâr of Junâgaḍh ... 24

Note 1. On Junâgaḍh, by the Editor... 33

Translations of the Aśoka edicts........... 36

Note 2. Neminâtha 47

Mahâls which pay all the Land and Customs Revenue Rights to Junâgaḍh...... 48

The Kaṣbah of Kutiânâ 49

Bântwâ 51

The Kasbah of Mângrol .. .. „

Note 3. On Ghumli or Bhumli 58

Kesod 62

Mâliâ .... „

Chorvâḍ .... „

Paṭṭan Diva 63

Note 4. On Paṭṭan Somanâtha 66

„ 5. On Ahilyâbâi 78

Account of Koḍinâr........................... „

Unâ and Delvâḍâ 77

Account of Rânpur 79

Visâvadar.......... .... „

Muzaffarâbâd .... „

The island of Diva, which formerly belonged to Junâgaḍh.......................... „

Account of Kâṭhiâwâḍ....................... 81

PAGE

Account of Amrêli 82
Account of the Mahâls which pay tribute to Junâgaḍh 83
Description of Gondal 93
Rajkoṭ 94
Morbi .... „
Description of Bhâvanagar 95
Description of Jhâlâwâr 98
The Râjas of Junâgaḍh 101
Rao Dayat and Kuvar Naughan 102
Naughan conquers Sindh 105
Râja Khengâr 109
Mularâja and Naughan 111
Fight of Râja Maṇḍalika with Maḥmud Ghaznavi .... „
Hamiradêva, Vijayapâla, Naughan, &c. ... 113
Jayasingh, &c. 114
Sulṭân Maḥmud captures Râja Maṇḍalika. 116
The story of Mehtâ Narsî 118
Râja Bhupat Singh bin Maṇḍalika 124
Râja Khengâr, Râja Naughan, Râja Śri Singh, Râja Khengâr 125
Note 6. On the Chuḍâsama dynasty ... 127
Governors on behalf of the Pâdishâhs of Aḥmadâbâd 131
Navâb Bahâdur Khân Bâbi 137
Navâb Mahâbat Khân 143
Captivity of the Navâb Mahâbat Khân ... 144
Shekh Miyân takes Verâval 146

PAGE

The Divânship of Amarji 147
Demolition of Dilkhâniâ........................ 149
Acquisition of Kutiânâ .... ,,
Conquest of Talâjâ 150
Conquest of the four forts of Mangrol ... 151
Liberation of the Mutasaddis of Kachh Bhuj 152
Punishment of the Vâghars and Mâliâs .. 153
Punishment of the Bâbriâs and of the Unâ Qasbâtis .... ,,
Kumbhâji attacks the Divânji........................ 154
Imprisonment of the Divânji and murder of Jamadâr Sâlmin the Arab 155
The Navâb marches against Mangrol and recalls the Divânji 156
Conquest of Sutrâpâḍâ........................ 159
Conquest of Positrâ........................ ,,
Navab Hâmid Khân (A.D. 1774-1810) ... 160
Victory over the Subahdars of the Peshvâ and Gâekvâḍ........................ 161
March to Pâlanswâ in Vâgaḍ, &c. 163
Victory over Jâm Jasâji, Râṇa Sulṭânji, and Kumbhâji 168
Murder of the Divân Amarji 1784, &c ... 172
Verâval taken from Divân Raghunâthji ... 177
The Navâb instigates the Arabs against the Divân 178
Gul Khân slain; marriage of the Navâb, &c. 179
Taking of Sutrâpâḍâ 180
Conquest of Kesôj 181

PAGE

Divân Raghunâth takes Chorvâd and Verâval, &c. ... 182
The Divânship of Kalyâṇ Seṭh ... 193
March of the Navâb against Bhâvanagar... 194
Jamâdâr Âmin cannonades Manjâvaḍi ... 195
Divân Raghunâth recalled from Nagar ... 196
Reduction of Kutiânâ, &c. ... 197
Navâb Bahâdur Khân (1810-1839 A.D.)... 205
Jamâdâr Omar and his expulsion by British aid ... 209
The taking of Kutiânâ ... 210
Marriage of Śambhu Parsâd ... 212
Dismissal of Jamâdâr Omar ... 213
Dismissal of Divân Raghunâth, and slaughter of Atits ... 215
Divânship of Sundarji (1809-10 A.D.) ... 218
Death of Divân Raghunâth... 219
Wedding of Kesarbâï ... 220
Interviews of Ranchoḍji and Governor Elphinstone ... 221
Capture and release of Captain Grant... 222
Expulsion of Mr. Anderson from Dvârkâ, and punishment of the Waghers by the English... 223
Chastisement of the Khumân Kâṭhis by the English ... 224
Defeat of Kesarbâï, and murder of Âḥmad Khân Faqir ... 227
Events of Saṁvat 1880 (A.D. 1823-24) ... 228

PAGE

Note 7. Capt. Grant's Narrative of his captivity ... 235
CONCERNING the HISTORY of NAGAR ... 240
Concerning the Jâm ... „
Founding of the city of Navânagar... 243
Jâm Raval bin Lâkhâ... 246
Jâm Vibhâji (A.D. 1561-1569) ... „
Jâm Satrasâl (A.D. 1569-1616) ... „
Jâm Jasâji (A.D. 1616-1624) ... 251
Jâm Lâkhâ (A.D. 1624-1645)... 254
Jâm Raṇmalji (A.D. 1645-1661)... „
Jâm Raisingh (A.D. 1661-1663)... 256
Jâm Timâchi Tagadh (A.D. 1663-1690)... „
Jâm Lâkhâji (A.D. 1690-1709) ... 257
Jâm Raisingh (A.D. 1709-1710) ... „
Jâm Timâchi (A.D. 1710-1743) ... „
Jâm Lâkhâji (A.D. 1743-1768) ... 259
Jâm Jasâji (A.D. 1768-1814) ... 260
Jâm Jasâji makes a friend of Râo Sâheb Bhânji ... 271
The laying waste of Gondal in Saṁ. 1850. 273
Meeting of Navâb Hâmid Khân with Merâman Khawâs ... 275
The Wâghêrs of Okhâ... 276
Flight of Jâm Jasâji ... 277
Arrival of Fateh Muhammad Notiyâr... 279
Râo Sâheb Râiḍhanji comes to Nagar and returns disappointed... 280
Attack on Bhânwâḍ ... 282

PAGE

Jâm Jasâji collects *aspverá* (horse tax) from Kâṭhiâwâḍ, &c. 285
Capture of Kandornâ fort 286
The English and Gâekwâḍ Governments send armies to Nagar (A.D. 1812) 287
A Kachh army crosses over to Hâlâr...... 288
Jâm Satâji (A.D. 1814-1820) 292
Jâm Raṇmâlji 297
Account of Okhâ 299

INTRODUCTION.

The peninsula of **Kâṭhiâwâḍ** or **Saurâshṭra**, lying between the gulfs of **Kachh** and Cambay or Khambhât, and surrounded on the south and west by the Arabian Sea, is the holy land of Western India. It was known to the Greeks and Romans under the name of Saurastrēnē; the Muhammadans called it by the Prakritized name of **Soraṭh**, and to this day a large district in the south-west, a hundred miles in length, still retains that name. Another district, quite as large, to the east of the centre, however, has long been known as **Kâṭhiâwâḍ**, from having been overrun by the **Kâṭhîs**, who entered the peninsula from **Kachh**, perhaps first in predatory bands in the thirteenth or fourteenth century; in the fifteenth the whole tribe was driven out of Kachh, and in that and the following century conquered a considerable territory. The **Marâṭhâs**, who came into contact with them in their forays, and were sometimes successfully repelled by them, extended the name of **Kâṭhiâwâḍ** to the whole province, and from them we have come to apply it in a similar wide sense; but by Brâhmaṇs and the natives it is still spoken of as Saurâshṭra.

The extreme length of the peninsula, from Goghâ in the east, to Jagat or Dwâraka in the west, is nearly 220 miles; its greatest breadth is about 165 miles, and its area 22,000 square miles, with an estimated population of about two and a half millions.

It is divided into 188 separate states, large and small, of which thirteen pay no tribute; ninety-six are tributary to the British Government, seventy to that of the Gaikwâḍ as the representative of the Marâṭhâs, and nine pay tribute to both; while of the latter three classes one hundred and thirty-two pay a tax called *Zortalabi* to the Nawâb of Junâgaḍh. The states are arranged in seven classes, with varying civil and criminal powers,—five of the larger belonging to the first class.

Kâṭhiâwâḍ is usually divided into ten provinces or *prânts*, of very unequal size:—

(1.) Jhâlâwâḍ, in the north, containing about fifty states, of which Dhrângadhrâ, Limbḍî, Waḍhwân, Wânkanêr, Sâelâ, Chuḍâ, and Thân-Laktar, are among the largest; originally it included Viramgaum, Mândal, and part of the Dhandhukâ district now uuder Ahmadâbâd.

(2.) Machhukâṇthâ, comprising Morbî and Maliâ, lies to the west of Jhâlâwâḍ.

(3.) Hâlâr, in the north-west, derives its name from the Hâlâ branch of Jâḍejâs from Kachh, and embraces twenty-six states, of which Jâmnagar or Nawânagar is the largest; Râjkoṭ, Gondal-Dhoraji, Dharol, Drâphâ, &c., are smaller.

(4.) Okhâmandal, in the extreme west, belongs to Barodâ.*

(5.) Baraḍâ or Jetwâḍ, along the south-west coast, is known also as P u r b a n d a r.

(6.) Sorath, in the south, is occupied by the Junâgaḍh State, and the two small holdings of Bâṇṭwâ and Amrâpur; but the sea-coast from Mângrol to the island of Diu or Div is also known as N â g h e r.

(7.) Bâbriâwâḍ, so called from the Babriâ tribe of Kolîs, is a hilly tract in the south-east, divided into many very small states, or village holdings, and includes many villages belonging to the Gaikwâḍ of Barodâ.

(8.) Kâthiâwâḍ, near the middle, is a large district comprising Jeṭpur-Chital, Amrelî, Jasdhan, Choṭilâ, Ânandapur, and fifty other smaller estates.

(9.) Und-Sarveyâ, lying along the Śatruñjî river, and divided into small holdings.

(10.) Gohilwâḍ, in the east, along the shore of the gulf of Cambay, is so named from the Gohil Râjputs, who are the ruling race in it. It comprises the Goghâ district, belonging to the Ahmadâbâd Collectorate,—Bhaunagar, a first-class state, Pâlitâṇâ, Walâ, Lâthî, and

* The island (*bêt*) of Śankhodâr belongs to Okhâmandal. It was long famous for its pirates.

many others; and it includes the old division of the province called W â l â k.

Generally speaking, with the exception of the Thângâ and Mâṇḍhav hills in the west of Jhâlâwâḍ, the Âlech and Dalâsâ ranges in Hâlâr, the hill of Gop, and others, the northern portion of the country is flat; but in the south the Gîr range runs nearly parallel with the coast, and at a distance of about twenty miles from it, along the north of Bâbriâwâḍ and Soraṭh, turning northwards towards Girnâr. Opposite this latter mountain, again, is the solitary Ośam hill, and then still further west is the Baraḍâ group between Hâlâr and Baraḍâ, running about twenty miles north and south, from Ghumli to Râṇâwâv, near which iron ore was dug in early times. After the limits of Babriâwâḍ are passed a low range of hills succeeds the Gîr; these hills join those of Und Sarveya. There is also a fine cluster of granite peaks at Chamârdi, and the Śihor and Khokhrâ ranges in the south-eastern portion of Gohilwâḍ.

The principal river is the Bhâdar, which rises in the Mâṇḍhav hills and flows south-west, falling into the sea at Navî-Bandar, in Baraḍâ, after a course of about a hundred and fifteen miles in a direct line, everywhere marked by the lands near its banks being in a high state of cultivation. It is a saying in the districts through which it passes that it receives ninety-nine tributary streams. From the same hills rises another Bhâdar, which flows eastwards past Râṇpur and Dhandhukâ into the gulf of Cambay or Khambhât, and in its short course attains a considerable size.

The Âjî, perhaps the prettiest stream in the province, rises near Sardhâr and runs northwards past Râjkoṭ, receiving the Mari from the left, and falls into the gulf of Kachh near Bâlambâ, in Hâlâr. It is noted for the excellence of its water, and the gold dust found in small quantities in its bed.

The Machhu, from near Sardhâr, flows north-west, through the district to which it gives name, past Wânkanêr and Morbî, into the gulf of Kachh, near Mâliâ.

The Wadhwân and Limbḍi Bhogâwâs both rise in the Thângâ range, and flowing past Waḍhwân and Limbḍî respectively lose themselves in the Raṇ to the north of the gulf of Cambay

The Śatruñjî, from the Gîr range, receives a large number of tributaries, and passes Palitâṇâ and Tâlâjâ on its way to the entrance of the gulf of Khambhât.

Saurâshṭrâ was doubtless at a very early period brought under the influence of Brâhmaṇical civilization, and, from its position at the extreme north of the coast line of Western India, it was the most accessible to influences from the West. As early as the reign of the great Aśoka of Magadha (B.C. 265-229) we find him inscribing his famous edicts upon the huge granite boulders at the entrance of the pass that leads from Junâgaḍh to Girnâr. If the reading in Strabo of *Saraostos* is really, as there is good reason to suppose, a corruption of some form of Saurâshṭra, then it was included in the conquests of the Indo-Skythian kings, Demetrios the son of Euthydemos (B.C. cir. 190), and Menander (B.C. 144), who, he says, pushed their conquests eastwards and "got possession not only of Patalĕnĕ, but of the kingdoms of Saraostos and Sigerdis (or Sigertis) being the remainder of the coast."

Its shores were well known to the Alexandrian merchants of the first and second centuries, but there is considerable difficulty in identifying the places they mention. Dr. Vincent,† Lassen,‡ and Col. Yule§ have each attempted the task.

Lassen places the city of Surastra at Junâgaḍh, and this is as probable a conjecture as perhaps any other that could be formed. Yule places it at Navi-bandar, which is very doubtful. If not Junâgaḍh or Vanthali, then Virâwal and Sîhor are the only two other sites that seem likely.

Bardaxima is located by Yule at Purbandar, perhaps from the resemblance of the name to Baraḍâ; but Śrînagar, in the same

† *Periplus of the Erythræan Sea.*

‡ Map of Ancient India in his *Indische Alterthumskunde.*

§ In Smith's *Ancient Atlas*, pp. 22-24, and map 31.

district, is a much older place, and near it is a small village named B a r d i y â, which may possibly be a reminiscence of the Greek name.

Yule places the B a r a k ē of Arrian at J a g a t or Dwârakâ ; Lassen also identifies it with D w â r a k â, which he places on the coast between Purbandar and Miyânî, near Śrînagar. M u l a-D w â r a k â, or the original site, was further east than this, but is variously placed near M â d h u p u r, thirty-six miles north-west from S o m a n â t h-P a ṭ ṭ a n, or three miles south-west from K o ḍ i n â r, and nineteen miles east of S o m a n â t h. This last spot is called Mula Dwârakâ to this day.

A s t a k a p r a, or A s t a k a m p r a, Yule has quite recently identified with Hastakavapra, mentioned in a Valabhi copper-plate grant, and believed to be the old name of Hathab, to the south of Goghâ; at G o p n â t h, Yule would have P a p i k é promontory.

The H o r a t æ are doubtless the people of S o r a ṭ h, who have an inveterate propensity to sound the letter *S* as an *H;* and the P a n d æ are the P â ṇ ḍ a v a, dwelling in the north of the peninsula, in the district traditionally known as P a n c h â l or D e v a-P a n c h â l, in which the chief town was T h â n, possibly the same as T h e o p h i l a, which Yule places doubtfully a little further east, about T a l s â n â, which, however, is situated in the sub-division of Jhâlâwâḍ known as the Nal Kâṇṭhâ, and not in Panchâla.

Piram island is probably rightly identified by Yule with the Baiones Insula of the ancients; Monoglosson he identifies with Mangrol.

Among the sacred places in the province, Prabhâsa Paṭṭan or Somanâth in the south, and Dwârakâ in the extreme west, are famous shrines of the Śaiva and Vaishṇava forms of Brâhmaṇism,—the former, one of the twelve great Śaiva Mahâliṅgas of India, and the account of whose destruction by Maḥmûd of Ghaznî is so familiar to every reader of history, is also the spot where tradition says the great Yâdava hero and demigod Kṛishṇa was slain; whilst Dwârakâ is one of his most celebrated shrines, where he is fabled to have saved the sacred books. Thân, in the north, is an old site of sun-worship, and in the neighbourhood are several snake-shrines; and in the Gîr is Tulasî Śyâm, a noted Hindû shrine, with a hot spring. There is also the shrine called Ghelâ Somanâth in Jasdan territory, which probably was the city of Somâpur said by Ferishtah to have been destroyed by Sultân Âhmad on his return to Gujarât after warring at Junâgaḍh.

Among their "high places" the Jains reckon Śatruñjaya as their great *tîrtha* or holy place, on the isolated mountain south of Pâlitâṇâ; Tâladhvaja, commonly known as Tâlâjâ

Tekrî, the isolated hill at Tâlâjâ; Ujjayanta or Raivata, the famous Mount Girnâr in Sorath; and Dhañka in Hâlâr. Perhaps the Lor or Lauhar hill in Bâbriâwâd is also intended by the Lauhitya of their sacred books. The Lonch and Kâmlo hills too in Und Sarveya are known to the Jains as Hastâgiri and Kadamgiri respectively, and are usually visited by pilgrims to Pâlitânâ.

Of the early history of the country we have but scanty notices. It was probably governed by satraps under Aśoka and the great Maurya kings. From coins that have been found pretty abundantly in different parts, it appears that for a period of about two centuries a dynasty known as the Kshatrapas, Sâhs, or Siñhas ruled,—perhaps at old Sîhor, Siñhur, or Siñhapura. Of this dynasty we learn from coins the names of some twenty-four princes, many of them with dates ranging from 72 to 250; the late Dr. Bhau Dâji, reckoning these dates from the Śaka era of A.D. 78, placed them between about A.D. 140 and 380.

Besides coins of the Kshatrapas, however, we have at least two inscriptions, unfortunately both somewhat defaced.

The first of these is on the famous rock between Junâgadh and Girnâr, recording the repair of the dam there by Râja Mahâkshatrapa Rudra Dâman in the year 72 of their era. His father's name is obliterated, but that of his grandfather is given as Mahâkshatrapa Chashṭaṇa.

The second is a short one on a pillar on the bank of the lake at Jasdhan, in the north of the Kâṭhiâwâḍ division. It has been translated by the late Dr. Bhau Dâji, and yields the names of five of the Sâh kings, viz. :—

1. Râja Mahâkshatrapa Bhadramukha Svâmî Chashṭaṇa;

2. Râja Kshatrapa Svâmî Jayadâmân his son ;

3. Râja Mahâkshatrapa . . . Rudra Dâmâ, his son ;

4. Râja Mahâkshatrapa Bhadramukha Svâmî Rudra Siñha, his son ;

5. Râja Mahâkshatrapa Svâmî Rudra Sena, his son, ruling in 127.

Coins supply the remainder of our knowledge of these princes, but fortunately the first of them is mentioned in the inscriptions on some of the caves in the Bombay Presidency : as at Kârlen, Nâsik, and Junnar.

From these materials Mr. Newton framed the subjoined Kshatrapa list of the kings, which is given, with the dates approved by Dr. Bhau Dâji, Professor Râmkṛishṇa G. Bhâṇḍârkar, and others :—

1. Nahapâna, A.D. 70.

2. The unknown king whose coin is given as figure 10 of the plate (p. 4, *Jour. Bo. Br. R. As. Soc.* vol. IX.).

3. (Syamo? tika.
4. Chashṭaṇa, son of Syamotika, A.D. 90.
5. Jaya Dâmâ, son of Chashṭaṇa.
6. Jiva Dâmâ, son of (Dáma?)Śrî, A.D. 113.
7. Rudra Dâmâ, son of Jaya Dâmâ.
8. Rudra Siñha, son of Rudra Dâmâ, A.D. 180-182.
9. Rudra Sâh or Sena, son of Rudra Siñha, A.D. 205.
10. Śrî Sâh, son of Rudra Sâh.
11. Sangha Dâmâ, son of Rudra Sâh.
12. Dâmâ Sâh, son of Rudra Siñha.
13. Yaśa Dâmâ, son of Dâmâ Sâh.
14. Dâmajata Śrî, son of Rudra Sâh, A.D 212.
15. Vira Dâmâ, son of Dâmâ Sâh.
16. Îśvara Datta.
17. Vijaya Sâh, son of Dâmâ Sâh (140-154), A.D. 218-232.
18. Dâmajata Śrî, son of Dâmâ Sâh.
19. Rudra Sâh, son of Rudra Dâmâ, A.D. 266, 276, 270.
20. Viśva Siñha, son of Rudra Sâh, A.D. 278.
21. Atrî Dâmâ, son of Rudra Sâh, A.D. 288, 292.
22. Viśva Sâh, son of Atrî Dâmâ, A.D. 295, 303.
23. Rudra Siñha, son of Svâmî Jiva Dâmâ, A.D. 328.
24. Yaśa Dâmâ, son of Rudra Sâh.

25. Svâmî Rudra Sâh, son of Svâmî Satya Sâh.||

From an inscription in the Bauddha caves at Nâsik, it appears that the Kshatrapas were overthrown by Gautamîputra, the Andhrabhṛitya king of the Dekhaṇ, about A.D. 330. Anartta or Saurâshṭra must have belonged to them for a short time. But the Guptas of Kanauj were then rising into power.

"The bards relate that Râma Râjâ, son of Vâḷâ Varsingji, reigned in Junâgaḍh and Vanthalî. . . . Râma Râja was of the Vâḷâ race. It is said in Saurâshṭra that, previous to the rise of the kingdom of Junâgaḍh-Vanthalí, Valabhînagar was the capital of Gujarât. The rise of Valabhî is thus told by the bards:—'The Gupta kings reigned between the Ganges and Jamunâ rivers. One of these kings sent his son Kumârapâla Gupta to conquer Saurâshṭra, and he placed his viceroy Chakrapalita or Chakrapâṇi, son of Parṇadatta or Prândat, one of his Amîrs, to reign as provincial governor in the city of Vâmanasthalî (the modern Vanthalî). Kumârapâla now returned to his father's kingdom. His father reigned twenty-three years after the conquest of Saurâshṭra and then died, and Kumârapâla ascended the throne. Kumârapâla Gupta reigned twenty years and then died, and was succeeded by Skanda Gupta, but this king was of weak intellect. His *senâpati* Bha-

* *Jour. R. As. Soc.* vol. XII., 1848, p. 32.

ṭârka, who was of the Gehlotî race, taking a strong army, came into Surâshṭra, and made his rule firm there. Two years after this Skanda Gupta died. The *senâpati* now assumed the title of king of Saurâshṭra, and, having placed a governor at Vâmanasthalî, founded the city of Valabhînagar. At this time the Gupta race were dethroned by foreign invaders."¶

The Junâgaḍh inscription represents Parṇadatta as Skanda Gupta's viceroy; Chakrapâlita as governor of a certain town, appointed to that place by his own father; and Bhaṭârka is mentioned in the Valabhî copper plates as Senâpati, while they represent Droṇa Siñha, his second son, as having first assumed the title of king: *Ind. Ant.* vol. III. (1874).

The G u p t a s introduced an era of their own, usually regarded as commencing in A.D. 319, but possibly about A.D. 185-195. They doubtless arose to considerable power before they added K â ṭ h i â w â ḍ to their dominions: indeed, according to tradition, the conquest of the country was only effected by K u m â r a p â l a G u p t a early in the reign of his father. This was probably between 80 and 85 of the Gupta era.

V a l a b h î, identified with the buried city at Walâ, in the east of the peninsula, eighteen miles north-west of Bhaunagar, now became the capital of the new dynasty; and when the Gupta

¶ Major J. W. Watson, "Legends of Junâgaḍh," *Ind. Ant.* (Nov. 1873) vol. II. p. 312.

race were dethroned the Valabhî kings extended their sway "over K a c h h, Lâṭ-d e ś a,* and M â l w â."

B h a ṭ â r k a must have established himself at V a l a b h î about 160 Gupta Saṁvat; and of the dynasty he founded we have numerous copper plates, discovered at Walâ and elsewhere in the peninsula, which, in recording grants to Brâhmaṇs and Bauddha ascetics, give also the genealogy of the family and important dates in their reigns. From such of these as have been translated† we gather that—

I. B h a ṭ â r k a Senâpati was followed by four of his sons in succession.

II. D h a r a s e n a Senâpati, eldest son of Bhaṭârka.

III. D r o ṇ a s i ñ h a, Mahârâja, a second son of Bhaṭârka, "whose royal splendour was sanctified by the great gift, his solemn coronation performed in person by the Supreme Lord, the Lord Paramount of the whole earth."‡

IV. D h r u v a s e n a I., a third brother, whose sister's daughter D u ḍ ḍ â was a Baud-

---

* The collectorates of Surat, Bharoch, Khêḍa, and parts of Barodâ territory.

† *Ind. Ant.* vol. I. pp. 14, 18, 45, 60; vol. III. pp. 335, 303; vol. IV. pp. 104 and 174; *Jour. As. Soc., Beng.* vol. IV. pp. 401, 475ff.; vol. VII. pp. 349, 966ff.; *Jour. Bo. Br. R. As. Soc.*, vol. III. pt. ii. pp. 313ff.; vol. VII. p. 116; vol. VIII. pp. 230, 245; vol. X. pp. 66ff.

‡ Copper plates, *Ind. Ant.* vol. I. p. 61; vol. IV. p. 106; *Jour. As. Soc. Beng.* vol. IV. p. 481.

dha devotee, and founded a monastery. The plate mentioning this is dated Saṁvat 216 (evidently of the Gupta era), other two bear dates 207 and 210.

V. Dharapaṭṭa, the youngest son of Bhaṭârka, who was succeeded by—

VI. Guhasena, his son, of whom there are copper plates dated respectively 250, 256 (or 266), and 258. The second grants four villages to "the community of the reverend Śâkya monks belonging to the eighteen schools [of the Hînayâna], who have come from various directions to the great convent of Duḍḍâ, built by the venerable Duḍḍâ."

VII. Śrî Dharasena II., the son of Guhasena, of whom we have also grants, dated 272 and 277.

VIII. Śîlâditya (Dharmâditya) I., son of Dharasena, also made a grant to a Bauddha community dated G. 286.

IX. Kharagraha, his brother.

X. Śrî Dharasena III., son of Kharagraha.

XI. Dhruvasena II., younger son of Kharagraha.

XII. Śrî Dharasena (Balâditya) IV., second son of Dhruvasena, of whom there are two grants, both dated G. 326,—one to priests of the Mahâyâna school, belonging to a monastery erected by Divirapati Skandabhaṭṭa; and the other to Brâhmaṇs of Siñhapura,—the modern Sihor. A third grant is dated S. 329.

XIII. Dhruvasena III., the son of Derâbhaṭṭa and grandson of Śîlâditya I.

XIV. Kharagraha II., the brother of Dhruvasena III.

XV. Śîlâditya II., son of Śîlâditya, the brother of Dhruvasena III. and Kharagraha II.

XVI. Śîlâditya III., his son, of whom there are two grants dated 356, and one 358.

XVII. Śîlâditya IV., son of Śîlâditya III., of whom a plate has been found dated S. 403.

XVIII. Śîlâditya V.

XIX. Śîlâditya VI.

It was either during the reign of Dhruvasena II., or of this last Śîlâditya, who was surnamed Dhruvabhaṭṭa, that the Chinese Bauddha pilgrim Hiwen-Thsang visited Western India, and apparently Valabhî itself (cir. A.D. 635-638). His account§ runs thus:—"The kingdom of *Fa-lapi* is about 6,000 *li* (1200 miles) in circuit; the capital has a circumference of 30 *li* (6 miles). As to the products of the soil, nature of the climate, the manners and character of the people, they are like those of *Ma-la-p'o* (Mâlwâ). The population is very numerous, and all the families live in wealth. There are a hundred whose wealth amounts to a million. The rarest

§ Stanislas Julien's *Mémoires sur les Contrées Occidentales*, tom. II. pp. 162 ff.; *Histoire de la Vie de Hiouen-Thsang*, pp. 369-71, 358, 447.

merchandize from distant countries is found here in abundance. There are a hundred convents, where nearly 6,000 devotees live, who for the most part study the doctrines of the *Ching-liang-pu* (school or *nikâya* of the Sammatîyas) which adheres to the 'lesser translation' (*Hînayâna*).|| We count several hundred temples of the gods; and the heretics of various sects are exceedingly numerous.

"When the Tathâgata (*Buddha*) lived in the world he travelled often in this region. Wherefore in all the places where the Buddha rested King Aśoka raised pillars in honour of him, or constructed *stûpas*. We observe at intervals the monuments that mark the places where the three past Buddhas had sat, performed deeds, or preached the law.

"The kings of the present age are of *Tsa-ti-li* (Kshatriya) race; all are nephews of king *Shi-lo-'o-tie-to* (Sîlâditya) of Mâlvâ. At present (about A.D. 636) the son of king Śîlâditya of *Kie-jo-ka-she* (Kanyakubja), has a son-in-law called *T'u-lu-p'o-po-tu*,¶ Dhruvapaṭu.* He is of a quick and passionate nature, and his intellect is weak and narrow: still he believes sincerely in 'the three precious things.'† For seven days every year he holds a great assembly

|| In Chinese, *Siao-ching;* Sans. *Hînayâna*.
¶ En Chinois *Ch'ang-jui*, "constamment intelligent."
* Or Dhruvabhaṭṭa, *Jour. R. As. Soc.* vol. VI. p. 329.
† Sans. *Triratna*.

at which he distributes to the multitude of recluses choice dishes, the three garments, medicine, the seven precious things, and rare objects of great value. After giving all these in alms, he buys them back at double price. He esteems virtue and honours the sages, he reverences religion and values science. The most eminent holy men of distant countries are always objects of respect with him.

"At a little distance from the city there is a great convent, built long ago by the care of the Arhat '*Oche-lo* (Áchâra). It was there that the Bodhisattvas *Te-hoe* (Guṇamatî), and *Kien-hoeï* (Sthîramatî) fixed their abode and composed several books which are all published with praise."

"On leaving this country he went about 700 *li* (140 miles) to the north-west, and arrived at the kingdom of '*O-nan-t'o-pu-lo*. The kingdom of ('*O-nan-t'o-pu-lo*) Ânandapura has a circuit of about 2,000 *li* (400 miles); the circumference of the capital is a score of *li* (5 miles). The population is very numerous, and all the families live in wealth. There is no (*native*) prince. The country is dependent on *Ma-la-p'o* (Mâlwâ), which it resembles in the products of its soil, nature of the climate, written character, and laws. There are a dozen convents, counting somewhat under a thousand devotees, who study the doctrine of the *Ching-liang-pu* (*nikâya* or school of the Sammatîyas) belonging to the lesser translation' (*Hînayâna*). There are many dozen temples of the gods; heretics of different sects live intermixed."‡

Such is the account of the Chinese pilgrim. The convent of '*Oche-lo*, which he mentions as being in the vicinity of Valabhî, Dr. Bühler has found mentioned in a grant of Dharasena II., as founded by Aṭharya, not "Âchâra," as Julien has transliterated the Chinese name.

The Anandapura here mentioned is probably the same as that referred to in the *Kalpa-Sûtra* of the Jainas, as one of their early centres of learning, and where that work was composed by Śrî Bhadra Bâhu Svâmî, in the year 980 of their era, during the reign of Dhruvasena II., who had just then been deeply afflicted by the loss of his beloved son Senâgaja. M. Vivien de Saint-Martin, following Stevenson, places it outside the peninsula —at Baḍnagar, or Vaḍanagar, in northern Gujarât, about twenty miles east-south-east from Siddhpur. From the connection in which it occurs, however, we might expect it rather to to be within the peninsula; and, though the distance does not agree with Hiwen-Thsang's, there is still a place called Ânandapura, fifty miles (250 *li*) north-west from Valabhî, which was very probably in early times the capital of a province including parts of the modern

‡ See continuation of Hiwen Thsang's narrative in *Note* 1, pp. 33, 34.

Jhâlawâḍ, Kâṭhiâwâḍ, and Hâlâr. This gains support from the mention of Dhruvasena of Valabhî, who must have been closely connected with Ânandapura to lead the writer of the *Kalpa-Sûtra* to refer to his family afflictions; and the accuracy of the latter is corroborated by Dr. Burns's copper plate, stating that Śrî Dharasena IV. was Dhruvasena's *second* son.

How the Valabhî dynasty ended we do not exactly know. We see that in the eighth century it still held Soraṭh, and even northern Gujarat. Tradition is almost unanimous in asserting that a Śîlâditya was overthrown and slain by a foreign invader. Merutunga, the Jaina chronicler, gives a legendary account of its destruction. A Mârwâḍì, he says, from Pâli had settled at Valabhî and attained to great wealth. Śilâditya forcibly took the jewelled comb of this man's daughter to give to his own daughter, which so offended the Mârwâḍi that, to be revenged, he went to 'the Mlechha country' and offered the king an immense reward to destroy Valabhî. The Jaina priests had warning and took to flight, carrying their favourite idols with them, and by this Mlechha lord Valabhî was utterly destroyed in Saṁvat 375. But this date cannot be correct, whatever be the epoch from which it is reckoned. Moreover, Śîlâditya VI. may not have been the last of the dynasty, so that if

Valabhî was destroyed by a foreign it was probably by a Muhammadan invader, from or through Sindh—not earlier than 750 A.D., and possibly later. In an inscription from Barodâ of Râja Karka II., dated Śaka 734, or A.D. 812, it is said that under Karka I. Saurâshṭra had "lost its appellation of Saurâjya from the ruin that had fallen upon it." This destruction of the country may refer to forays by the same invaders in the eighth century, about the time when Vana Râja founded the Châvaḍâ kingdom of Aṇhillavâḍa, in northern Gujarât.

Tradition says that on the fall of Valabhî the Vâlâ governor of Vâmanasthalî became independent. Râja Râma had no son, but his sister was married to the Râja of Nagar Ṭhaṭhâ, in Sindh, who was of the Sammâ tribe. This sister's son was named Râ Gârio, and Râma Râja bequeathed the kingdom of Junâgaḍh-Vanthalî to this nephew, who was the first of the Chuḍâsamâ Râs of Junâgaḍh. This Râ Gârio, the grandson of Rai Chuḍa, is said to have extended his dominions into Upper India, conquering Kanauj, Gwâlior, and Dohad, in Mâlwâ.

There were petty kingdoms, however, established in various parts of the peninsula, as at Ḍhank, Deva Paṭṭan, &c., of the history of which we know but little. The Châvaḍâs and Solaṅkis of Anhillavâḍa Paṭṭan made frequent inroads against these chiefs, but do not seem to have ever permanently subjugated the western portions of the country, where the Jeṭhvâs and Chuḍâsamâs held sway, the latter till the fifteenth century, when they were reduced by Maḥmûd Begaḍa in 1469-70.

The narrative of Ranchoḍji son of Amarji, the Diwân of Junâgaḍh about the commencement of the present century, begins at a much latter date, but cursorily notices the dynasty of the Chuḍâsamâs. It is in reality a chronicle of his own times, and will be found not devoid of interest.

TÂRIKH-I-SORAṬH.

Śaṅkara Jagat Pati.

The Lord of lords descriptions cannot laud ;
In all attempts our weakness we confess.
Every plant whereon the zephyr of his love once breathes must flourish, and whatever his wrath touches withers for time and eternity.
Whoever enjoys his favour attains happiness, but he abideth in misery from whom the rays of his light are turned away.
This Sovereign to all monarchs grants power,
The face of the earth is his board—
As a banquet of dainties to friends and to foes.
To diadems the meanest of men he can raise,
And Sulṭâns to the dust can abase ;
All-powerful is he and worketh his will.

This poorest of Nâgars, Ranchoḍji, the son of Amarji Diwân, humbly informs those who examine histories and peruse chronicles that, as many accounts written concerning the Shâhs of India and of Gujarât are well known, it seemed useless to repeat what has already been narrated. Accordingly, from a feeling of attachment to his native country, he will confine his account to the states of Junâgaḍh and Hâllâr, and the affairs of other Râjâs as it has come to his knowledge from the oral statements of intelligent men, and from written information.

Description of the Sirkâr of Junâgaḍh.

The fort of Junâgaḍh is called in Sanskṛit Karaṇa Kubja,* but as an account of it is given in the *Prabhâśa Khaṇḍa* of the *Skanda Purâṇa* I shall describe its present state only. The citadel, called Uparkoṭ, is strongly built of stone, and is situated in a valley at the foot of Mount Girnâr; it has eighty-four turrets, two gates, and two *wâvs*†—one of the latter called Aḍi, and the other called Chaḍi,—built by Râja Noṅghan's slave-girls.‡ There is also a *kuvo* (or draw-well) excavated by Noṅghan and named after him. The stone dug out to form the fosse around the fort served for the construction of the towers and battlements; and, in case of a siege, there is a subterranean passage leading into the fort on the east side, which might be used to convey provisions to the garrison.

There is a tradition that the Uparkoṭ, or

* The Persian MS. has here Karankonj, the Gujarâti Karaṇa Kuvira: Jirangaḍh is given by Major Watson, *Ind. Ant.* vol. III. p. 43. See *Note* 1, page 33.

† Wells with descents to the water by flights of steps.

‡ The Gujarâti reads, 'by a Pâsavan (slave-girl or kept mistress) of Râja Noṅghan.'

fort, was built by the Yâdava Râja Ugarasena,§ when he fled from Mathurâ in dread of Kâla Yavana Shâh of Khorâsân, and came to the Sorath country. It is said that in Saṁvat 1507 (A.D. 1450) Râja Mandalik repaired the fort of Uparkot.|| Afterwards, in the reign of Shâh Akbar, A'isa Khân came from Sindh to be the Subâhdâr, and built the wall of the city in Saṁvat 1690 (A.D. 1633) with a hundred and fourteen turrets and nine gates,—four of which

§ The Gujarâti translator, Manishankara Jatashankara Mujamundâr, adds a note here, that 'he had learnt from Rânî Magâ, the Vahivanchâs (or keeper of the genealogies) of the Chudâsamâ kings, that at Junâgadh, on the Revatâchal, there ruled a king Revata, who gave his daughter Revati to Baladeva, the brother of Śrî Krishna, and bestowed this fort in *kanyâdân*, or marriage dowry, on the Yâdava Baladeva.' This was doubtless derived from the *Harivaṁśa*. It is there said that Ânartta was the son of Śaryâti, and Ânartta's son was Reva, who ruled the country of Ânartta—a part of Surâshtra, 'bounded on one side by the sea and on the other by Arûpa, with Girivara (Girnâr?) for its fortress.' Raivata Kakudmin was the eldest of the hundred children of Reva, and succeeded him on the throne of Kuśasthali. This prince went one day, accompanied by his daughter Revatî, to the abode of Brahma, where for a little while (of the gods, but really many human ages) he assisted at a concert of Gandharvâs. On returning he found his capital occupied by the Yâdavas and named Dvâravatî. Raivata thereon gave his daughter to Balarâma and retired as a devotee to Mount Meru. (*Harivaṁśa*, ch. 10, 93, 111, 112, and 155.) As Raivata is the proper name of Girnâr, this reads as if intended to be understood as an allegory.—Ed.

|| This is shown by an inscription over the gate, now much defaced.

4

were kept open, and five closed. In Saṁvat 1718 (A.D. 1661) the fort was renovated and improved by Mirzâ A'isa Tor Khân.

Round the city are tanks bearing the following names:—Khokhariyâ, Jhâbariâ, Pari, Setha, Vâgheśvari, Jamiyal Śâ, Kunvâra, Varśâ, Vandrâvana, &c.; there are also *kuṇḍs*, as the Brahmakuṇḍ, Sarasvatikuṇḍ, [Dâmâkuṇḍ, Pâtâkuṇḍ,] Khâsî Kuṇḍ, and others.

The suburbs around the city are named Khamadrol, Harâ, Mâdaṇpur, Jośipur, Daulatpur, Tenbawâḍi, Dhârâgar; there is also the place Bâra Shahîd, or graves of the ṭwelve martyrs who fell in the battle with Râja Jayasiñha¶ in the year S. 1395 (A.D. 1338). There are also gardens, such as the Baśâratbâgh, Sirdârbâgh, the Bahâdurbâgh, and others, which are always fresh, blooming, and noted for their excellent fruits, as *rayaṇas*,* custard-apples, guavas, and especially mangoes.

The Nâgar Brâhmaṇs,—who commit to memory the glorious *Veda*, study religious books, and, if so minded, are able by a single glance of protection to preserve others from destructive calamities,—in consequence of the vicissitudes of the times, the attacks of the Musalmân and the Dekhani armies, are themselves now fallen from their former rank of zamindârs of

¶ This was Jayasiñha Chuḍâsamâ, who ruled from A.D. 1333 till 1345.

* *Mimusops hexandria*,—Roxb.

Vaḍanagar, Viśalnagar, Tharâd, Sâṭhodar, &c. to that of beggars. These, as well as the Brahmakhâtris, who were as skilled with the sword as they themselves with the pen, were brought hither by the Râṇâs of Junâgaḍh. Both these castes enjoyed special privileges secured by *parwânâs*, and by a stone inscription set up in the middle of the bâzâr, exempting them from paying various taxes. These rights are still continued, [but the stone inscription is not now to be seen].

In this country have been settled from time immemorial—Girnâra Brâhmaṇs, Ahers, Khânts, Kolîs, Parmâr Râjpûts, Vâghelâs, Vâjâ Râjpûts, Chuḍâsamâ Râjpûts, Sarasvatî and Soraṭha Brâhmaṇs, as well as the Surṭhî people. There are also Lohânâs and Bhâṭiâs, whom king Noṅghan brought from Sindh. The governors and Nâibs of the Ahmadâbâd and Dihli Sulṭâns maintained Sayyids, Baluchîs, Lodîs, and Afghâns in various offices, paying them salaries and pensions; but the cultivating classes immigrated from Gujarât.

Mount Girnâr lies to the east of the city: it vies with the sky in height, and its huge mass causes the earth to tremble under it:—

Its pinnacles touch heaven's lofty face,
Its rocks the earth's foundation form;
Ever in bloom are the bushes that wave on its sides,
With fruits its trees are laden heavily.

The top of the mountain is adorned by the temple of Śri Girnârî Nâth, which is visited by Hindus from all quarters. There are abundant springs of water, many fruits, and various and useful vegetables, as well as countless medicinal plants. The springs of Gaumukh and Kamandala vie with Kawther, and Bhîmâkuṇḍ Sâkara-kuvo, and Hâthipaglâ with the Salsabil of Paradise in sweetness.

The three temples opposite the fort or Devakoṭ were erected by two Baniâ brothers, Vastupâl and Tejaḥpâl. Tradition runs that a widow, on paying a visit to her *guru*, was told that she would give birth to two famous sons; but a person present objected that as she was a widow she could have no offspring. A camel-driver, however, who was sleeping near, happening to overhear the conversation, immediately got up, seated the woman on his camel, and took her to his home, where in due course of time she was delivered of two infants, one of whom was named Vastupâl, and the other Tejaḥpâl, who built these temples in Saṁvat 1288† (A.D. 1231).

The large temple near the Bhîmâkuṇḍ was built in Saṁvat 1519 (A.D. 1462), and consecrated on 15th Kârtik by Râja Satarath. The fort and the chambers were built of black stone by Râo Khengâr of Junâgaḍh. He built also

† One copy has S. 1277, *i.e.* A.D. 1221; both dates occur in the inscriptions on the triple temple built by the brothers. See *Report on the Antiquities of Kâṭhiâwâḍ and Kachh*, p. 169.

an idol-house with eighty-four *dukhâns* (small rooms) for pilgrims; and, though it cannot be called a house of God, no one is outside God's house.

It is said that five thousand years ago, when Neminâth‡ of the Yâdu tribe heard the cries of the sheep, pigs, and buffaloes that had been collected for a banquet, he imagined they were calling for justice, and accordingly he set them at liberty, but himself retired from this wicked world to Mount Girnâr, where he became an ascetic, on the spot where a temple was afterwards built in Saṁvat 1333 (A.D. 1277), during the reign of Râja Maṇḍalik.

From Junâgaḍh to the Chillah of Datâtri on the mountain, which pilgrims call Guru Datâtri, and the Musalmâns the shrine of Shâh Madâr, the Jogis the footprint of Gorakhnâth, the Śrâvaks the seat of Neminâth, and others that of Pârśvanâth, a road was constructed in Saṁvat 1882§ (A.D. 1826) by a merchant of Diva (*Diu*) bandar named Sanghaji. From the gate of the fort up to the *maṇḍap* of Śrî Girnâr Mâtâ there are 1096 stone steps, and from Gaumukh to Hanumândvârâ there are 968.

To the south of Girnâr is the Chillah of Jamiyal Shâh, which is visited by pilgrims from great dis-

---

‡ See note 2 at page 47.

§ The MSS. read 1682 and 1683, but the road was under construction when Col. Tod visited Junâgaḍh in 1822.

tances, who profess to derive great benefits from their visit. The Sûrajkuṇḍ to the north, the cell of Kâlikâ, the Oghaḍ Pâduka, and the Maddhi Bhârathi on the east side, are noted for their miracles, and at each devotees sit like lions intent on hunting the gazelle of salvation.

At the foot of the mountain on the west side, which may be compared to the approach to the throne for the constant worship of God, is the temple of Śrî Bhavanâth, Paitheśvar, or Mahâdeva, which is visited twice a year by bands of Atîts and pilgrims, who walk round it, and bring to the fair, as articles of trade, arms, shawls, jewels, and other goods.

There are various rest-houses for travellers along the ascent to the mountain, which are named Pânchapâṇḍava, Chodiya Parab, Kâli Parab, Dholi Parab, Mâli Parab, Suvâvḍi Parab, so called because a female pilgrim was there delivered of a son, the name signifying "the Rest-house of good delivery."

To the west of Girnâr are also situated the temples of Śrî Vâgeśvarî Mâtâ and Dâmodar Râya, with the Vageśvarî Kuṇḍ and Dâmodar Kuṇḍ. In the latter the bones of corpses melt. The Revati Kuṇḍ is always full of water, and from the sands of the Suvarṇarekhâ gold was washed in ancient times.* It flows from the mountain, and it is also the common belief that

* This belief probably arose from the reddish-yellow grains of mica with which the soil abounds.

there exists on the mountain a spring concealed from human eyes, called Raskup, which possesses the property of changing everything into gold, and the following legend is told of it:—Not very many years ago, a Brâhmaṇ having lost his way, and being thirsty, tied his gourd to a rope when he arrived at this spring, intending to draw water, when all at once he heard the words "*Bhar Rañkâni nâmin*," *i.e.* "Fill in the name of Rañkâ." In spite of astonishment he quenched his thirst, again filled the gourd, went to the town, and, suspending it on a nail in the house of a blacksmith, an old acquaintance of his, who lived on the public way, he went off on some business. It happened that a few drops of the water fell on the anvil and hammer, which were beneath the gourd, and changed them into pure gold; whereupon the blacksmith made good use of so splendid an opportunity of bounty from the invisible world, by transmuting into gold every piece of iron he had in the shop. In this way he became as rich as Qârûn.¶ When the Brâhmaṇ returned he perceived that his gourd was empty, but the house full of gold; and on asking the blacksmith for his name the reply was Rañkâ. Accordingly he said, "Your deposit you have received."

Hemistich:—What is your fate will overtake you, sure!

¶ The Gujarâti has Kubera, the god of wealth.

It is said that the blacksmith gave a nugget of gold to the Brâhmaṇ; but God knows best.

In the fort there are two large cannon, taken with other spoils from the Portuguese of Diu; they were cast in Egypt A.H. 937; one of them is eleven, and the other nine cubits long.

On the top of the mountain the following localities also are remarkable:—Hanumândvârâ, the Pâduka of Râmânand, Bhairavajap, Borâdevî, Jata-Śaṅkara-Mahâdeva, Jadeśvara, Siddhakarani Mâtâ, Muchhakanda Râjrâjeśvara Mahâdeva, and many others not necessary to mention.

During the lapse of time, the fort of U p a r k o ṭ was deserted, but was taken possession of in Saṁvat 1804 (A.D. 1747) by Mânsiâ Khât, who became the source of much trouble. Afterwards it was made a *choki*, but was on several occasions occupied by Arabs, whom the Navâb Sâheb succeeded in expelling.

The length of this Subâh, from the port of Ghoghâ to Arâmrâ, is one hundred and two *kos;* and its breadth, from the port of D i v a to S a r d h â r a, is seventy-two *kos*. Some say that the government of the C h u ḍ â s a m â Râjputs extended as far as the town of B u r a d, situated on the banks of the Sâbarmatî near Khambayat, and that it was called the government of S o r a ṭ h.

In this Sirkâr there are 500 *mâlguzâri* villages (with 37,200 houses and 120,060 men), paying *chauth*, which are well established, and the neighbourhood of the fortress is also populous. The forts of Majewaḍi and Kadiâ are flanked by four towers. The revenue, including Bântwa, amounts to eight lâkhs of rupees. In most of the *mahâls* the revenue was assessed by a rough guess (made by inspecting the standing crops), which system is in Hindi called *dhâl;* but in a few mahâls the Government share of the produce is taken in the grain-yard. *Bero* [*vero*, land-tax] is levied on every plough. Sipâhis and Sayyids and Nâgars pay no *zakât* [customs dues]. The current *kori** Nâgher Parganâ is the *Chândshâhi* or Pâdshâhi and the Divi rupee. The Parganâs are Sâlem, Banthali, Kutiânâ, Bhaḍ Miârî, Aliah, Biârej, Chorvâḍ, Bandar Verâval, Patan Div, Sutrapâḍa, Kodiânâ, Una, Delwâḍâ, and collective Parganâs :—Mangrôl, Jetpur, Bandar Jhânâpoli, Rânpûr, Bagasrâ, Bilkhâ, Śil Bandar, Verâval, and Amreli.

Note 1 at page 24.

[Junâgaḍh, 'the old fort,'†—anciently *Girinagara,*—is a place of great antiquity and historical interest. We find it visited in the seventh century by the indefatigable Chinese Buddhist traveller Hiwen Thsang,‡ whose journal runs thus :—

---

* A rupee is equal to 3½ *korîs*.

† Not *Yavanagara*, as erroneously supposed by Lassen.

‡ *Vide ante*, pp. 16-19.

"Leaving the kingdom of Valabhi (near Bhaunagar), Hiwen Thsang went about 100 miles to the west, and reached the kingdom of *Su-la-ch'a* (Saurâshṭra). This realm is nearly 800 miles in circuit. The capital has a circumference of six miles, and upon the west side (*the country*) touches the river *Mo-hi* (Mahi). Its inhabitants are very numerous, and all the families are wealthy. The country is subject to the kingdom of Valabhî. The soil is impregnated with salt, and its flowers and fruits are few. Though heat and cold are equally distributed over the year, storms of wind never cease. Indifference and coldness characterize the manners; the people are superficial, and do not care to cultivate learning (*nor the arts*). Some follow the true doctrine, and others are given to heresy. There are some fifty convents, where they count about three thousand recluses (*the most part of the school Shang-tso-pu*), who study the doctrines of the (*Ârya*) *Sthavira* sect, which holds by the 'greater translation' (*Mahâyâna*). There are a hundred temples of the gods (*Devalayas*), and the heretics of different sects live together. As this realm is on the way to the Western Sea, all the inhabitants profit by the advantages the sea affords, and give themselves to trade and barter."

"At a short distance from the (*capital*) city rises Mount *Yeu-shen-ta* (Ujjanta§) upon the top of which a monastery is established. The chambers and galleries have been mostly hollowed out in the face of a scarped peak. The mountain is covered

§ Ujjayanta, one of the names of Raivata or Girnâr.

with thick forests, and streams from the springs surround it on all sides.|| There holy men and sages walk and fix their abode, and thither resort crowds of Ṛishís endowed with divine faculties."

Of the Buddhist convents he speaks of there are still evidences. On the Uparkoṭ there is a very large half-ruined masjid, near which a curious excavation was discovered about ten years ago and opened up. It consists of a hall and a neat tank or bath, with a second story or galleries above. The hall has six principal pillars with very elaborate capitals ornamented with groups of human figures, mostly females. And again, outside the Uparkoṭ, both to the north and south, in the sandstone of which it is formed, there are numerous excavations of great age; whilst, at a short distance, the masjid at *Mahi Ghaḍechi* is built above a Buddhist cave-temple having still two pillars and two pilasters in front, with lions rampant as brackets outside the scarcely formed capitals. There are also numbers of Bauddha caves near Bâwâ Pyârâ's Maṭh.

But about half a mile to the westward of the town, at the entrance of the dell or valley leading in between two of the hills that girdle the mighty and sacred Girnâr, is *the* antiquity of Junâgaḍh—the rock inscribed with the edicts of Aśoka Skandagupta and Rudra Dâma. This remarkable lapidary monument of antiquity seems to have been first described by Colonel Tod, who saw it in 1822, and remarked the similarity of the characters

|| Or—"and one hears the murmur of gushing fountains."—*Vie de Hiouen-Thsang. Documents Géographiques*, p. 448.

upon it to those of the Dilhi Lâṭ and the Buddhist caves; but his *Travels* were not published till 1839, and it was the Rev. Dr. J. Wilson who first obtained a transcript of it, a copy of which was forwarded to Mr. James Prinsep, of Calcutta, early in 1837, who translated it.

These inscriptions contain fourteen paragraphs, tablets, or 'edicts' of Aśoka, the great Buddhist emperor of India, who ruled about 262 to 226 B.C., and who constantly styles himself "Râja Pṛiyadarśi."

They have since been retranslated and commented on by Professors H. H. Wilson, E. Burnouf, C. Lassen, and Dr. H. Kern. The following are the best translations now available. Those who wish to see full transcripts, &c. must consult the *Antiquities of Kâṭhiâwâḍ and Kachh* (pp. 95 to 127), or *Indian Antiquary* (vol. V. pp. 257-276).

Translations of the Aśoka Edicts.

I. "This is the edict of the beloved of the gods, the Râjâ Priyadasi. The putting to death of animals is to be entirely discontinued, and no convivial meeting is to be held: for the beloved of the gods, Râja Pṛiyadasi, remarks many faults in such assemblies. There is but one assembly, indeed, which is approved of by the Râja Pṛiyadasi, the beloved of the gods, which is that of the great kitchen of Râja Pṛiyadasi; every day hundreds of thousands of animals have been slaughtered for virtuous purposes; but now, although this pious edict is proclaimed, that animals may be killed for good purposes, and such is the practice, yet, as the practice is not determined, these presents are proclaimed, that hereafter they shall not be killed."¶

II. "In the whole dominion of king Devânâmpṛiya Pṛiyadarśin, as also in the adjacent countries, as Chola, Paṇḍya, Satyaputra, Keralaputra, as far as Tâmraparṇî, the kingdom of Antiochus the Grecian king, and of his neighbour kings, the system of caring for the sick, both of men and cattle, followed by King Devânâmpṛiya Pṛiyadarśin, has been everywhere brought into practice; and at all places where useful healing herbs for men and cattle were wanting he has caused them to be brought and planted; and at all places where roots and fruits were wanting he has caused them to be brought and planted; also he has caused wells to be dug and trees to be planted on the roads, for the benefit of men and cattle."*

III. "King Pṛiyadasî says: This was ordained by me when I had been twelve years inaugurated in the conquered country—that among those united in the law, whether strangers or my own subjects, quinquennial expiation shall be held for the enforcement of moral obligations, as duty to parents, friends, children, relations, Brâhmaṇs, and Śramaṇas. Liberality is good; non-injury of living creatures is good; and abstinence from prodigality and slander is good. The Assembly itself will instruct the faithful in the virtues here

¶ The above is Wilson's—*Jour. R. As. Soc.* vol. XII. p. 164. The translation of this edict has not been revised by either Burnouf or Kern.

* Kern, *ut sup.* p. 91.

enumerated, both by explanation and by example."†

IV. "In past times, during many centuries, attacking animal life and inflicting suffering on the creatures, want of respect for Brâhmaṇs and Śramaṇas, have only grown greater. But now, when King D e v â n â m p ṛ i y a P ṛ i y a d a r ś i n practises righteousness, his kettledrum has become a summons to righteousness : while apparitions of chariots of the gods, and apparitions of celestial elephants, and fiery balls, and other signs in the heavens showed themselves to the people. In such a manner as has not been the case in many centuries previously, now, through the exhortation of King D e v â n â m p ṛ i y a P ṛ i y a d a r ś i n to cultivate righteousness, has the sparing of animal life, the gentle treatment of creatures, respect for relatives, respect for Brâhmaṇs and monks, obedience to father and mother, obedience to an elder, grown greater. This and many other kinds of virtuous practices have grown greater, and King D e v â n â m p ṛ i y a P ṛ i y a d a r ś i n shall cause this practice of virtue to increase still more, and the sons, grandsons, and great-grandsons of King D e v â n â m p ṛ i y a P ṛ i y a d a r ś i n shall also cause this culture of virtue to increase; standing steadfast in righteousness and morality until the destruction of the world, they shall exhort to righteousness; to exhort to righteousness is surely a very ex-

---

† This is Wilson's translation of this tablet, proposed 'subject to considerable doubt." M. Burnouf observes that this last sentence is more literally—" 'D'après la cause et d'après la lettre;' à peu près comme quand on dit, *au fond et dans la forme*."

cellent work, while from him who is immoral no practice of righteousness is to be expected. Increase, therefore, in these things, and no diminution, is good; for this end has this been written; may they attend heartily to the increase hereof, and not aim at the diminution of it! King Devânâmpṛiya Pṛiyadarśin has caused this to be written twelve years after his inauguration."‡

V. "The beloved of the gods, King Pṛiyadasi, thus proclaims: Virtue is difficult of performance, therefore much good is to be done by me, and my sons and grandsons, and other my posterity (will) conform to it for every age. So they who shall imitate them shall enjoy happiness, and those who cause the path to be abandoned shall suffer misfortune. Vice is easily committed; therefore Dharma Mahâmatra (*or* great officers of morals) are appointed by me, in the thirteenth year of my inauguration, for the purpose of presiding over morals among persons of all the religions, for the sake of the increase of virtue, and for the happiness of the virtuous, among the people of Kamboja, Gandhara, Râshtṭṛika, and Pitenika. They shall also be spread among the warriors, the Brâhmaṇs, the mendicants, the destitute, and others, without any obstruction, for the happiness of the well-disposed, in order to loosen the bonds of those who are bound, and liberate those who are confined, through the means of holy wisdom disseminated by pious teachers; and they will proceed to

‡ This and the VIth are from Dr. Kern's version.

the outer cities and fortresses of my brother and sister, and wherever are any other of my kindred; and the ministers of morals, those who are appointed as superintendents of morals, shall, wherever the moral law is established, give encouragement to the charitable and those addicted to virtue. With this intent their edict is written, and let my people obey it."§

VI. "King Devânâmpṛiya Pṛiyadarśin saith: In past times there has never yet existed care for the (civil) interests, nor official superintendence; therefore have I instituted the same; all the time that I have been reigning there have been everywhere inspectors over the women, sanctuaries, travelling pilgrims(?), traders (or trade-markets), and parks for walking, in order to attend to the interests of my people,|| and in all respects I further the interests of my people;¶ and whatever I declare, or whatever the Mahâmatra shall declare, shall be referred to the council for decision. Thus shall reports be made to me. This have I everywhere, and in every place, commanded, for to me there is not satisfaction in the pursuit of worldly affairs; the most worthy pursuit is the prosperity of the whole world. My whole endeavour is to be blameless towards all creatures, to make them happy here below, and enable them hereafter

---

§ This has not been revised by Dr. Kern. The above is Professor Wilson's version, slightly modified by later commentators.

|| The Dhaulî redaction reads: "All the time that I have been reigning, the inspectors over, &c. have had to communicate to me the interests of the people."

¶ Thus far Kern's version, *ut sup*. pp. 75, 76.

to attain *Svarga*. With this view this moral edict has been written : may it long endure, and may my sons, grandsons, and great-grandsons after me also labour for the universal good ! but this is difficult without extreme exertion."*

VII. "P ṛ i y a d a s i, the king dear to the gods, desires that everywhere the ascetics of all persuasions should remain [*in peace*]; they all desire the regulation that they exercise upon themselves, and purity of the soul; but people have different opinions and different likings, [*and*] the ascetics obtain, whether the whole, or whether a part only [*of what they ask*]. Nevertheless, for himself, to whom there reaches not a large alms, the empire over himself, purity of mind, knowledge, and firm devotion which lasts for ever, this is good."†

VIII. "In past times the kings went out on journeys of pleasure; stag-hunting and other such-like recreations were in vogue. But king D e v â n â m p ṛ i y a P ṛ i y a d a r ś i n, ten years after his inauguration, came to the true insight. Therefore he began a walk of righteousness, which consists in this, that he sees at his house and bestows gifts upon Brâhmaṇs and monks, he sees at his house and presents elders with gold, he receives subjects of town and country, exhorts to righteousness and seeks righteousness. Since then, this is the greatest pleasure of king D e-

---

* Lassen, *Ind. Alt.* vol. II. p. 268, note 1, Burnouf (*Lotus de la Bonne Loi*. p. 654) translates the last sentence, "mais cela est difficile à faire si ce n'est par un héroisme supérieur."

† From Burnouf's version.

vânâmpṛiya Pṛiyadarśin in the period after his conversion."†

IX. "King Devânâmpṛiya Pṛiyadarśin speaks thus: It is a fact that men do all kinds of things which are thought to assure luck, as well in sicknesses as at betrothals and marriages, at the getting of children, or at going from home. On these and other occasions men do all kinds of things which are thought to bring prosperity. But he is a great fool who does all those manifold, multifarious, vain, and useless things. This, however, does not indeed remove the necessity of a man's doing something which will bring prosperity, but such a kind as has been named is of little use, while of great use is true piety. To that belongs proper treatment of servants and subordinates, sincere reverence for elders and masters, sincere self-restraint towards living beings, sincere charity to Brâhmaṇs and monks. These and other such-like actions—that is called true piety. Every man must hold that forth to others, whether he is a father or a son, a brother, a lord; this is noble; this must a man do, as something that assures luck, until his aim has been fully attained. Mention was made just now of 'sincere charity:' now there is no charity, no affection to be compared to charity or affection springing from true piety. It is just this which a well-meaning friend, relative, or companion must, at every occurring opportunity, impress on another, that this is duty, this is proper. By doing all this a man can merit heaven; there-

† This and the next four are from Dr. Kern's versions.

fore let him who wishes to gain heaven for himself fulfil, above all things, these his duties."

X. "King Devânâmpṛiya Pṛiyadarśin does not deem that renown and great name bring advantage greatly, if, at the same time, his people, for the present and afterwards, were not practising right obedience, and following exhortation to virtue. In so far only king Devânâmpṛiya Pṛiyadarśin desires renown and great name. All, therefore, that King Devânâmpṛiya Pṛiyadarśin strenuously strives after is for the life hereafter, so that he may be wholly and altogether free from blemish. Now blemish is the same as sinfulness. But such a thing is, indeed, difficult for anyone whatever, be he a person of low degree or of high station, unless with the utmost exertion of power, by sacrificing everything. But this is, indeed, most difficult for a person of high station."

XI. "King Devânâmpṛiya Pṛiyadarśin speaks thus: There is no charity which equals right charity, or right conversation, or right liberality, or right relation. Under that is comprehended proper treatment of servants and subordinates, sincere obedience to father and mother, sincere charity towards friends and acquaintances, Brâhmans and monks, the sparing of animal life. This is to be commended as good, whether by father or by sons, by brothers, by friends, acquaintances, and relatives, nay, even by neighbours: thus it is *good;* thus must men act. He who acts thus makes this world a friend to him, and hereafter a man obtains for himself an imperishable reward through all that true charity."

XII. "King Devânâmpṛiya Pṛiyadarśin honours all sects, and orders of monks, and conditions of heads of families, and honours them with love-gifts and with marks of honour of all kinds. To be sure, Devânâmpṛiya does not attribute so much value to love-gifts or marks of honour as to this, that the good name and intrinsic worth of all sects may increase. Now intrinsic worth can grow greater in many ways, but the foundation thereof, in all its compass, is discretion in speaking, so that no man may praise his own sect, or contemn another sect, or despise it on unsuitable occasions; on all manner of occasions let respect be shown. Whatever of good, indeed, a man, from any motive, confers on any one of a different persuasion, tends to the advantage of his own sect and to the benefit of a different persuasion; by acting in an opposite manner a man injures his own sect and offends a different sect. Though every one who praises his own persuasion may perhaps do all that from attachment to his own sect, for the purpose of glorifying it, nevertheless he shall, by so doing, greatly injure his own persuasion. Therefore concord is best, so that all may know and willingly listen to each other's religion. Because it is the wish of Devânâmpṛiya that the members of all persuasions may be well instructed, and shall adhere to a doctrine of benevolence. And to them who are inclined to all that, let the assurance be given that Devânâmpṛiya does not attach so much value to love-gifts or show of reverence as to this, that all sects may increase in good name and intrinsic worth, and be reverenced. For this end sheriffs over legal proceedings, magistrates entrusted with the superintendence of the women, hospice-masters (?), and other bodies have been appointed. And the result of this is, that Devânâmpriya's persuasion has increased in prosperity, and that he causes the Righteousness to come forth in full splendour."

XIII. " . . . . . Whose equality and exertion towards that object, exceeding activity, judicious conduct . . . . . . afterwards in the Kalinga provinces not to be obtained by wealth . . . . . . the decline of religion, murder and death, and unrestrained license of mankind; when flourished the (precious maxims) of Devânampiya comprising the essence of learning and of science: dutiful service to mother and father; dutiful service to spiritual teachers; the love of friend and child, (charity) to kinsfolk, to servants, (to Brâhmaṇs and Śramaṇas, &c., which) cleanse away the calamities of generations; further also in these things unceasing perseverance is fame. There is not in either class of the heretics of men, not, so to say, a procedure marked by such grace, . . , . . nor so glorious nor friendly, nor even so extremely liberal as Devânampiya's injuntion for the non-injury and content of living creatures . . . . . and the Greek king besides, by whom the kings of Egypt, Ptolemaios and Antigonos, and Magas, ... Both here and in foreign (countries), everywhere the religious ordinances of Devânampiya effect conversion wherever they go; . . . . , conquest is of every description; but, further, the conquest which bringeth joy springing from pleasant emotions becometh joy itself; the victory of virtue is happiness; the victory of happiness is not to be overcome; that which essentially possesses a pledge of happiness,—such victory is desired in things of this world and things of the next world."§

XIV. "King Devânâmpṛiya Pṛiyadarśin has caused this righteousness-edict to be written, here concisely, there in moderate compass, in a third place again at full length, so that it is not found altogether everywhere worked out; for the kingdom is great, and what I have caused to be written, much. Repetitions occur also, in a certain measure, on account of the agreeableness of various points, in order that the people should in that way (the more willingly) receive it.

If sometimes the one or other is written incompletely or not in order, it is because care has not been taken to make a good transcript, or by the fault of the copyist (*i.e.* the stone-engraver)."||

In one place only, namely, the signature of the Girnâr inscription, is Buddha referred to. Of this signature there remains—

. . *va sveto hasti savaloka sukhâharo nâmaṁ.*

What is left means—

"The white elephant whose name is the bringer of happiness to the whole world."

"That by this term Śâkya is implied," Dr. Kern thinks, "there can be no doubt, since the

---

§ Mr. Prinsep's translation—*Jour. R. As. Soc.* vol. XII. pp. 227-233. A large part of the original of this edict has been broken off from the stone, which renders the translation very difficult.

|| Dr. Kern's version.

legend says that the B o d h i s a t t v a, the future Buddha, left heaven to bring happiness to men, and entered his mother's womb as a white elephant."¶

Note 2 on page 29.

[N e m i n â t h a or A r i s h ṭ a n e m i, who gives his name to one of the summits of Girnâr, and to whom the Jainas consider the whole mount as sacred, is the twenty-second of their *Tîrthaṅkaras* or deified saints,—men who, through successful austerities, they imagine, have entered *nirvâṇa*, and have done with the evils of existence. This one is the favourite object of worship with the Digambara or naked Jainas. His complexion, they say, was black, and most, if not all, of his images here are of that colour; like all the other Tîrthaṅkaras, he was of royal descent, being the son of Samudravijaya, king of Ś a u r y a n a g a r a or Soriyapuri, in the country of Kuśavarta, and of the Harivaṅśa race—his paternal uncle being Vasudeva, the father of the famous Kṛishṇa. At the age of three hundred he renounced the world, and leaving Dvârakâ went to Girnâr to spend the remaining seven hundred years of his long life in asceticism; he received his 'Bodhi,' or highest knowledge, whilst meditating at Ś e s h a v a n a, to the east of the Bhairava-jap, where footprints (*pâglâṅ*) are also carved—some say Neminâtha's, others Râmânanda's. His first convert was a king D a t t â t r i, to whom he became *guru*, after which he gradually rose to the exalted rank of a Tîrthaṅkara, and finally attained *nirvâṇa* on this lonely pinnacle of rock which retains his

¶ Kern, *ut sup*. p. 43.

name. He had as tutelary goddess, or familiar *devî*, Ambikâ Mâtâ, the same to whom the old temple on the first summit is dedicated. The Mango tree is also appropriated to him by the Śrâvakas as his 'Bo-tree,' whilst the *śankha* or conch-shell is his cognizance. He is, in fact, the Kṛishṇa of the Jainas.

But it is not to them alone he is sacred here; the Vaishṇavas who come from the pilgrimage to Dvârakâ consider they only reap the fruit of their toils when they have paid their respects to Guru Dattâtraya.]

Mahâls which pay all the Land and Customs Revenue Rights to Junâgadh.

Vanthali has two stone forts, washed on different sides by the rivers Ojhat and Obin. The palace of Vâmanrâja is in the town, as well as the Sûraj Kuṇḍ. The Tomb of Bhalla Shâh, with the Asrâm of Kapilamuni, is celebrated in this kasbâ. The kasbâtis, who in former times became Musalmâns, immigrated to this country from Naghor, and occupy themselves with cultivation.

Vanthali was for a long time known by the name of Patan, but Vahudipal Dhundhlimal the Yogi, who lived in the hills of Dhank, in his wrath pronounced the curse "*Patan so datan!*" "Patan, be buried!" upon it; whereupon eighty-four towns bearing that name were swallowed up by the earth, and Patan shared the same fate, as may be seen even in our days, since, wherever excavations are made, foundations of buildings, and various things, are dug up. During the tenure of power of the author in this town, two stone horses, each one cubit high, were dug up, with a stone box in which they were, and also other more valuable things in Saṁvat 1842 (A.D. 1785).

As the rivers swell greatly during the rains, it is difficult to cross them, and there is a great deal of mud, but the soil is good, and produces excellent sugar-cane, mangoes, and great quantities of guavas; they sow three times every year.

In the Saṁvat year 1803 (A.D. 1746) Kahuji with the Navâb Fakhr-al-daulah unsuccessfully besieged the town, but in 1835 Jabbâr Khân treacherously obtained possession of the fort, which, however, was again taken from him after a siege by Divânji Amarji Sâleh; but again it fell into the possession of the Jamadârs Sharf-al-din and O'mar for some years, and was captured in 1851 (A.D. 1794) by Madhurâya Ben Khoshkhâl, to expel whom the author was called from Nâgar by the Navâb Sâheb Hâmed Khân, and he succeeded in doing so by negotiation in 1860 (A.D. 1803). Afterwards Madhurâya with Bâbâji Sâheb, the Kârbhâri of the Gaikvâḍ, again besieged it, but ineffectually.

THE KASBÂ OF KUTIÂNÂ.

This place has two stone forts, and is situated

on the banks of the Bhâdar river. It is said that for a long time a Chârani woman whose name was Kuntî used to pasture her cattle on this spot, which in course of time became a village. The governor, Kalidâs, who was a Baniâ and had built a fort for himself in the vicinity of Aḥmadâbâd to which he gave his own name, constructed here also a square fort of considerable strength so as to control Purbandar and Hâllâr. During the government of the Musalmâns, Afghân Sipahis, Maliks, Khokhars, Jundrâns, &c., settled here, and gradually became so strong as to be independent, and appointed Nia'mat Khân Lodi as their governor; but afterwards, growing dissatisfied, they surrendered the fort to Râṇâ Sulṭânji, from whom they likewise revolted, and gave it to Hâshem [Hasan] Khân, the adopted son of Navâb Bahâdur Khân, from whom it was taken by Amarji, the father of the author. In Saṁvat 1840 [A.D. 1783] the Divân Govindji rebelled, and the Navâb Sâheb, having besieged the fort for a month, afterwards made peace. In the year 1858 [A.D. 1801] Kalîyândâs Hirji, a Baniâ, revolted from the Navâb Sâheb, but after a month's contest the author took the fort from him.

The Khâgasri fort, which was formerly at the head of the Parganâ, with twenty-four villages, was given to Maluk Muḥammad Sindhi as a jâghir, for his services as Qâzi, of which also the fort of Devara is an appanage from the time of the Divân Sâheb Amarji.

The temples of Vageśvarî Mâtâ and Amareśvara were built by Dalpatrâm, the younger brother of the author. The place of pilgrimage (*mezâr*) of Chaman Jellâl is the ornament of this town at a distance of about three *kos* from which also' are Gokarṇatîrtha and Mahâdeva's Śivalaya. Most of the villages are joint property with Purbandar and Mângarol.

BÂNTWÂ.

B â n t w â has a strong fort, and the village of M a ṇ a r belongs to it; most of it at present belongs to P u r b a n d a r and M â n g r o l, and is inhabited by the Mehmans. Nawâb Sohrâb Khân, Governor of Khambâyat, waged war against Sher Zamân Khân and Diler Khan Bâbi, compelling them to evacuate Ghoghâ; but they obtained eighty [? 84] villages as a jâgir from the Navâb Sâheb Bahâdur Khân in 1779 [?1789], A.D. 1722.

THE KASBÂ OF MÂNGROL.

The port of M â n g r o l has two strong forts on the sea-shore with ditches, and is the residence of a governor or Hâkam. After annexing to B â n t w â eighty villages, two hundred and eighty-one still belong to Mângrol.

In ancient times Râṇâ B h â n, Râja of G u m l i,§

§ See note at p. 58.

forsome reason divorced his wife, and being desirous again to recall her he consulted learned men on the subject. They said that a dismissed wife might again be taken back if eighteen hundred virgins were given by him in marriage, he defraying the bridal expenses. Accordingly the Râṇâ built a bridal hall or *chauri*, of squared stone, in S. 1264, and gave these virgins in marriage, and this edifice existed for many years till the arrival of Shams Khân, the Nâib of the Sulṭân Firoz Shâh, who converted it into a Jamâ'a mosque, and left Sikandar Khân as Thânâdâr, in Saṁvat 1350 (A.D. 1293). In this place Makhdûm Jehaniah with other saints are buried, and at the tomb the spears of A'li, the garment of the prophet, and a goblet brought from the fourth heaven are shown to pilgrims.

In former times the zamindârs of these places were Râjpûts of the Vâghelâ tribe, but gradually various others obtained lands, *e.g.* Qâzis, Maliks, Sayyids, &c., and who, becoming powerful, expelled the Vâghelâs. These persons usually obeyed the governors of Junâgaḍh or Gujarât.

Under the government of Śrimant Peshvâ Bâji Râo, his Nâib Natâji distressed the Rayâs so much that many of them emigrated to Junâgaḍh and other parts of the country. Natâji also gave much trouble to the Musalmâns and Jats on account of the *Ekâdaśi* [11th of the Hindu month] fasting, and on account of the

Mondays, and the people in general were much dissatisfied with him; accordingly Shekh Miân, son of Qâzi Fakhr-ud-dîn, expelled Jâdav Jaswant, the Thânadâr of the Śrimant Peshwâ, by the edge of the sword, in the year Saṁvat 1805 [A.D. 1748], and taking the government into his own hands, levied tribute|| from Kesod, Chorvâḍ, Koḍinâr, Pâṭan, Purbandar, &c.; sometimes also he made raids into Kâṭhiâvâḍ, and carried away whatever property or cattle he could, from which he used to pay the wages of his Sipahîs; the *Deśâgiri* allowance of these places, however, still belongs to the Nâgars, Baniâs, and Khâtrîs.

Prosperity increased during the rule of Shekh Badr-ud-dîn bin Nur-ud-dîn bin Shekh Miân, son of the Qâzi. He also kept up the dignity of his position by waging a successful war against Purbandar and Chorvâḍ; he died, however, on the 8th Vaiśâkh Śuddh of the Saṁvat year 1871 (A.D. 1814), and was succeeded by his son Abâ Miân.

The grandfather of the author was a god-worshipping man adorned with every good quality; his name was Kuṅwarji bin Prâgji bin Gopâlji bin Vekunṭh bin Śripat bin Śivâji, and he was the hereditary agent of the Chief, and possessed several pieces of land in this Kasbâ, partly irrigated from wells and partly by the

|| The original has *khirâj*, properly *land-tax*, but here used, as it often is, for *tribute*.—J. W. W.

rains, the produce whereof constituted his support. He worshipped the *Liṅga* of the lord Śrî Buḍhâbâvâ, which was a gift from the Sulṭân Farukhsiyar Shâh of Dihli, and with reference to it the following legend is current:—

It is related that one day when the Sulṭân Akbar was walking on the banks of the Jamunâ he perceived two women going home from the river with full waterpots on their heads, when all of a sudden a mouse carried by a kite flying above them fell down; and one of the damsels immediately exclaimed disparagingly to her companion, "Just see what times of weakness have set in, when a kite is unable to carry such a little mouse! Four thousand eight hundred years ago, when the Kauravas and Pâṇḍavas were waging a great war against each other, I was a kite, and flew away with the arm of Râja Jydrat, the Shâh of Sindhu, which had two armlets on it." The Sulṭân happened to overhear these words; accordingly he stopped; and to his inquiries the woman replied without further ceremony as follows:— "I had been created a kite, and having, after picking it up from the ground with my beak, flown away with the arm of Râja Jydrat, which the arrow of Sâtaki [Bhuri Śrava, a descendant of the Svâtaki Yâdavas] had severed from his shoulder, I sat down on the top of a tree. After I had consumed all the flesh, I dropped the bones, together with the gold, into the well beneath the tree ; and I dare say that if the heap of dirt which has accumulated on the spot during the lapse of ages were to be removed, the truth of my statement would be confirmed by the discovery of the bones and armlets." The Shâh despatched servants, who dug up the spot, and brought from the depth of the well two Śiva-lingas which were set in the gold armlets just mentioned. It is related that the arm-bone of that râja was eight spans long. The two Śiva-lingas were kept in the Shâh's private apartments, and were day and night placed in contact with fragrant substances, such as attar and water of roses, sandal, saffron, and aloes ; camphor-lights, food, beverages, garments, and jewels were placed before them, and he secretly worshipped them, away from the eyes of weak-minded critics, as the Musalmâns had already become accustomed to accuse his majesty of idolatry and irreligiousness because he was in the habit of saying—

(*Distich*)—

> " In idol forms I worship God,
> Not idols separate from God."

This custom was kept up till the time of 'Azim Shâh ; but afterwards when the turn of the Shâhzâdâh Farukhsiyar came and he began to reign, he presented his Vazîr, the Râja Chabilârâm Bahâdur, who conquered the Dekhan and was a Nâgar, as a reward for his services, with the two Śiva-liṅgas, a dress of honour, and a Rudrâksha rosary the beads of which were made of pearls. On this occasion he said with his own blessed tongue, "O Râja Bahâdur! This is Buḍhâbâvâ" (*i.e.* "old father," which is a metaphor for Eternal Creator), "worship it!" When he took the *Liṅgas* home, he gave one of them, which was of emerald colour, to Dayarâm, who was a highly respected Nâgar and a *jâgirdâr* in the pargaṇâ of N â g i n â p û r and district of M e v â t. Some time afterwards the conquests of the Dekhanis, the dissensions of the Amirs, and the invasions of the Persian armies disturbed the comfort of the *jâgirdârs* and royal servants, so that Dayarâm established himself at Banâras, where he became so intimate with the grandfather of the author that he betrothed to him his own daughter, and after a while, when they returned to Mângrol, the wedding was consummated there; on that occasion he presented his daughter also with the Śri Buḍhâbâvâ as a portion of her dowry, which is the source of endless blessings and of divine favours. Then becoming a *sanyâsi* he went to Nâsik, and finally to Banâras, where he died, whilst the Mehtâ kept and continued to worship the Śiva-liṅga. Lastly, Sulṭân Zufar Khân and Tâtâr Khân came with troops from Mângrol, altered the Sûraj temple and called it the Râvali mosque; they also spoilt the Râvali Wâv. About two hundred years ago [1510], on the staircase of the Gomati Wâv, the image of Ranchoḍ Râya was found by Parbat Mehtâ, and is to this day worshipped in a Vaishṇava temple of Junâgaḍh.

Here are places of pilgrimage, such as that of Merân Shâh and others, and, at a distance of three *kos*, the temple of Kâmnâtha or Kâmeśvara. In the town itself may be seen the temples of Kâśi Viśvanâth, Hâtkeśvarâ, Siddheśvara, Nîlakaṇṭha, Mâtâ Hinglâj, Mangalâj, Appâchharâdevi, Navadurgâ, Saptamâtri, Ranchoḍ Râya, and Raghunâtha Râya.

In this zillâ there is much garden cultivation, and fine water-melons and *vâls* [*oliyas*] are produced. Here the Nâgars are Jâgirdârs, Kârbhârîs, Kanûngûis, Desâyas, and they follow all the occupations in which penmanship is required; they were invited by the râjas and governors from all sides, and employed in civilizing the country.

Merchandise from Arabia, the Koṅkaṇa, from Sindh, and from the coasts arrives in the port of Mângrol, and is the occasion of much trade. On a certain occasion some Bokhâri Sayyids entered the town in carts in the disguise of a marriage procession, and treacherously took possession of Mângrol, and fourteen wives of the Hâkim of this place preferred being consumed by fire in the tower of Sakotri to losing their honour.

The parganâ of Mângrol is the joint property of the Navâb of Junâgaḍh and of the Râja of Mângrol. It contains the following forts with four towers, viz. Mahiâri, Bagasrâ, Śil, Diwâsa, Sepa (?), Meswana (?), Lâthodrâ, and Shergaḍh. Some of the lands are under cultivation, and others are neglected.

Note 3 on Ghumlî or Bhumli, page 51.

[In the south of the Navânagara territory, and about forty miles west from Ḍhânk, is Ghumlî, an old deserted capital of the Jeṭwâs—now of Purbandar. It lies about four miles south of Bhanvâḍ, in the last valley facing the north, in the north-eastern end of the Baraḍâ hills, and concealed from the north by a low ridge, which bends round in front of the opening to the valley or dell, shutting up the town in a sort of *cul-de-sac*, open only through the narrow valley to the north-west, by which it is approached from the modern village of Mukhânâ. Up both sides of the dell its ruined walls wind in various directions along the shelving ridges which overlook it, up to the summit of the mountain, where was a fortified citadel, still containing the walls of many of the houses in a tolerable state of preservation, but entirely deserted except by wild beasts. The very vertex is occupied by a small temple of Mâtâ Âsâpurî—a favourite object of superstitious reverence with the Jeṭwâ Râjputs.

According to the traditions of the province, the earliest seat of the Jeṭwâs was at Śrînagara, a few miles from their present one of Purbandar. Soon afterwards it was at Bhimor or Mordvajpurî, now a ruined site opposite to Morvî and six generations later—probably early in the tenth century—Ghumlî or Bhumlî was made the capital, and adorned with imposing buildings by Râjâ Sâl Kumâra; but in Saṁvat 1369 (A.D. 1313) it fell, after a desperate siege, by an army from Sindh. From Ghumlî the Jeṭwâ chief then removed to Chaya, near Purbandar,—the latter being its port, which has since supplanted Chaya.

This ruined and deserted capital was visited by the indefatigable Colonel Tod in 1822, and described by him in his *Travels*¶ in his usual glowing and exaggerated style. In 1837 Captain (now General Sir G.) Le Grand Jacob gave an account of a visit to it with much more accuracy and detail.*

"All is now jungle," says the latter, "where once multitudes of human beings resided; within and without the ruined ramparts so thick is it as to make it difficult to trace them even from a height. The ground-plan of Ghumlî resembles a wide-spread fan, the two sides of which are formed by the gorge of the valley, leading up to the peak on which the fort is built, the circular portion being represented by the ramparts."

"The extreme breadth from the eastern to the western wall," he adds, "is about three-quarters of a mile; its length from the north wall to the narrow of the gorge less than half a mile; there are two flanks of about two hundred and fifty yards' length, joining the northern face to the natural flanks offered by the hills; the eastern one with

---

¶ Tod's *Travels in Western India*, pp. 404ff.

* *Jour. R. As. Soc.* vol. V. pp. 73ff.

its semi-arched battlements, reaching halfway up the scoop of the hill, is in a tolerable state of preservation, but the remainder is in ruins, the bastions have fallen in, and are only faintly to be traced through the jungle. A ditch, of the usual Hindu dimensions, surrounds the wall; the masonry I was surprised to find for the major part of well-chiselled stone, dove-tailed grooves for clamps; the iron or lead which may have been used for this purpose has doubtless been long since pilfered. There were originally two gateways to the north and west." The last only was still standing till within a few years ago, and bears the name of Râmapoḷa, but only a fragment of it now remains.

"The area contained within the limits I have above described is now tenanted only by wild beasts, and other jungle inhabitants; mounds or lines of rubbish faintly pourtray the lines of streets, though I am disposed to consider the houses were chiefly of frail materials; nothing remains as witness of its former state save an insignificant temple near the eastern wall, two small flat-roofed ones of the earlier age of Brâhmaṇism, a splendid well, itself worthy of description, and the ark or royal citadel, the contents of which peculiarly merit notice; wells of good masonry are sunk here and there, which the traveller should take heed not to stumble into. This ark occupies the centre of the area, and contains, originally guarded by a wall all round, the palace† and its adjuncts;

---

† The palace is probably represented by a mound of stones in front of the splendid ruin of the Navalâkha Temple.

a large bathing-reservoir, surrounded with small apartments as if for dressing-rooms to the zanâna, if not the zanâna itself, is separated from the palace by a court."

Various accounts and dates are given of the destruction of this city; it seems most probable, however, that some time during the first half of the fourteenth century, Jâm Unâḍ invaded Baraḍâ and besieged the Râṇâ in Ghumlî. After a long contest, Unâḍ, despairing of success, returned with his army to Kachh. Here, according to tradition, his son Bâmani,‡ ashamed of the disgraceful termination of his father's expedition, assumed the command of the army and conducted it back to Ghumlî, which place he reduced after an obstinate siege of twelve months. The Sammâs destroyed the city, which the Jeṭvâs, from superstition, did not attempt to rebuild, but removed their capital to Chaya, near the sea-coast. Purbandar, said to be on the site of Sadamapura, mentioned in the *Bhâgavata Purâṇa*, was at first the port of Chaya, but has since become the seat of government of the Jeṭvâ chief.§

Probably owing to the resistance made by the Baraḍâ Râṇâs, the Sammâs, after reducing Ghumlî, returned to Kachh, without establishing their authority in the country. Jâm Unâḍ, however, is said to have given his territory in Sindh in charity to the Chârans before setting out to conquer another, and on Bâmani's arrival in

‡ May this not have been Manâi, mentioned in the Kachh annals?

§ Conf. *Bombay Selections*, XXXIX. (N.S.) pp. 166, 207.

Kachh on his way back he formed the design of establishing himself there, and succeeded in doing so.||]

KESOD.

This place is situated on the banks of the Kesod river, and has two strong forts. After the taking of Junâgaḍh, it together with Chorvâḍ became a jâgir of the Râizâdâhs. In this district the Râjpût Lâthias, Sarvaiyas, and others, who are descendants of the Chuḍâsamâ Râjpûts, originally Zamindârs of Sindh, hold jâgirs.

MÂLIÂ.

Mâliâ has a fort with towers, and is situated on the river Mekal. The Zamindârs are of the Hâṭhi tribe. The parganah is small, but abounds in mangoes.

CHORVÂḌ.

Chorvâḍ is situated near the sea-shore, and has two strong forts; and several villages belong to it. At a distance of one *kos* from Chôrvâḍ the river Birjâmi falls into the sea, but though it is so near to the sea there is no bandar, on account of the paucity of inhabitants; there are, however, fine gardens and beautiful fields. Betel-leaves unequalled in agreeable taste and pungency are grown in this place, and are even exported to Hâlâr, Kachh, and Soraṭh; also all kinds of vegetables grow. The total revenue is 50,000 *koḍîs;* there are thirteen

|| From *Antiquities of Kâṭhiâvâḍ and Kachh*, pp. 178, 185.

villages under it. The forts with four towers of Kukasvaḍâ and Visâval are also on one side of Chorvâḍ.

OF PAṬṬAN DIVA.

This is a strong fort situated on the sea-shore, surrounded by a fosse full of water. The rivers Hiran, Sarasvatî, and Kapilâ flow near the base of the fort. In ancient times the zamindâri of this place belonged to Parmâr Râjpûts. The slaughter of the Yâdavas and of Śrî Krishṇa in this locality is recorded in the *Prabhâsa Kathâ*. Here great quantities of mangoes, water-melons, and *gunda* fruits are produced, which are exported. Verâval is the seaport of this district. Nia'mat Khân Lodhi, an adherent of the Navâb Bahâdur Khân, built a strong fort, which in the Saṁvat year 1824 (A.D. 1767) was repaired by the Divânji Sâheb Amarji, and was repaired for the second time in 1845 (A.D. 1788). Divân Raghunâth, son of Amarji and Dulabhaji, brother of Amarji, were besieged here by Râṇâ Sulṭânji of Purbandar in one of his warlike expeditions, as will be narrated in the proper place.

Śrî Sômânâthâ* of Paṭṭan the adherents of Islâm believe to have been brought from Mekka during the time of Abraham the Friend of God; but the Hindus hold that it existed here from all eternity, as a *Śiva-liṅga* by Chandramâ.

¶ See Note 4 at page 68.

This place was devastated by Sulṭân Maḥmûd the Ghaznavide in the Saṁvat year 1078 (A.D. 1021), by Shams Khân in 1375 (A.D. 1318), by Zufar Khân the Shâh of Gujarât in 1568 (A.D. 1511), and by Tâtar Khân bin Zafar Khân nine years later, who forcibly converted many persons to his own religion.

During the time of Sulṭân Maḥmûd the Ghaznavide, the Ghuri Pâdishâhs, and the Sulṭâns of Gujarât, nobody could prosper without adopting Islâm. Accordingly many became Muhammadans here, as for instance the Kasbâtis, who are to this day called Paṭṭani, and are mostly subject to the governor of Junâgaḍh, but they revolted often and erected forts, such as Sutrâpâḍâ, Hirâkoṭ, Dhâmlej, Lodhvâ, Pushnâvara, Lâthi, &c., trying to assert their independence.

Gorakhmaḍi is a place belonging to the Kânphaṭâ Yogis, and noted from ancient times in all parts for hospitality both to travellers and refugees, and its charitable daily meal (*sadâvrat*) was well known throughout the country. It was for a long time under the protection of many successive governments; gradually, however, the Paṭṭanîs began to drive away horses from the place and commit robberies, wherefore Madaninâtha, who was the chief Yogi, buried himself alive. This event brought on the ruin of the Paṭṭanîs, who commenced to live in discord among themselves and with the people whom they hated; accordingly they appointed Nia'mat Khân Lodi as their governor, from whom they afterwards again revolted, but he slew some of them, and then, at the invitation of the inhabitants, went to Kuṭiânâ. The Lodhi tower is a monument of his rule. His history is this :—Nia'mat Khân used to live at Ahmadâbâd in Sheikpûra, on the bank of the river Sâbarmati, and obtained Upletâ,* Kuṭiânâ, Paṭṭan, and Koḍinâr as a *jâgir* from the Shâh of Gujarât, and after he had properly settled the affairs of all those places he betook himself to Paṭṭan and peopled Verâval, which the Paṭṭanîs had laid waste, and there he also built a fort. Now, since the Paṭṭanîs would not suffer him to enter Paṭṭan, he removed in the space of seven months all the thorny bushes and trees which obstructed his movements between Paṭṭan and Verâval, and, commencing the war in earnest, established a *thánah* at Sutrapâḍa. The Paṭṭanîs marched against him, but were put to flight after great slaughter, and compelled to submit to Nia'mat Khân's government A few days afterwards Nia'mat Khân obtained a chance and marched with his troops into the town, and, having also obtained aid from Verâval, put many Paṭṭanîs to the sword, and on this occasion his Divân, Iśvaradâs, was wounded, but many Paṭṭanîs were beheaded by the executioner, and many thrown into the sea. Nevertheless the Paṭṭanîs

* Upletâ is an important mahâl now belonging to the Gondal State.

again assembled to the number of three thousand men, and, under the leadership of Sayyid Miân, scaled the walls of the fort by means of ladders, but Nia'mat Khân routed them again, and after encountering much opposition remained ruling in the city. Some time afterwards Mânâji Ângriâ made a descent on Verâval in ships, and, after fighting during three days and nights, he made peace and received the gift of a horse as *nazarânah.* The Portuguese of Diva also made some attacks, but retired disappointed.

He plundered the villages of Kâlâwad and Bântwâ, in Hâlâr, and defeated his pursuers, and established a right to tribute over certain villages.

Sulṭâna Bibî, the paternal aunt of the Navâb Sâheb Mahâbat Khân, obtained possession of the fort, and ruled for sixteen years. After some time the Paṭṭanîs considering Shekh Miân—who was one of the Kasbâtis of Mângrol—a man of good disposition, allowed him to enter the fort, and he commenced to conduct the government. Seeing the pride and insolence of Pahâḍji and Chand and Fîroz Shâh, however, and, fearing lest they might expel him, he drove the Paṭṭanîs from their native country into hell and the flames, and made them food for alligators and jackals.

The temple of Somanâtha, which the Musulmâns had converted into a mosque, was in ruin, and was not repaired till Saṁvat 1840 (A.D. 1783), during the government of Sheikh Miân [the successor of Nia'mat Khân], when it was rebuilt by a most excellent lady, Âhilyâ Bâi,† the wife of the Holkar Malhâr Râo Bahâdur. After thirty years the Divân Viṭhal Râo Devâji, who was a Subahdâr of Kâṭhiâwâḍ under the government of the Gaikwâḍ, built high *nagâra-khânas*, travellers' houses, *harams*, and repaired the temples of the Jain and Kaneśvara and of Jânkiśvara.

The following are some of the temples in this city :—The temples of Daitsudan, Narsing, Mahâkâli, Anapurṇa, Gaṇapati, Shashi-Bhukhan, and Pragteśvara, which last was built by the Divân Raghunâthji [a brother of the author]. The Râṇatalâo, Rudreśvara, Sûraj, Banéśvara, and Hatkeśvara are some of the sacred places much visited by Hindus. Bhalkâkuṇḍ, Kadamkuṇḍ, Bangañgâ, Râma-Pushkara, Gaurikuṇḍ, Vishṇukuṇḍ, Brahmâkuṇḍ, Rudrakuṇḍ, Sûrajkuṇḍ, and Jalprabhâs are some of the sacred tanks where the people are cleansed from their sins.

The places of pilgrimage to Mângrol-Shâh, Chandkattâl, Maghrabi-Shâh, Mâhi-Hâjat and Godar-Shâh are noted. At a distance of five *kos* from Paṭṭan is the Prâchi Tîrtha, celebrated far and near, and visited by pilgrims from great distances ; here the *śrâddha* ceremonies are performed, whereby the spirits of the departed are propitiated and evil genii warded off.

In Saṁvat 1849 (A. D. 1792) the Navâb Sâheb Aḥmad Khân, with the aid of the Paṭ-

† See Note 5, page 76.

ṭaniṣ, scaled the walls of the fort during the night by means of ladders, and expelled Sheikh Bedr-al-din.

This country, situated on the sea-shore, produces annually three crops, consisting of great quantities of red rice and *vallânak* [*kâng*], but unfit for the consumption of wealthy persons; from Purbandar as far as Mahwah and Sâbar,‡ these crops are very abundant.

Without the fort of Sutrapâda the temples of Navadurgâ, Bhavâni, the Sûrajkuṇḍ [Châmankuṇḍ], may be seen. In the same pargaṇah also the *tîrthas* of Gayâtrikuṇḍ, Brahmâkuṇḍ, Vishṇu-Gaya are celebrated places for ablution. The revenue amounts to three and a half lâkhs of *koḍis*.

Note 4, *on Paṭṭan Somanâth*, at page 64 of the text.

[Paṭṭan Somanâth, or Prabhâsa Paṭṭan, is a place full of interest to the antiquarian. It is a walled town of considerable size, famous in the annals of Hindu history on account of its temple containing one of the *dvadâśajoti lingas*, or twelve symbols of Mahâdeva, which, like the Ephesian Diana, were said to have fallen from heaven. It is one of the *ratnani*, or inestimable jewels, for which Surâshṭra is celebrated in the *Purâṇas*,—the other four being the river Gomati, beautiful women, good horses, and lastly Dvârakâ. The fame of the great temple of Someśvara fired the fanatic zeal of Maḥmud of Ghazni, who led an army of thirty thousand men lightly equipped against it in 1025 A.D., and re-

‡ This is Sâbar Kundlâ.

duced the fort after an obstinate resistance on the part of the Hindu chiefs, who had leagued to defend their shrine. "Fifty thousand infidels and more," says the *Rozat us-safa*, "were slain round this temple, which was of vast dimensions." But at length Maḥmud prevailed, destroyed the sacred *liṅga* by a fire lighted round it to break the hardness of the stone, plundered the temple of its immense wealth, and carried off its gates to Ghazni (to appear again in history after a lapse of more than eight centuries,—when gates were brought from Kâbul as trophies—believed by some to be those of S o m a n â t h a). The temple, it is said, was supported by fifty-six pillars, ornamented with rubies, emeralds, and other precious stones; and each of these pillars bore the name of a different king of India as its embellisher. Whether Maḥmud destroyed the temple also we do not know, but it is pretty certain that not a vestige of it now remains, unless it be in the capitals and columns strewn all about and built into the walls of the present temple, of the town and its houses.

It was too profitable to the Brâhmaṇs, however, not to be soon restored by the Hindu princes under their influence. Among these its greatest benefactors were probably the Solaṅki princes of Anhilapaṭṭan, and accordingly there is evidence of its having been restored by Bhima Deva I. (A.D. 1021-1073). We find Siddha Râja (1093-1142) visiting it about a century after its desecration by Maḥmud; and again, in A.D. 1168, the great Kumârapâla, in search of a way to manifest his piety, is advised by the wily Jaina Âchârya Hemachandra to restore the temple of Someśvara. And with this is connected a tale that is perhaps worth repeating:—In two years the restoration was completed,—the temple "once more resembled Meru," and the Brâhmaṇs, jealous of the influence of the Âchârya over the king, tried to entrap him, proposing to Kumârapâla that he should accompany the royal retinue to the dedication. When the proposal was made, the Jaina at once replied, "What need of pressing the hungry to eat? Pilgrimage is the life of the ascetic; what need is there of an order from the king?" He then started on foot to visit the holy places of his own creed, and met Kumârapâla at Somanâtha. At the inauguration of the new temple the Jaina astonished the spectators by his devotions to Śiva. At the threshold of the temple he exclaimed, "In the splendour of this shrine Mahâdeva, who dwells in Kailâsa, is surely present." Then entering and going through the prescribed gesticulations before the *liṅga*, he said, "Thou existest, whatever be thy place, whatever be thy time, whatever be thy name, of whatsoever nature thou art. Thou art he in whom is no guilty act, no guiltiness consequent upon the act,—one only god. Praise be to thee! He who has destroyed the affections, which are the seeds that produce the bud of existence, be he Brahmâ, be he Vishṇu, be he Śiva, to him be praise!" Then falling flat on the ground he worshipped Śiva in the *dandavata*. All this was done with an object; and after the ceremonies were over, Kumârapâla and Hemachandra entered the shrine alone, closing the door behind them.

Here, the story says, the Âchârya made Someśvara reveal himself to the king and address him thus :—"O king, this monk is an incarnation of all the gods; he is free from deceit; to him it is given to behold the divinity as a pearl in his hand; he knows the past, present, and future; understand that the path he shall show you is, without doubt, the road to liberation." The credulous king was caught, and there and then the Jaina administered to him a vow to abstain from animal food and fermented liquor to the end of his life. The temple of Somanâtha was then left in charge of Vṛihaspati Gauḍa, a Kanauj Brâhmaṇ; but, perhaps chagrined at the victory of Hemachandra, he reviled the Jaina religion, for which he was deprived of his place, and only restored to it after making the most humble submission to the influential Âchârya.

If the remains that still exist are not those of the temple of Bhima Deva and Kumârapâla, it is difficult to say to whom we owe them. It seems probable that for more than a century after Kumârapâla's time it was unmolested; but the Muhammadan had cast his eyes on the rich province, and at length, in 1297, the Śulṭân, Âlau' d-dîn Khilji, sent his brother Alaf Khân, and Nusrat Khân, his prime minister, to effect the conquest of Gujarât. Then it was that the idol shrines suffered, and the famous idol of Somanâtha was again destroyed. A century later, in 1395, Muzaffar Shâh I. led an expedition against Paṭṭan, and, destroying all the Hindu temples, he built mosques in their places,—or more probably he converted them into mosques; and again, in 1413,

Ferishṭah tells us that his grandson and successor, Aḥmad Shâh I., on his return from an expedition against the Râ of Junâgaḍh, "destroyed the temple of Somapur, wherein were found many valuable jewels and other property." Later still Maḥmud Shâh I., surnamed Begara (1459-1511) is named by Hindu tradition as having sent an army to reduce the place, when he built a mosque on the site of the temple. The building, however, still attests that the Muslim only desecrated the Hindu temple, defaced its sculptures, and converted it into a place of worship for the followers of Islâm, but did not raze it.

This famous ruin occupies a rising ground, probably a rock with a coating of soil upon it, close to the sea-shore. It faces the east, and on the south side there are still considerable remains of the old Hindu sculptures, much resembling those at Amaranâth, near Kalyâṇa, but on a larger scale. On the other sides, the outer facing of the walls has been almost entirely removed: indeed, until a few years ago, this fine old ruin was used as a sort of quarry from which to obtain building-stones. The outer pyramidal roof of the *maṇḍapa* and the great spire over the shrine had been destroyed by the Muhammadans, and hemispherical domes substituted in their place. Over the eastern entrance they erected two clumsy minarets, and threw arches in between the pillars of the central octagon which support the dome. The diameter of this octagon is about 33 feet, and the greatest width of the *maṇḍapa* inside is 64 feet, its length up to the door of the shrine being nearly 70 feet. The shrine itself is 18 feet 9 inches square inside, and there has been a *pradakshiṇa* round it; but behind this all is destroyed. The floor has been of polished black stone or marble, some fragments of which are still found. Both the domes are now open above, and the whole has evidently been for long the haunt of cattle rather than of devotees—Muslim or Hindu.

To compensate for its loss to her religion and its local attendants the Somapada Brâhmaṇs, the famous Ahilyâ Bâî, widow of Khaṇḍe Râo Holkar, built another temple—*New Somanâtha*—in the town; but if the hand of time only has to do with both, it will be a neglected ruin before its aged predecessor is greatly changed.

In the town is the *Surya Kuṇḍa*, as the Hindus call it,—a remarkable remnant of their architecture. It has been defaced, and patched, and altered now, but when first completed it must have been a work of much elegance, forming the colonnade round a large tank—long ago filled up except a small pond about nine yards square in one corner of the enclosure. This colonnade has had at least three rows of pillars on three of its sides, and seven on the fourth,—in which are five octagonal areas each about 20 feet across. The columns still standing, some of them imbedded in the outer walls, are about two hundred and fifty in number, and nearly all of them have been carved in the most elaborate style of Hindu art. A wall has been built in, connecting the outer row of pillars, and a *mimbar* and *mihrabs* have been formed to adapt it to Muhammadan worship.

Near this is a plain building, its walls outside covered with plaster, and apparently an ordinary

Muhammadan house with scarcely any windows; inside, however, it proves to have been a Jaina temple of an interesting type, and said to have a cellar (*bhoinorun*) under it. It is now used as a storehouse by a Muhammadan, who says it has been in his family for at least a hundred and fifty years.

A little to the north of Paṭṭan Somanâtha there is a large cluster of sacred places, many of them very unpretending in appearance, but each with its legend or associations. First is T r i v e n i— 'three plaited locks'—the junction of the three rivers Hiraṇyâ, Kapila, and Sarasvatî,—a *tîrtha* for pilgrims bathing, and without a visit to which the pilgrimage to Dvârakâ would scarcely be considered complete. Further out is the temple of Rudreśvara, built on the site of an older temple of Kedâreśvara destroyed by the Muhammadans,—some of the columns and sculptures of which, however, have been employed in the restored building. Beside it is the *dargah* of Muḥammad Shâh;—for Islâmite superstition is fond of thrusting itself into notice in the scenes where it has displayed its iconoclastic fanaticism. This *dargah* and that of Abbi Shâh, a little further out, are but miserable places, scarcely worth a visit, unless it be to half suffocate one's self in the labyrinth of little cells at the back of the first. Beyond some quarries is the old temple of Sûrya Nârâyaṇa, whose dome and spire have suffered at the hands of violence, but have been plastered over to keep out the rain. Under it is a cellar or cave.

On the banks of the river Hiraṇyâ we find D e v asarga or Dehotsarga—an old *pipal* tree with a very small temple beside it, and some huts forming a monastery ; this is a place of great sanctity, for under the *pipal*, of which the present one is a traditionary scion, Kṛishṇa lay down to rest at noon, when a Bhiḷḷa—mistaking his tawny coverlet for a deer, or the mark on his foot for the eyes of one—sped an arrow with such mortal force as bereft his godship of life. Islâmite devotion here consecrates a place of prayer for its votaries under their sacred tree, and desecrates its vicinity by making it a place of graves. The Hindus have, many a time since its erection, had the power to destroy the offensive and ugly wall, but they do not seem possessed of such aggressive and iconoclastic propensities. South from this are the small shrines of Koṭeśvara,—or the million *liṅgas*, containing only large fragments of the symbol,—and Bhimeśvara or Bhimanâtha, now much dilapidated. Not far from these is Bhalka Kuṇḍa, a reservoir—empty at least in the dry season—in excellent repair, about three hundred and eighty yards in circumference, and forming a regular polygon of sixteen sides, with three oval apertures on one for the entrance of the water. To the west of Paṭṭan, the spire of the Śeshi Bhushan or Bhidiyo temple attracts the eye by its height—owing principally, however, to the higher level on which the temple stands : it is a restoration, rather than a renewal, of an old temple, and is of similar style to that of Sûrya Nârâyaṇa.

It is curious to find here remnants of the Brâhmaṇical monasteries. There are several of them in this neighbourhood, not apparently of any great extent or with numerous inmates, nor are the buildings in any way pretentious—they are mere collections of huts.§

[*Note* 5:—*on Ahilyâ Bâî.*]

The famous Ahilyâ Bâî was born in 1735 of a family of the name of Sindhia, and was married to Malhâr Râo Holkar's only son *Khaṇḍe Râo,* who was killed at the siege of Kambhîr, near Dîg, in 1754. By him she had a son *Malli Râo,* and a daughter *Muktâ Bâî.* Malli Râo succeeded his grandfather Malhâr Râo, but nine months after died mad, when Ahilyâ Bâî succeeded to the administration of the Holkar government, 1765, and ruled with great wisdom, firmness, and talent till her death in 1795. She was a most devoted Hindu, and built sacred edifices at Jagannâtha, Nâsik, Elurâ, Nimâr, Maheśvara, Somanâtha, Dvârakâ, Gâyâ, Kedarnâtha, Rameśvaram, &c. Her daughter Muktâ Bâî became a *sati* with her husband, Yasvant Râo Panśiya, and Ahilyâ Bâî built a beautiful temple to her memory at Maheśvara, on the Narmadâ.

Account of Korinâr.

This town is the residence of a governor or *hâkam,* and is situated on the banks of the Shingora. The temple of Muta Dvârakâ and the port is on the sea-coast. The Bokhâri and Qâderi Sayyids obtained it in *wazifah* from the Amirs and Shâhs of Gujarât, and dwell here; but in

§ *Notes of a Visit to Kâṭhiâvâḍ in* 1869, pp. 17 *et seq.*

Sâmvat 1780 the Dekhaṇîs [Marâṭhâs] prevailed, and obtained a moiety of the revenue. In course of time a *peshkash* of five thousand rupees was paid through the management of the Divânji Sâheb Amarji, and the Gâikvâḍi official (*mutasaddi*) was not admitted to a share in the management, after whose death his younger brother the Divân Dulabhji paid a fixed sum by way of farm. Now, in Saṁvat 1871 (A.D. 1814), Govind Râo Gâîkvâḍ has, by the aid of the English Government, obtained possession of the whole parganah. In it is also situated Rudrâkya, a place of ablution for Hindus.

The revenues amount to two lâkhs of Jâmîs [2,00,000 *koḍîs*].

Unâ and Delvâḍâ.

The forts of Unâ and Delvâḍâ, built of white stone, are two *kos* distant from each other.

The residence of the governor looks over the river Machundri. The Talâo and the Châcheria Wâv were built in Saṁvat 1515 (A.D. 1458) by a Kâyat named Somanâtha.

It is related that in ancient times, when this country was under the government of Brâhmaṇs, the Râṇi of a Râja whose name was Vejal, who was of the tribe of Wâjâ, happened to arrive on a visit to the temple of Sûraj, where the Musulmâns have a mosque at present, and that some Brâhmaṇs immodestly and boldly lifted up the curtain of her chariot, without any civility, and had a look at her beauty. This affront the Râjputs passed by at the time, but attacked the Brâhmaṇs on their great holiday, the 15th of Śrâvaṇa Śud [on which they put on the sacred thread], slew many, and took the fort. In course of time, however, the Kasbâtis again expelled the Râjputs, and occasionally lived in independence, but at times acknowledged the supremacy of Muzaffarâbâd, or accepted a governor from Junâgaḍh ; and for some time Manohardâs and Somaji Jikâr were the Mutasaddis in behalf of the Navâb Mahâbat Khânji, whom they accepted as their ruler.

In Saṁvat 1825 (A.D. 1768) the Divân Sâheb Amarji levied a fixed tribute from Unâ ; afterwards, in Saṁvat 1827 (A.D. 1770-71), on account of the evil conduct of the Kasbâtis, Latif Mian, a Sayyid of Delvâḍâ, conquered the place from them, and they were banished from their *vatan*, but through the aid of the Divân Sâheb Amarji they were again reinstalled in their former holdings.

The temple of Dâmodhar, the place of pilgrimage of Hazrat-Shâh, Raghunâth, Guptaprâyâga, and Mahâ Kâleśvara are the ornaments of this mahâl. Without the town is a tank of sweet water, and at a distance of twelve *kos* is the temple of Tulsi Syâm, with a spring of hot water ; and ten *kos* further, at Dohan, is a fine temple of Mahâdeva. In the woods are many wild plantain trees.

The revenues amount to three lâkhs of Jâmis.

ACCOUNT OF RÂNPUR.

This is a fort at the foot of Mount Girnâr, and is the *jâgir* of Muzaffar Khân II. Its produce amounts to thirty thousand Jâmîs.

VISÂVADAR.

This is a fort with four towers. Most of this pargaṇa is deserted, and on its frontier is nothing but jungle and forest of useful and of jungly trees. The Gir hills are forty *kos* in length and twenty-five in breadth; there is also cultivation in some parts.

The revenue of this parganah is 20,000 *koḍîs*.

MUZAFFARÂBÂD.

This country was colonized by Muzaffar Shâh Gujarâti in Saṁvat 1632 (A.D. 1575), who built the fort on the sea-shore and garrisoned it with Râjputs; they cultivate both dry and irrigated land.

The revenues amount to one lâkh of Jâmîs.

THE ISLAND OF DIV, WHICH FORMERLY BELONGED TO JUNÂGAḌH.

In ancient times the zamindârs of this island were Vâghelâ Râjputs; but Shams-al-din Khân took it from Vaghelâ Jayasingh in the Saṁvat year 1387 (A.D. 1330) and established a *thânah*, and during the reign of Sulṭân Bahâdur Shâh the Mutasaddis of this place were Kavâm-al-mulk and Malik Ṭughân Ben Ayâz. In Saṁvat 1588 (A.D. 1531) some Portuguese arrived treacherously in the guise of merchants, but they were captured and surrendered to the Sulṭân, who made Musulmâns of them; on that occasion also several cannon were taken, and the two which are [in the Uparkoṭ] at Junâgaḍh probably came from this place; afterwards, however, the Portuguese came into the possession of Div, and the manner in which this happened is as follows:—

When Bahâdur Shâh, who had come, on the second occasion, by way of Khambâyat to Div, the Portuguese who were there represented to him that they had brought three hundred *mans* of rose-water and of *aṭar*, which were in danger of being spoilt before merchants arrived from various parts to remove them, and requested to be allowed to build four walls. The Sulṭân agreed, but after his departure they erected a strong fort, which they provided with cannon and muskets, and prepared for war. When this news reached the Sulṭân, he determined to get possession of the fort by treachery and to expel the Portuguese; he arrived accordingly, but, being aware of his intention, they slew Sulṭân Bahâdur Shâh in Saṁvat 1593 (A.H. 943), and became masters of the island. The names of the six men who were killed together with Bahâdur Shâh are as follows:—Malik Amîn, Shuja'et Khân, Lashkar Khân [Âlp Khân], Sikandar Khân, and Gaṇesh Râo the brother of Maidani

Râo. It is asserted that the fort of Divbandar and the buildings with gardens were all constructed by Malak Ayâz.

The revenues amount to one lâkh of Jâmîs (1,50,000 *koḍîs*).

Account of Kâṭhiâvâḍ.

For some reason or other, Kâṭhîs of thirty different tribes emigrated to this country from Khorâsân, and some also from Pâvar, a district in Kachh. The Wâlâ Kâṭhîs are of the stock of the Râjput Wâlâs, the lords of the district of Ḍhânk, one of whom married a Kâṭhiâni damsel, and was therefore expelled from the Râjput caste, and entered that of the Kâṭhîs. From this union resulted two sons, Khumân and Khâchar respectively, to whom the Râja of Junâgaḍh granted a small territory. And when this territory become populous that zillâ was called Kâṭhiâvâḍ.

It is related that Shams Khân slew the Wâlâ Râja in battle, and took possession of the town of Kileśvara, situated in the Baraḍâ hills; and when he conquered Okhamaṇḍal he demolished the temple of Jagat, placed over the spot a sort of mosque, and returned. Châmparâj, son of Ebhal the Kâṭhi, happened to have a daughter of wonderful beauty, whom Shams Khân coveted without having seen her, but Châmparâj refused all his offers, as no marriage is to be contracted with persons following a different religion; accordingly he was attacked by Shams Khân and slain, with his daughter, and 1,800 adherents all of whom died fighting bravely.

Some time afterwards V e r â W â l â, a Kâṭhi, with the permission of the Navâb Bahâdur Khân, built the fort of J e ṭ p u r. The Kâṭhîs pay a great deal of tribute and annually one horse likewise to Junâgaḍh; but they live on plunder and make raids to the extreme limits of Gujarât.

The beauty of the Kâṭhi women was remarkable in former times, and the Khumân Kâṭhîs used to carry off by force handsome women from amomg the lower classes; now, however, Kâṭhi women are frightful to look at, like demons and *ghûls*. The Kâṭhîs are brave and hospitable, and their principal towns are the forts of J e ṭ-p u r, M e n d a r d â, B i l k h â, B a g a s a r â, K u n d a l â, J a s d â n, C h i t a l, S u d â m r â, Â n a n d a p u r, B h â d l â, D h â n d h a l p u r, and P â l i y â ḍ [with large or small forts]. G a-ḍ h a r â is also a fort, but not a strong one.

Account of Amreli.

After the demise of the Navâb Sâheb Hâmid Khân, the Gâikvâḍ's Nâib Divân Sâheb Viṭhal Râo, by the aid of the English, took from his son the whole of Amreli, by way of *nazarânah*, though formerly the Gâikvâḍ had but a third-share in the revenue; now, however, in Saṁvat 1869 (A.D. 1812-13), the Gâikvâḍ took the whole parganah, and built a fort and ruled independently.

The revenues amount to six lâkhs of Jâmîs (about Rs. 2,00,000).

Account of the Mahâls which pay Tribute to Junâgaḍh.

Purbandar, situated on the sea-shore, has a well frequented port and a strong citadel. Here the zamindâr is a Jeṭhvâ Râjput who is a descendant of Makaradhvaja, son of Hanumân. The town contains numerous gardens, and both sweet and brackish water; and the inhabitants, who trade with the ships, are Vâṇiâs and Bhâṭiâs. The temples of Kedârnâtha Mahâdeva, of Sudâma, of Verâvalimâtâ, of Porabhavâni, and the Kedârkuṇḍa, are much visited by the inhabitants.

The Râjas here bore the title of Râṇâ, and in ancient times the fort of Ghumli,|| situated in the Baraḍâ hills, was the capital of the state; it was, however, deserted seven hundred years ago, on account of the devastations committed by the army of the Jâm which he had brought from Sindh, and which demolished the fort. The citadel of Bhânvâr obtained its name from the Râṇâ Bhâna (Jeṭhvâ).

The government of the Râṇâs extended as far as Nâgnah, founded by the Râṇâ Nâga, and the temple of Nâganâtha is also one of his memorials. About three hundred years ago the Râṇâ was put to flight by the army of the Jâm Râval, and took refuge with the Mer tribe.

|| See above, p. 58.

The rule of the Jâm extended as far as R â ṇ â W â v and the creek of Bhokirah; but by his liberality, justice, and distribution of food the Râṇâ attached that wild tribe to himself, and they conquered for him with their swords the country on the west side of the Baraḍâ hills, and acknowledged him as their sovereign.

In course of time Nâgars from all sides were invited and settled at the places of Chhâya, Râṇâ Wâv, Mokal, Dhebar, &c., which became their *jâgirs;* and the Râṇâ entrusted the management of his affairs to them, and to this day a tribe of Nâgars is called after the name of those villages.

In Saṁvat 1789 (A. D. 1722) Mubâriz-al-mulk made his appearance at M â d h a v p u r in order to collect *peshkash,* and with the assistance of the Navâb Bahâdur Khân of Junâgaḍh the fort of M â d h a v p u r was taken. In this contest [Ranchoḍdâs] Nâgar, the Thânahdâr of the place, was slain, and after the locality had been plundered the inhabitants paid forty thousand Jâmi *koḍis* as a ransom for the image of P â r a s-n â t h a.

It is related that there was a lady named Sôn, of the lineage of a râja of B â l a m b h â. She composed a hemistich in Hindî, and giving it to a Brâhmaṇ informed him that she would be ready to take any man for her husband who could compose the other hemistich. The Brâhmaṇ started on his journey according to her direction, but was disappointed until he arrived in G h u m l i, where he met the Kunwar Halâman Jeṭhvâ, the son of Sehyâ Râṇâ, who wrote a hemistich as required, and handed it to the Brâhmaṇ. On his return the Brâhmaṇ delivered the line to Râṇî Sôn, who, intent on keeping her promise, mounted a chariot and arrived in Ghumli; but alas! alas! for times in which females do not break their promises, but men in one hour turn away from their oaths and written obligations, like the revolving sphere! The Râṇâ Sehyâ heard of the bride's beauty, and himself became enamoured of her and desired to obtain her favours; but he had apprehensions as to Halâman, and therefore immediately banished him for a term of twelve years from his realm. Halâman departed to Anjâr, a town in Kachh, where his paternal aunt dwelt; but Sôn likewise returned to her country, and Sehyâ Jeṭhvâ reaped only sorrow and disappointment. One day, however, Halâman was rocking himself in a hammock slung to the branch of a tree, when some fairies perceived his beauty and took him up into the air; when they discovered, however, that he was only a human being, they dropped him to the ground. The fall almost killed Halâman, but as his aunt knew that his very life was bound up with his love for Sôn she despatched a ship with the news to her; and Sôn, whilst embarking in it, exclaimed—

"A ship I mount, O wind of mercy blow,
Perchance my love again will greet my sight!"

The ship arrived more quickly than the fleeting cloud, and when Sôn took Halâman into her arms he recovered consciousness, and although discarded by fairies he was soon joined to one as beautiful.

In 1790 (A.D. 1733) Mubâriz-al-mulk, the Subâh of Gujarât, and his commander of the forces, Safdar Khân Bâbi, arrived with an army at Purbandar, and the Râṇâ, being unable to offer any resistance, fled and embarked everything he could, with his family, in ships and put to sea. The army took possession of seven cannon, with all the baggage which had been left behind, and was ready to demolish the fort, when the helpless Râṇâ made his appearance and saved the fort from destruction by paying one lâkh and twenty-five thousand Jâmis.

In Saṁvat 1805 (A.D. 1748) Kuṭiânâ was taken by the Râṇâ from the Qasbâtis, and held by him for ten years, after which time it fell into the power of Hâsham Khân, with the coöperation and aid of the Qasbâtis. In Saṁvat 1782 the Râṇâ bought Mâdhavpur from the Desâis of Mângrol, and incorporated it with his possessions. In Saṁvat 1830 Sheikh Miân from Mângrol took, under cover of night, possession of the fort of Nayi, situated on the sea-coast, by scaling its walls with ladders, but the Râṇâ Sulṭânji called to his aid Jâḍejâ Kumbhoji, Zamindâr of Gondal, who was a connection of his by marriage, and erected batteries against the fort, and Shekh Mian obtaining quarter surrendered the place.

In the Saṁvat year 1834 he built the fort of Bhetâli, on the limits of the country of Nagar (the borders of Hâllâr); it was beleaguered by Mehrâman, a Khavâs of the Jâm, for some time, with a native army. To make short work of the matter, he constructed a moveable fort called Rângaḍh, and making an assault reached the walls, against which he placed ladders; but the assailants had not ascended to the middle of them when such a fire of musketry poured upon them from the fort, and fiery projectiles were thrown upon the Musulmâns, that they became unwilling fire-worshippers and retreated, while burning the slain Hindus became superfluous. In spite of this disgraceful repulse, Mehrâman Khavâs did not raise the siege, and Ṭhakar Premji Lohâna, Kâmdâr of Râṇa Sulṭânji, opened negotiations for aid through a paternal uncle of the author, whose name was Govindji, for a long time Faujdâr of Kuṭiânâ. When the victorious army approached nearer, Mehrâman Khavâs raised the siege and made peace; whereupon the army marched from that place towards Okhâ to subdue the robbers of Positarâ, who robbed the people by land and by sea, and those events have already been narrated. The account of this will be given in connection with Junâgaḍh.

In the Saṁvat year 1839 Ṭhakar Premji,

Kâmdâr of Purbandar, having become haughty and fat like a tumour, in the exuberance of his power, made an alliance with Mehrâman Khavâs of Navânagar and Kumbhâji of Gondal :—

A tree which has scarcely yet taken root
A strong brave man will soon eradicate ;
But if you leave it long to thrive and grow
No strength of windlass will pull up its root.

As the Divân Amarji, like the brilliant sun, was day by day prospering more, the three tâlukdârs just mentioned attempted to break his power ; they attacked him, but were quickly put to flight with their troops.

In Saṁvat 1843 the Divân Amarji took Chorvâḍ from Sanghâji Raizâdâh, a relative of Râṇâ Sulṭânji, who, on account of his quarrels with Pîthâyet Hâthi, the Zamindâr of Mâlya, was unable to pay the wages of his troops. After accomplishing this object, the army of Junâgaḍh marched to Verâval, held by the Jamadârs Rakhia Banhura and Ibrâhim Khân Paṭṭani, who were disloyal towards the Navâb Sâheb ; the fort walls were scaled by ladders, and Diler Khân, the cowardly Thânâdâr, took to his heels ; so that the Divân Sâheb Raghunâthji was able in a very brief time to conquer both the forts.

In Saṁvat 1855 Kalyâṇ Sheṭ, the Divân of the Navâb Sâheb at Junâgaḍh, fled to Kuṭiânâ, where he raised the standard of revolt, and plundered the country of Drâphâ, but the

Râṇâ Sulṭânji prepared an army to encounter him, and the author being in the Râṇâ's service was appointed to march with cannon and troops to punish Kalyâṇ Sheṭ.

The beginning of Divân Ranchoḍji's remaining in the service of Râṇâ Sulṭânji was as follows :— The author had taken his departure from Nagar to Mângrol with some horsemen to celebrate the wedding of his younger brother Dalpatrâm, whilst the Divân Sâheb Raghunâth had himself remained in Nagar; and Mehrâman Khavâs, perceiving the field free, and disregarding politeness, imprisoned the Nâgar Kârkuns of the tribe of Buj who dwelt in the same street as we did. The Divân Sâheb being helpless, the Sirbandi attached to the Divân's house having gone to Mângrol, despatched a letter to the author, which reached him whilst he was encamped at Devrâ, on his return journey from Mângrol; accordingly he sent all his men to Navânagar, and went himself to the Râṇâ Sulṭânji at Purbandar.

In fine, when I arrived in the vicinity of Kuṭiânâ, Kalyân Sheṭ, Jamadâr Nâsar bin Yamani, with Yahya and others, also Gangâsingh Purbhiâ with Qasbâti and other troopers, marched out to the sound of kettle-drums with banners and cannon, drawing their troops up in battle array near the Idgâh of Kuṭiânâ. On perceiving this display I slowly approached the foe with my troops till we could almost touch them with our swords and spears, but they ran like a herd of sheep from brave lions, and did not stop till they reached the bâzâr of the town, and their cannon and some of their men were taken. As a reward for this victory the Râṇâ presented me with a necklace of pearls and a palanquin.

In Saṁvat 1864 [A. D. 1807] Hâlâji Kuṅvar made Jamadâr Omâr his secret partner, and by promises of gifts of pearls, &c. he obtained possession of the fort of Khirasrâ from Subadâr Khân Afghan. He then plundered Mâdhavpur and took possession of the fort of Navîbandar by scaling its walls with ladders in the darkness of the night; his intention was to take Purbandar also, but it was not fulfilled. Râṇâ Sultânji called to his aid the Divânji Sâheb Viṭhal Râo, who, through the intervention of the Divân Sâheb Raghunâthji, under whose protection Omâr the Jamadâr was, suppressed the rebellion by paying one lâkh of Jâmîs [*koḍîs*]. In the Saṁvat year 1865 (A. D. 1808) Hâlâji Kuṅvar, through the Divân Raghunâthji, under pretence of requiring protection, but in reality to capture his own father, had taken into his service the Jamâdâr Murâd Khân, Faqir Muḥammad Mekrâni, and Sheikh Muḥammad Zobaidi the Arab, and again rebelled, but, being unable successfully to oppose the Râṇâ, they fled to Kandornâ, which was in their possession, where they took refuge, but surrendered it after a few days to the Jâm Sâheb Jasâji, who promised them their former service and gave them the sum of one lâkh of

Jâmîs [*koḍîs*]. Hâlâji despatched his Vakils to implore assistance from the Huzûr Alexander Walker Sáheb, who had accompanied the Subah of Kâṭhiâvâḍ, Divân Sâheb Viṭhal Râo, in aid of the Gâikvâḍ, and who, levying tribute, had established their fear amongst the zamindârs. The noble-minded Sâheb immediately marched, took the fort in two hours, but granted pardon to the garrison; and, as Kuṭiânâ was near, by order of the Divânji Sâheb Raghunâthji, the author was admitted to the honour of waiting on the Sâheb Bahâdur, and offering as *nazaránah* a horse and a Yemani sword set with jewels; he met Ballantine Sâheb and Robertson Sâheb twice, and twice received a handsome dress. On that occasion the Colonel said, "You are well disposed towards the Sarkâr Company Bahâdur, and you will be much regarded. Be of good cheer, and if you come with me to Baroda you will obtain an honourable post in the Company's service." But, as I did not think proper to separate from the country of Kuṭiânâ, I took leave at Pâl and returned.

On this occasion I had gone in the company of the Amir-like Alexander Walker to see the fort of Ghumli, but I saw only ruins, a burnt and fallen temple, a deep *wáv* full of limpid water, some ancient dilapidated edifices, two tanks, and a wall on the hill which is called the fort Âbâpurâ.

In Saṁvat 1866 (A.D. 1809) the Râja assigned

a share in the revenues of Purbandar to the servants of the Sarkâr Company Bahâdur, and the farm of the revenue to Sundarji Khatri; Prathirâj Kuṅvar resisted, but on aid coming from the Company Ṣarkâr the fort of Chhâyâ was evacuated in two hours and made over to Hâlâji. The Kuṅvar, being wounded, was captured, with his wife, but the *sipâhis* were so greedy to have the golden anklets of his grandmother that they cut off her feet.

After the demise of Hâlâji the reign of Prathirâj began, and the old inhabitants, who were Lohânâs and Nâgars, emigrated. Râṇâ Sulṭânji himself was, after the death of his son, received into the mercy of God in Saṁvat 1869.

The *mandir* of Mâdhavarâî is situated in the fort of Mâdhavpur, in the tâlukâ of Purbandar; and the *kuṇḍa* named Sita-mundri, which is very well known, is situated at a distance of two *kos* therefrom. In this zillâ—*mung* (pulse), *kashiya* (*Phaseolus radiatus*), and sugar-canes are produced; most of the soil is alluvial and produces three crops annually. The forts of Chhâyâ, Râṇâwâv, Adwânâ, Miâni, Navî, Kandorna, and Mâdhavpur are dependencies of this mahâl; on the west is the sea; on the east are Kuṭiânâ, Mahiâri, and Mângrol; on the south the sea; and on the north the hills of Baraḍâ and the district of Hâlâr. There are two seaports, namely Purbandar and Navî, and the revenues amount to eight lâkhs of *koḍîs*.

Description of Gondal.

This is a district of H â l à r; it was deserted for some time, but Amîn Khân ben Tâtâr Khân Ghorî took charge of it in 1647 (A.D. 1590), for Muzaffar the Sulṭân of Gujarât, and cultivated it. Kuṅvar Vibhâji obtained it as *jâgir* from his father; but Kumbhâji bin Hâlâji, by his good fortune and his cunning, having got the zamindârîs of D h o r â j i and U p l e t â from the Navâb Sâheb for service done and for a little money, and having taken B h â y â v a d a r from the Desâîs Govind Râî and others, besides some villages from the Kâṭhîs and Râjputs, he built forts and established an independent *râj*. His good and mild government was extensively praised. By the help of the army of the Gâikvâḍ his own attacked Trimbakrâo with a number of Kâṭhîs and Girâsiâs, firing some cannon at the fort of Navânagar; but the Nâgars of the vanguard of the army were slain. The fort in G o n d a l was built on the banks of the Gonḍli river in ancient times, and up to our days graves may be seen there. In the year 1828 the Marâṭhâ army attacked that of Junâgaḍh, which was encamped at Majhevaḍî, and captured the Arab Jamadâr Sâlmîn, who was, however, afterwards released again.

The forts of M o v i â, of D h o r â j i, of U p l e t â, of B h â y â v a d a r, of G a n o d, of A n a l a g a ḍ h, and of M e n g n i belong to Gondal, which is bounded on the west by Ḍhank, on the east by the parganah of Râjkôṭ, on the west by the parganah of Dhrol, on the south by the parganah of Jeṭpur. These were formerly the limits, and the revenue amounts to ten lâkhs of Jàmîs.

Description of Râjkot.

This is a dependency of H â l â r, and was given as a *jâgir* to the holders by the Jâm Râval instead of Kâlâwad. He bestowed S a r d h â r on Masûm A'li Khân, who treacherously slew the Kâṭhîs that were the zamindârs of it. The fort of R â j k o ṭ was built of white stone by Lakhâji Jâḍejâ on the banks of the river Ajî. He divided scattered villages among his brothers, but Kotḍâ and Râjpura still belong to him. In Saṁvat 1875 (A.D. 1818) the English Sarkâr, the paramount power in Kâṭhiâvâḍ, built a handsome camp here. Râjkoṭ is bounded on the east by the Panchâl, on the west by Pardhari, on the north by Wânkâner and Thân, and on the south by Kâṭhiâvâḍ.

Description of Morbi.

Morbi was given as an *inâm* to Rao Bhârâ by the Dehli Sulṭâns in Saṁvat 1627 [A.D. 1550], for his surrender of Sulṭân Muzaffar into the hands of Âzam Humaiyun. After Râyaji had been slain by his younger brother Kâyaji, the latter, much as he tried, could not obtain full power, and was obliged to be content with M o r b i, A d h o î, and W â g a ḍ. In Saṁvat 1508 (A.D. 1451) the Faujdâr on the part of the

Shâh of Gujarât was Toghlak Khân, who built a strong fort on the banks of the Machhu river. The revenue of this district amounts to three lâkhs of Jâmîs; it produces good *jowâri*, and it is bounded on the east by Jhâlavâḍ, on the west by Dhrol, on the north by the Salt Raṇ, and on the south by Wânkâner.

Description of Bhâvanagar.

In ancient times most of the zillâs of this region were in the possession of the Audich string-wearers (Brâhmaṇs). Mokherâji, a Gohel Râjput, governed the island of Perim, and made a firm stand against the royal army which attacked him near Gundi. He obtained four *chorâsîs*, viz. those of Lâthi and others, from the Râja of Junâgaḍh on account of the connection with his daughter. It is said that the Sulṭân of Gujarât, having taken the Râja, kept him prisoner in a stable for horses. A potter having arrived there from Gohelvâḍ was gratuitously supplying water during the fasting month (Ramazân) to the guards, who considered themselves obliged thereby; in the mornings and evenings they were engaged in breaking the fast; on such an occasion the potter took the Râja, and, placing him on his donkey instead of the water-bag, carried him out of the town to a place where a party of Atîts was encamped, who received him in a handsome and kind way, dressed him as a *jogi* and took him to Śihor, where one of his cousins reigned. The Atîts sent in their Vakil with the following message :—"We are travellers and are in the habit of waiting on râjas ; we have brought arms, jewels, and shawls ; if orders are issued we will display these things and also offer presents." The Râja, who had no experience, agreed, and the Atîts, who entered the fort with their arms, seated the former Râja on the *masnad* and removed the new one. It is related that when the people saw the Râja in the state of a Darvaish, wearing red garments, they said, "This is a Râval," *i.e.* a darvaish ; and from that day he obtained the title of Râval. I have also heard that when the Râja fled from this captivity he went to Dungarpur, where his maternal uncle was reigning, and where he remained for several years. As the Râja of Dungarpur was one of the brothers of the Râja of Udaipur and had the title of Râval, he bestowed it also on his nephew ; but God knows best.

In Saṁvat 1779 (A.D. 1722) Bhâvâsing Râval built the fort of Bhâvanagar, of which he assigned a part of the revenues to the English and to the Peshvâ on the 3rd Vaiśâkh Śud. After him his grandson Vakhatsingji enlarged his territory by taking possession of some localities belonging to the Kolîs and Kâṭhîs, and obtained Goghâbârah and Râjula from the Navâb Sâheb Aḥmad Khân, and became very strong and prosperous.

The tâlukâ G o g h â was given by the Sulṭâns of Gujarât to the Bâbis, and afterwards in Saṁvat 1810 (A.D. 1753) it came into the possession of Momin Khân, and then into that of the Śrimant Peshvâ. When in course of time Sohrâb Khân and Momin Khân removed Sher Zamân Khân from Goghâ, it fell into the hands of Vakhatsingh, and he is still the joint possessor of it with the English.

The fort of T a l â j â was taken by the aid of the Divânji Sâheb Amarji; and, Saṁvat 1850 (A.D. 1793), Wakhatsinghji took C h i t a l, which from the number of the Kâṭhîs, and the aid of the Navâb Sâheb Hâmid Khân Bahâdur, was very strong, and he destroyed the fort of J a s d a n. In the Saṁvat year 1852, after the fighting was over, the Navâb Sâheb granted a *parvânâ* for K u n d l â and other places on condition of paying tribute. The parganahs Mâhuva, Talâjâ, Râjulâ, Kundlâ, Sihor, Dihor, Trâpaj, Umrâlâ, Pâtana, and Botâd are dependencies of Bhâvanagar. The fort of Ṡ i h o r is the capital, and is situated between two mountains. The temple of R o v â p u r i in Bhâvanagar is a celebrated one. The three ports are M â h u v a, G o g h â, and B h â v a n a g a r, to which numerous merchants resort in ships. Here fine *âmbas* (mangoes), *gundâs*, and oleanders (*kanár*) are produced.

P â l i t â n â belongs to one of his *bhâyâd*. The fort is situated at the foot of Mount Ṡ a t r u ñ j a y a, which contains many ancient temples visited by pilgrims from distant places. The limits of Bhâvanagar are the sea on the east, on the west the parganah of Amreli, on the north Jhâlâvâḍ and Śrî Bhimnâth; on the south the parganah of Unâ Bâbriâvâḍ and of Muzaffarâbâd. The produce amounts to eight lâkhs of rupees.

Description of Jhâlâvâḍ.

This zillâ began to pay tribute during the time of the Divânji Sâheb Amarji, in Saṁvat 1832 (A.D. 1795), and was for some time the *jâgir* of Umdat-ul-Mulk. Chroniclers narrate that in Saṁvat 1320 (A.D. 1263) Siddhrâo Jayasiñha, the Râja of Gujarât, reigned in the capital city of Piran Paṭṭan, who had a wife beautiful as a fairy; it happened that a Deva or Râkshasa fell in love with her, and had intercourse with her every night after tying the Râja her husband up in a corner.

Hemistich:—An uncongenial consort is great misery.

The Râja had a confidential and faithful servant, a Râjput of the Jhâlâ tribe, whose name was Makwânâ Harpâl Valad Kesar, and to whom he promised a fine *jâgir* if he would relieve him from this enemy. The said Râjput agreed, kept his word and removed the Bhut; the Râja on his part was also desirous to fulfil his promise, and asked the Râjput how he wished to be rewarded. The latter replied, "Let every village be mine where I can bind a *toran* or string of green leaves during one night." The Râja agreed, and in one night Jogini—whose devotee the Râjput was—tied 1799 *torans* to as many villages, but when the Râjput arrived at the gate of Digsar the morning began to dawn. Accordingly the Râja gave all the villages thus marked to the Jhâlâ Râjput, and seven villages to the Chârans. As the Jhâlâ had adopted the Râṇî of Râja Siddhrâo Jayasiñha to be his sister, he gave her the five hundred villages of the Bhâl as a present, and kept the others for himself. Halwad and Dhrângadra were constituted seats of government, and the other parganahs were distributed among his sons and cousins. In course of time such places as Limbaḍi, Sailâ, Vânkâner, Lakhtar, Vaḍhvân, Thân, Chuḍâ, and others became separate tâlukâs, and were adorned with strong forts. Pratâpsingh Râja, in order to aid Jâm Tamâchi bin Râi Singh, who was his nephew, had given his own daughter to Mubâriz-al-mulk, and the daughter of one of his cousins, who was the Zamindâr of Mâthak, to Salâbat Khân Bâbi, by whose support he seated the Jâm on the throne of Nagar.

Sadâśiv Râmchandra captured the fort of Halwad in Saṁvat 1816 (A.D. 1758) and captured Râja Bâbhâ, who paid ransom and was released. Mubâriz-al-mulk laid siege to the fort of Vaḍhvân, which was so reduced by scarcity of water that by the intervention of Chatarsingh, Râja of Nârvar, an arrangement was come to by which a payment of *peshkash* or tribute was made in its behalf, so that Râja Arjan Singh remained in safety. In Saṁvat 1862 (A.D. 1805) Bâbâji Sâheb assailed the fort of Vaḍhvân with cannon and besieged it, but marched away disappointed. Fateh Singh Gâikvâḍ besieged the fort of Limbaḍi in Saṁvat 1831 [1834], but the Divânji Sâheb Amarji sent an army from Junâgaḍh to the aid of the Râja Harbhamji, whereupon Râo Sâheb Fateh Sing thought proper to make peace and depart.

In this country there is a great deal of alluvial soil ; it produces good *jowâri* and cotton, but no trees except *nim*.

Vânkâner is a strong fort on the banks of the Machhu river. Here the Râja Bhârâji Jhâla reigns, who was at first the *tilât* (or heir to the throne) of Halwad. When his father died, Tilât Sulṭânji went out of the town to perform the funeral ceremonies, but his brothers closed the gates and shut him out ; accordingly he went to Nagar, and with the aid of the Jâm took possession of Vânkâner, Thân, and 108 villages belonging to Mahyas and Bâbriâs, and thence he ravaged Jhâlâvâḍ ; he was afterwards slain in the battle of Màthak, but his descendants still reign at Vânkâner. The Râjas of Halwad and Vânkâner unite in Chandra Singh, the fifteenth ancestor of their line.

This country is mountainous ; the temple of Jadeśvara Mahâdeva, which has been repaired by the Divânji Sâheb Viṭhalrâo, is a famous one. In the mountains green, white, and black stones are quarried, and the Panchâl parganah adjoins them. Jhâlâvâḍ contains some celebrated temples, among which is that of Śrî Bhimnâth, the Atîts whereof are rich and esteemed, and also the temple of Somanâth.*

The total revenue of Jhâlâvâḍ is 5,00,000 rupees.

On the east of Jhâlâvâd are the parganahs of Pitlâd and Baroda, and on the west Morbi and Vânkâner, on the north Dhandhukâ and other parganahs and Viramgâm, and on the south the parganahs of Bhâvanagar and Khambâlâ.

The Râjas of Junâgaḍh.

An account of Mount Girnâr, of the excellencies and blessings of the temples of Śrî Girnâr, of Bhâvanâth, of Mahâdeva, of Mṛigikuṇḍa, of Dâmodarkuṇḍa, &c. is given in the *Prabhâsa-khaṇḍa,* which is a portion of the *Skandapurâṇa,* a book of great authority among the Hindus. Be it known that the great Râjas of the Solar and of the Lunar race who have passed away are countless :—

Distich :—How many heroes buried under ground
On earth no vestige of them can be found !

During the space of 2350 years Junâgaḍh was governed by Chuḍâsamâ, *i. e.* Lunar

* This is Ghelo Somanâth, and not the one near Prabhâsa Pâṭṭan.

Râjputs who were descendants of Śrî Sadâśiv, and who are said to have come in former times from Sindh, the throne devolving in regular succession to nine men of the name of Naughan, ten of the name of Jakhrâ, eleven of the name of Âlansingh, and to other individuals with various names, who became Râjas. As no chronicles exist of this dynasty of high lineage, and it would not be worth while to repeat mere tales, only a short account will here be given.

Râo Dayat and Kuvar Naughan.

A caravan of the Râja of Gujarât, whose capital was Pirân Pâṭṭan, happened to go on pilgrimage to Śrî Girnâr and Dâmodarakuṇḍa, and arrived in Junâgaḍh. It so happened that on this occasion Râo Dayât expressed his desire to marry the daughter of Râja Siddha Râo of Gujarât, who was extremely beautiful, and wanted her to be surrendered to him in lieu of the tax which was to be levied from the travellers. When the leader of the caravan perceived that there was no other way of getting out of the difficulty than by stratagem, he proposed that permission should be given first to go to Pirân Pâṭṭan, and then to return for the wedding in due state and with the customary presents. In this manner the Râja was deceived, and the caravan was allowed to depart.

When they had arrived in their own country, Râja Siddha Râo conceived the idea of getting possession of J u n â g a ḍ h and of enjoying the pleasures of Mount G i r n â r. Accordingly he took a girl of unparalleled beauty, clothed her in royal garments and placed her in a sumptuous chariot to represent his daughter the princess. She was accompanied by several young men dressed as females to attend upon her, as well as by five hundred carts supposed to be loaded with her dowry, but in reality each containing four valiant armed men. There was also a powerful vanguard preceding the large party, and announcing everywhere its arrival. Dayât, who suspected nothing, was so joyful that he adorned the city, opened his treasury liberally, and went out in great joy to meet his bride, in whose chariot he took his seat; when, however, this train entered the city, the gatekeeper, whose eyes were blind but whose mind was wide awake, exclaimed when he heard the heavy rattle of the carts, "The load of these wagons consists of able-bodied men, and not of tender girls." When the guards perceived that the secret was revealed, they quickly leaped out of the carts, shouting, "Boys, throw off your female garments! Use your swords; we are not women!" Accordingly they slew Dayât and took possession of the fort of Junâgaḍh.

On that frightful occasion a girl carried N a u g h a n K u ṅ v a r, who was a small boy, to a place called Alidhar, in the parganah of K o ḍ i n â r, to the house of an Ahir called D e v â i t, who was the Mukaddam or Pâṭîl of that place. In course of time certain scouts, glad to foment disturbances, informed the governor left by Siddha Râo at Junâgaḍh of this circumstance; accordingly men were despatched from Junâgaḍh to take Naughan forcibly away; but, as it is against the Hindu religion to surrender a person who has taken refuge in a house, Devâit preferred to give up his own son, whose head the malefactors immediately cut off, and Devâit exclaimed—

Hemistich:—If me you do not fear, fear God!

When the hard-hearted wretches were informed of their mistake, they shouted for Naughan, but Devâit brought another son, and another, until those butchers had killed all his seven sons; and, to his eternal honour, Devâit preserved the life of Naughan.

Distich:—He never dies who his religion keeps;
The moon is shining always in the world.

As it was the will of the omnipotent and most glorious Creator, the universal Benefactor, that the world-illuminating sun of Râja Naughan should rise with a horoscope of felicity, illuminating the world with the conquests and victories of his reign, and imparting eternal glory and freshness to the delightful country of Sindh, and to purge it from the thistles and chaff of rebellion, the executors of the divine commands had preserved his life from this wrathful dust of his cruel foes. In proof of this it may be stated that Devâit had a lovely daughter of tender age, for a long time the playmate of Kuṅvar Naughan; they lived with each other as sister and brother. When that girl, whose name was Jâsal, became of age, Devâit made a wedding feast for her on a large scale, but as the grief for his murdered sons was yet deep in his heart he invited all his tribe-fellows the Ahirs, who were extremely numerous, and consulted them on the subject; and they finally came to the determination to invite many of the followers of Siddha Râo and to slay them. Accordingly Devâit went to Junâgaḍh with great ceremony, and induced the Nâib of the Râja, with all the Amirs and grandees of the locality, to come to the wedding feast. The Râja himself was not aware of the proverb that it is folly to trust in the politeness of foes, and that the waves which lick the feet of the wall will overthrow it: accordingly they went; at the time of the repast Devâit caused them to sit in rows, and the Ahirs, at asignal from Râo Naughan, who had also the murder of his own father to deplore, fell upon the guests, all of whom were slain, and became themselves a splendid repast for the crows and vultures, whereas Naughan was carried to Junâgaḍh and placed on the throne in the Saṁvat year 874 (A.D. 817).

Naughan conquers Sindh.

There was a great famine in Saṁvat 895 (A.D. 838) in the country of Soraṭha, so that many persons died of hunger. The Ahirs, who had much cattle, heard that corn was cheap, and grass as well as water plentiful in Sindh, and went there; and among them also Devâit, with his beautiful daughter Jâsal, took up his abode in a beautiful fresh, pleasant, and green prairie. According to the hemistich:

The rose's beauties cannot be concealed.

Jâsal's attractions had reached the ears of Hamir Sumrâ, who, under pretence of hunting, went quite close to her dwelling.

Distich :—Not sight alone will love beget;
But speech will contribute to bliss.

He beheld a maiden beautiful beyond all description, and in comparison with whom even fairies would be plain-looking.

Verses :—Her form a palm, made by Mercy's hand;
The charms of grace her head adorned;
Her features Irem's garden's samples were,
With various hues of roses blooming;
Her chin so wonderfully beautiful,
Its dimple a well of immortality;
Her waist so slim and thin and accurate;
No one was ever born here beneath
To see her face and not to lose his heart.

At the sight of Jâsal's beauty the Sulṭân of love took possession of the Shâh's heart, and erected the flag of affection towards her in his breast, captivating him like a bird in the lasso of her curls.

The charms of love find entrance through the ear,
They rob the mind of peace, the heart of sense;
But sight makes grow the seed which speech has cast,—
Yes, hearing is but seeing's seed.

In short, the Shâh's passion was so fervent that he immediately asked for the hand of Jâsal, but the Ahir abhorred the uncongenial union of a Hindu maiden with a Muhammadan, and Hamir Sumrâ became angry.

Distich :—Patience abides not in a lover's heart,
Nor water in a sieve.

Accordingly he ordered the guards of the road to allow no one to pass in the direction of Soraṭha ; nevertheless Jâsal managed to send the following lines by means of a courier, who was quick as the lightning and rapid as the wind, secretly to her friend Naughan :—

Verses :—" My lord, have pity with my case :
I am in great calamity ;
I have no helper thee beside ;
Thou wilt distressed persons aid ;
My shame and honour do defend ;
Show me the road to our own land."

In conclusion, she besought Naughan to protect the honour of his adopted sister, in the same way as Śrî Kṛishṇa had protected Draupadi from her persecutors. As soon as Naughan had received these lines and perused them, he immediately collected an army consisting of Râjputs, Ahirs, Kolîs, Kâṭhîs, Khânts, Bâbriâs, and Mers in order to punish the godless Sumrâ, and marched by the way of Kachh through Lakhpatnagar to Sindh.

Distich :—

His numbers of the army when they took
The coats of mail three lâkhs they found to be.

When the Shâh of Sindh heard from his spies that Râja Naughan was approaching—

Distich :—

His tongue he from his mouth protruded ;
His breath had missed the way, and fast it stuck.

He coiled himself up like a snake in his rage, and roared like a famished lion, and was impatiently expecting Naughan, who was meanwhile approaching with an army reaching from the boundary of Kaśmîr to the mountains of Mekrân, turbulent like the waves of the ocean, countless in nnmbers, with fire-vomiting cannon, lightning-throwing guns, blood-shedding muskets, and all sorts of engines. The battle was fought on a fine morning, and the forces of Sumrâ were so arranged that his left flank consisted of Sammâs and Sumrâs, whilst his right consisted of Kâbulîs and Kaśmîrîs ; with the van were Mir Behrâm, Ibrâhim Kulikhân, and Jangiz Khân, while Mirza Kuli, A'li Haidar the lord of the Subâh of Peshâwar, and Shâdâdkhân Ghaznavi who kindled the flames of war, were with the centre ; whilst on the opposite the foe-breaking Mahârâja Sakatsing and Jakatsing Jâdu, Nâg Jeṭwâ and others, with a multitude of Kâṭhîs, such as Harsur Khâchar, and Devsur Wâlâ, and Nâgdân Khumân, and Râo Nunsar and Bahru Lâkâ, and Hirâ Kachhân on the left, and Pâṇḍurang Apâ, and Gaṇpat Râo Nimbalkar, and Bhujang Râo Bhonslâ were placed in the van, and with crowds of Ghâṭîs and others pushed on to meet the foe. When the opposite lines were arranged, a brisk cannonade opened the battle from both sides, followed by musketry fire* according to the Faranghi fashion, which sent many to their eternal rest and brought numberless heads to the ground. Afterwards the *mêlée* began, in which spears and swords were used promiscuously with darts, clubs, and arrows. The battle lasted from morning till evening, and Sumrâ was put to flight with his Baluchîs, leaving hills of corpses on the field. The Râjputs delivered Jâsal and took her, with all her friends, with many Lohânâs, Bhâṭiâs, Khatrîs, Sarasvatîs, and other Hindu castes, with some Sindhîs and Musulmâns, with their wives and children, whom they established in the country about Junâgaḍh. Chroniclers narrate that so many long-bearded but short-lived Sindhîs were slain that a bridge was made of their bodies across the Salt Raṇ, over which the army passed. Much plunder fell into the hands of the courtiers of the Râja, who obtained also a lâkh of gold ingots from his invasion of Sindh, and used them in building the temple of Petha Devî in Hálâr, but in lieu of one of them, which the brother-in-law of the Râja had kept back, his own head was inserted in the wall; God, however, knows best. Noghan Râja has passed away and left a good name.

Râja Khengâr, son of Naughan.

Râo Khengâr ascended the throne in Saṁvat

* The author evidently forgot, when writing this, that firearms were not in use in Naughan's time.

k

916 (A.D. 859), and marched with a large army intending to raze the fort of Pâṭṭan, in Gujarât, to the ground; as Siddha Râo happened at that time to be away on some business and at a great distance, Khengâr made use of the opportunity to carry off some stones from that fort, wherewith he built the Kâlva gate at Junâgaḍh. To take vengeance for this insult the son of Siddha Râo afterwards invaded Junâgaḍh, and Khengâr being pursued by his foes the thread of his life was snapped in the vicinity of Bagasara, but Râṇî Rânik Devḍî, his spouse, was captured, and the Amirs intended to make a present of her to the Mahârâja Siddha Râo. The Râṇî, however, endued with a keen sense of modesty peculiar to the innocent, took refuge in the temple of Śankara, lord of the world, situated on the Bhogâvâ river and exclaimed,—

Hemistich :—

Thou modesty hast granted, preserve my honour!

All of a sudden the surface of the earth was opened by the will of that Concealer, and she leaped of her own accord into the gap, which thus became her grave.

Distich :—

The bosom of the earth was quickly opened;
She entered, like the soul, the abode of dust.

Another account about Rânîk Devḍî is that she was originally the daughter of Râja Siddha Râo, and that by the aid of their knowledge of stellar influences astrologers made the statement that she would be married to her own father. This information so distressed the Râja that he exposed the infant girl in a lonely place to become the food of birds of prey. But, as everything decreed by fate must take place, it happened by the providence of God that a potter took the little maiden from the desert, and being much pleased brought her up ; afterwards he happened to go to Soraṭha, where he presented her to Râ Khengâr, and informed her that she was the daughter of Râja Siddha Rào, lest she might become imbued with hatred towards her own father, on account of which she afterwards sacrificed her life, which event took place in Saṁvat 952 (A.D. 895).

Mularâja and Naughan.

The reign of Khengâr lasted thirty-six years ; his son Mularâja ascended the throne in Saṁvat 952, and reigned thirty-five years and six months. Râja Jakhrâ, son of Mularâja, began to reign in Saṁvat 987, and he reigned for twenty-one years. Râjâ Ganrâj, son of Jakhrâ, became king in Saṁvat 1009, and reigned for thirty-eight years and four months. Râja Maṇḍalika, son of Ganrâj, mounted the throne of Soraṭha in Saṁvat 1047.

Fight of Râja Maṇḍalika with Mahmud Ghazńavi.

The hateful Sulṭân Maḥmûd Ghaznavi marched with an army from Ghaznin to Gujarât with the intention of carrying on a religious war. In Saṁvat 1078 (A.D. 1021, A.H. 414) he demolished the temple of Srî Somanâth and returned. This act so provoked the Mahârâja Maṇḍalika, who was a protector of his own religion, that he marched with Bhim Deva, the Râja of Gujarât, in pursuit:

> They ran like fawns and leaped like onagers,
> As lightning now, and now outvying wind!

The Muhammadans did not make a great stand, but fled; many of them were slain by Hindu scymitars and prostrated by Râjput war-clubs, and when the sun of the Râja's fortune culminated Shâh Maḥmûd took to his heels in dismay and saved his life, but many of his followers, of both sexes, were captured. Turkish, Afghân, and Moghul female prisoners were, if they happened to be virgins, considered pure according to their own belief, and were without any difficulty taken as wives; the bowels of the others, however, were cleansed by means of emetics and purgatives, and the captives were after that disposed of according to the command, "The wicked women to the wicked men, and the good women to the good men" [*Qorân*, xxiv. 26]; the low females were joined to low men. Respectable men were compelled to shave their beards, and were enrolled among the Shekâvat and the Wâdhel tribes of Râjputs; whilst the lower kinds were allotted to the castes of Kolîs, Khânts, Bâbriâs, and Mêrs. All, however, were allowed to retain the wedding and funeral ceremonies current among themselves, and to remain aloof from those of other classes; but God knows best.

During the reign of Maṇḍalika, *dharmaśálás*, temples, tanks, bridges, and *wávs* were constructed, and it lasted forty-eight years and two months.

HAMIRA DEVA, VIJAYÂPÂLA, NAUGHAN, &c.

Râja Hamira Deva, the son of Râja Maṇḍalika, began to reign in Saṁvat 1095; he exercised both justice and equity, and the country prospered more than under his father; he governed it during thirteen years and some days.

Râja Vijayâpâla, the son of Râja Hamira Deva, ascended the throne in Saṁvat 1108, and sat on it for fifty-four years and six months.

The reign of Râja Naughan, son of Râja Vijayâpâla, began in 1162, and lasted two years.

Râja Maṇḍalika, the son of Naughan, began to reign in 1184, and died eleven years afterwards.

Râja Alansingh, the son of Maṇḍalika, commenced to reign in Soraṭha in 1195, and his government lasted fourteen years.

Râja Dhanesh, the son of Alansingh, became Râja in the year 1209, and reigned five* years.

Râja Naughaṅ, son of Naughan, obtained the *ráj* in 1214, and reigned nine years.

Râo Khengâr came to the throne in 1224 (A.D. 1167), and reigned forty-six years.

---

* Some copies have 'nine.'

Râja M a ṇ ḍ a l i k a, son of Râja Khengâr, placed the diadem of râja-ship on his head in the Saṁvat year 1270, and reigned twenty-two* years three months and twenty-two days.

Râja M a h i p â l a, son of Maṇḍalika, began to reign in 1302; he reigned thirty-four† years five months and three days.

Râja K h e n g â r, the son of Mahîpâla, began to reign on the 12th Mâghasar in Saṁvat 1336 (A.D. 1279). He conquered eighteen islands such as Div Bheṭ, Śankhodar, and others, and repaired the temple of Somanâth, which the Musulmân Sulṭâns had destroyed; his reign lasted fifty-four years and thirteen days. During his time Shams Khân arrived, by order of Firûz Shâh, and took Junâgaḍh after a little struggle, whereupon Râja Khengâr took refuge on Mount Girnâr, and thus saved his life, but the town was plundered.

JAYASINGH.

J a y a s i n g h, son of Râja Khengâr, became Râja in Saṁvat 1390, and reigned eleven years eight months and eleven days.

Râja M u g a t s i n g h, son of Jayasingh, also called Mokalsingh, ascended the throne on the 6th Bhadrava in Saṁvat 1402, and retained it for fourteen years and thirteen days.

Râja M a d h u p a t, son of Mugatsingh, com-

---

* Some copies read 'thirty-two.'

† Some copies read 'thirty-four.'

menced to reign on the 4th of Ashvad in Saṁvat 1412.* He reigned five years one month and six days.

Râja M a ṇ ḍ a l i k a, son of Madhupat, began to reign on the 10th of Kârtika Śud in Saṁvat 1421. His reign lasted seventeen years six months and three days.

Râja M e l a k, the brother of Maṇḍalika, who was the son of a slave-girl, began his reign in Saṁvat 1439, and it lasted eleven years eleven months and twenty-four days.

Râja J a y a s i n g h, the son of Melak, became king in the Saṁvat year 1468. He reigned for eighteen years three months and fourteen days. He took the fort of Zanjirah (?) from the Musulmâns, who, asking for and obtaining quarter, evacuated the place.

Râja K h e n g â r bin Jayasingh mounted the throne in Saṁvat 1486. When the Pâdishâh Aḥmad Gujarâti marched his army to aid the Muhammadan religion and to overthrow the government of Junâgaḍh, Khengâr, the son of Jayasingh, and his Divân, Hira Singh, who was a Nâgar, being unable to resist him, took refuge in the fort of Uparkoṭ, and remained there in safety in Saṁvat 1470, but eventually they died, and the town was plundered, and Sayyid Kâsam and Sayyid Abul-Khair, who were left with a *thânah* to collect the *salâmi*, bestowed *jâgirs* on

* Some copies have S. 1412.

the Muhammadans both in the city and parganahs, and caused them to settle there, and also, with a view of advancing their own religion, they caused Musulmâns of the Sindhi, Baluch, and Jat tribes, as well as Khokhars, Maliks, Multânîs, Khuraishîs, Afghâns, and Ghorîs to settle there, and made them solemnly promise to shave their beards, and not to kill cows, and keep in their mosques painted or carved figures of the Jalâdhârîs and of the Śiva-*liṅga*, which custom is still observed in those parts. At that time Toghlak Shâh, the Sulṭân of Dehli, also devastated the town. His reign lasted for twenty years.

Sultân Mahmud captures Râja Maṇḍalika.

He began to reign in Saṁvat 1489. Kiwamu'-l-Mulk, Âmir of Sulṭân Maḥmûd, ravaged the country of Junâgaḍh in Saṁvat 1520, and in Saṁvat 1524 took from the Râja his gold umbrella, and after another two years had passed he again ravaged the city and country. Afterwards Sulṭân Maḥmûd Gujarâti conquered Junâgaḍh at the instigation of a Vâṇiâ named Visal, who was the Kâmdâr of the Râja. The Visal Wâv is a memorial of him. When the Sulṭân was about to invade Junâgaḍh, he ordered his treasurer to get ready five *krors* of rupees of ready cash consisting only of gold, the armourer to procure 1700 sword-hilts of Maghrabi, Yamâni, Egyptian, and Khorâsâni manufacture, each weighing from six *sirs* of gold, according to the weight of Gujarât, to four *śirs*; again 3300 hilts of Ahmadâbâd made of silver, and of weights varying between four and five *śirs*; 1700 large daggers, the hilt of each weighing from 2½ to 3 *śirs* of gold; and the chief equerry to get ready 2000 Arab and Turkish horses, and thus equipped he arrived at Junágaḍh and laid siege to the city.

The reason why Visal the Vâṇiâ instigated Sulṭân Maḥmûd to come with an army was this :—The Vâṇiâ Visal possessed a wife whose face was like that of a fairy, and whom to see was like beholding a *huri*; her waist was slim, her brows arched. Her name was Manmohan. One of her glances enfettered the heart of Râja Maṇḍalika with the chains of her amber ringlets, so that he, captive as he was in the net of her musked curls, having by the tricks of a crafty procuress obtained access to his mistress, fully enjoyed himself with her. When Visal the Vâṇiâ became aware that his conjugal happiness had been destroyed, he determined to avenge himself, and invited Sulṭân Maḥmûd Gujarâti to invade Junâgaḍh. The Sulṭân, who longed for such news as a fasting man longs for the sound "Allah Akbar," and who was desirous of this wealth which was to be got for nothing, at once marched in that direction with a powerful army. In a short time, by the advice of the base Visal, Râja Maṇḍalika fell captive into the Shâh's hands. During the siege the Sulṭân bestowed on the *sipâhîs* five *krors* of gold, besides houses, farms, and dresses of honour, and after the Râja had embraced Islâm he bestowed on him the title of Khân Jahân, and his tomb is in the Mânikchok in the bâzâr of Ahmadâbâd. The fortress of Junâgaḍh fell into the hands of Sulṭân Maḥmud in Saṁvat 1527 (A.D. 1470), and after two years he restored the country to his offspring in *jâgir*. And another account of the destruction of the kingdom of the Râos, who are also known by the title of Râizâdahs, is this.

The Story of Mehta Narsi.

The fame of the god-knowing devotee, the walker in the paths of righteousness and abstemiousness, Mehtâ Sâheb Narsi, the Nâgar, is known from pole to pole, and also the miracles performed by him have spread abroad in all directions. Offended at the ill-humour of his brother's wife, Narsi one day left the house and went to the house of his god, as represented by the temple of Mahâdeva Gopinâth, where he spent several days in fasting, penance, and prayer. At last the ocean of boundless grace was seething, the cloud of divine favour thundering and an invisible angelic herald conveyed these words to the ear of Narsi:—"I have placed the enjoyment of corporal desire and the pleasures of this world at the disposal of the lord Śrî Kṛishṇa. You shall behold the spectacle of the Râs Mandali, the dancing and the singing of the

Gopîs, with your bodily eyes. Put into poetry and declare again what you have seen, in order that those who listen to your songs may obtain eternal salvation." Narsi Mehtâ complied; since that time nearly 370 years have elapsed, but high and low still sing his hymns, and thus accumulate provision for their final beatitude:—

Hemistich—The moon is always present in the world!

Narsi Mehtâ was a man destitute of money, and associated with Vairâgîs and Bhaktîs, who tramp about the country; nevertheless when his son Sâmaldâs was celebrating his wedding with the daughter of a Nâgar, Madanji of Vaḍanagar, he miraculously came into the possession of various kinds of chariots, horses with gold ornaments, rich clothes and jewels. Kuvarabâi, the daughter of Narsi Mehtâ, was married to the son of Śrî Ranga Mehtâ, an inhabitant of Únâ (under Junâgaḍh), in Jhaveripûra street. Afterwards Narsi appeared with his two ears and nose in Ûnâ to attend the ceremony of pregnancy, and said to his daughter, "Ask your mother-in-law to prepare a list of the garments called *Mâmerû* in Hindi, that I may make arrangements for obtaining them." Kuvarabâî replied, with her eyes full of tears, her heart sad, and voice mournful, "In these bad times such a hope is impossible. Such things are at the disposal of wealthy people; be satisfied with having seen me, and depart in peace." Narsi Mehtâ replied, "Let not your heart be dismayed; the Most

High will take care of us, and will not allow us to despair. Get the list quickly, and be not down-hearted." Kuvarabâî obeyed, and a list was mockingly prepared, to realize which would have been beyond the means even of wealthy people. On that occasion Kuvarabâî's father-in-law said, "Let them also write for two make-weight stones of gold, that the wind may not carry away the garments of Narsi Mehtâ." The list made by the mother-in-law was given to Narsi Mehtâ, who prayed to the eternal Benefactor and universal Giver; when, lo, a merchant from the invisible world, whose name was Dâmodar Sheṭ, and his wife Lakhmi Bâî, arrived with several clerks and carts loaded with goods. This man exclaimed, "I am one of the Gumâshtas of Narsi Mehtâ, and having selected from various countries the articles he wanted for the *Mâmerû*, have brought them." The people of Śrî Ranga Mehtâ were amazed at what they saw, and at what was coming. The merchants proceeded immediately to open the packages, and to display to those who were present in the assembly more articles than had been written for, together with two golden stones, several suits of clothes, ornaments, and vessels, whereupon all praised the bounty of the universal Giver, and reviled the mockers and unbelievers. The women of the family had prepared water for the purposes of ablution before the repast, which was boiling hot; and as it was not possible to wash without the aid of cold water, which the unbelievers had removed by way of trial, such a rain began to pour, by the liberality of Śankara, that the water of shame was running down the countenances of the members of the family who had played this trick.

Once some jokers induced Narsi Mehtâ to write a *huṇḍi* for certain Vairâgis, who went with it to Dvârakâ, but were, after a great deal of searching, disappointed in their inquiries after the banker to whom the *huṇḍi* was addressed, and they began to revile Narsi, when, lo, a banker made his appearance, accompanied by two clerks, from the invisible world, and having taken the *huṇḍi* from the Vairâgis counted out ready money to them.

In spite of beholding so many evident miracles, Râja Māṇḍalika prohibited Narsi Mehtâ from propagating the Vaishṇava sect; but, not being able to obtain compliance, he convoked a meeting of Sanyâsis, who sever all connections, and utter no other formula except "He is one and has no partner," as well as of Veda reading Brâhmaṇs, to decide the controversy. The Sanyâsis opened the meeting with the declaration of the unity, the adoration, and praise of the god, who exists from all eternity, and said, "Listen to the words of truth, and abandon the path of Vaishṇava; if you pay not attention to it, you will at last hear what no one has ever heard. Abandon the worship of idols, the playing on musical instruments, singing poems, and the praise of love and beauty, which lead carnal men into error." Narsi Mehtâ, however, replied :—

Distich :—

"Each tribe its way, its faith and Qebla has.
To rosy cheeks my worship I address.

The way of lovers is unknown to angels, then what will be the case with you? O ye wearers of red rags, who retail nonsense, are emaciated by poverty and distress, and who have learnt nothing beyond sitting in deserted places and smearing yourselves with loam, what can you know about the pleasures and ecstasies of image-worship?

Distich :—

"Reflex of the Friend's face we see in cups!
O ye who do not know the bliss of wine!

What will these conversations about the Vedânta and arguments from the law avail you against those who are plunged in corporeal delights and carnal pleasures?

Distich :—

"That bitter drink the Sofi wicked calls
More sweetness gives to us than virgins' kisses."

By degrees the controversy went beyond mere words, and the disputants caught hold of each other's throats and hair, and Râja Maṇḍalika exclaimed, "What profit is there in this useless talk? If Hazrat Dâmodar Râî, whom this Nâgar worships, stone as he is, will take off from his own neck a flower-garland and give it to this Nâgar, we will leave him to his own ways; but if not, he is to be killed." Narsi Mehtâ was brought to the idol of Dâmodar Râî, whom he immediately began fervently to address, in fear of his life and of his honour, but at first ineffectually, because some delay had taken place in the bestowal of the garland. The reason was that Narsi had pledged the *Râg Kedârâ*, which he was to have sung for Dâmodar Râî, to the Mehtâ Dharanidâs in the Qasbâ of Talâjâ for eighty rupees, and therefore could not sing it on the present occasion. The Father of all goodness and succour of the needy was so bountiful as to assume the form of the debtor, *i.e.* of Mehtâ Narsi, and to pay the above-mentioned amount to the creditor, in return for which he received the bond, which he threw from the sky in the presence of the whole meeting, whereupon Narsi Mehtâ immediately began to sing the *Râg Kedârâ*, and obtained the garland of flowers, which the idol put upon Narsi. Some of the revilers became black in the face, whilst others felt their cheeks slapped. Mehtâ Narsi obtained the garland in Saṁvat 1512, and for the crime of insulting so innocent a worshipper of the god the Maṇḍalika dynasty lost the throne for ever.

It is related that a Nâghi Chârani, who was a modest woman, dwelt in the village of Moniyâ, in the parganah of Bagasarâ and tâlukâ of Junâgaḍh, in a virtuous and retired manner. Râja Maṇḍalika, who had heard of the beauty of her son Nâgâjan's wife, betook himself to the chase of that gazelle-eyed maiden. This Chârani girl rose to see the Râja pass, but when he caught sight of the unveiled countenance of that fairy he removed the curtain of modesty from his own heart, and, obeying his lust and passion, attempted to place his hand on her breast, but she guessed his intention, and, turning away her face, cursed him saying, "The bride of your prosperity will turn from you as I do now, and will associate you with Musulmân Pâdishâhs;" and this was the second cause why Mahârâja Maṇḍalika lost the throne.

Distich:—

Wherefore attach your heart to this world's beauty?
Of a thousand bridegrooms the bride she is.

It is said that Jamial the Darvaish,* whose *takia* or chapel is on the mountain, was present when this affair of the Nâghi Chârani took place. The duration of his reign was forty years; and for 128 years after Mahârâja Maṇḍalika, till the reign of Sulṭân Akbar, his descendants sometimes prospered and sometimes did not; sometimes they were conquered, at other times they were conquerors and reigned; at last, however, they obtained Chorvâḍ, Kesod, and other places as *jâgirs*, and became entirely tributary. Their names are here given:—

Râja Bhupat Singh bin Maṇḍalika

Became Râja in Saṁvat 1529 [1528]. The

* This is Jamial Shâh, whose shrine is on the Dâtâr at Junâgaḍh.

Sulṭân kept him as a *jâgirdâr* at Junâgaḍh, but the Thânahdâr on behalf of the Pâdishâh was Tâtâr Khân bin Zafar Khân, the adopted son of Sulṭân Muḥammad, and he levied the *salâmi* (land-tax). The reign of Bhupat Sing lasted 31 years. Mirza Khalil likewise beat the drum of dominion, and founded the place Khalilpur, near Junâgaḍh.

Râja Khengâr, son of Râja Bhupat Singh.

He began to reign in Saṁvat 1560, and his *râj* lated 22 years and 4 months; and the Thânahdârs of the Pâdishâh were Malik Ayâz and Tâtâr Khân Ghori, who collected the *salâmi*.

Râja Naughan, son of Khengâr.

He became Râja in Saṁvat 1581, and his *râj* lasted 28 years 11 months and 20 days; Sayyid Kâsam and Mujâhid Khân Behlim were the Pâdishâhi Thânahdârs.

Râja Śri Singh, son of Naughan.

He became Râja in Saṁvat 1608, and his *râj* lasted 34 years 1 month and 10 days. Khân Ázam Kokaltâsh, who became the Subahdâr of Ahmadâbâd in place of Khân Khânân, conquered Junâgaḍh in Saṁvat 1633.

Râja Khengâr, son of Śrî Singh.

He became Râja in Saṁvat 1642. In his time Sulṭân Maḥmûd and Bahâdur Shâh Gujarâti often came and sojourned at Junâgaḍh. In aid of Sulṭân Muzaffar Gujarâti this

Râja raised confusion in Gujarât in 1647. That Shâh bestowed Junâgaḍh in *jâgir* on Âmin Khân, son of Tâtâr Khân Ghori, Thânahdâr of Junâgaḍh, but he rebelled, whereupon Fateh Khân Shirwâni brought an army on the part of Mirza Khân, son of Bahrâm Khân, who had the title of Khân Khânân, and plundered the town of Junâgaḍh in Saṁvat 1633; but Fateh Khân himself died, while Âmin Khân remained safe under the protection of the fortress, which was, however, after the death of Fateh Khân, besieged by Khân Khânân, who led an army against it and erected batteries, but being unsuccessful he raised the siege and went to beleaguer Mângrol. Hereupon Âmin Khân sallied forth from the fort, and asking aid from Jâm Satarsâl marched to give battle; on this Mirza Khân raised the siege, and went forward and ravaged the Koḍinâr district, but his elephants were captured and carried off by Jâm Satarsâl's army. Âmin Khân bin Tâtâr Khân, and the untrustworthy Itimâd Khân, and the hapless Daulat Khân, had, in spite of their accepting a bribe of two lâkhs of Jâmis from Sulṭân Akbar, resolved to join Muzaffar Shâh and Khengâr. They now summoned Jâm Satâji from Nagar to their aid, and rewarded him with thirty-six villages, as will be related in the chronicles of Nagar. The reign of Khengâr lasted for 22 years, and Tâtâr Khân was for thirteen years the imperial thânahdâr, together with the Chuḍâsamâ Râis.

Note.—On the Chuḍâsamâ Dynasty.

The reigns of the first four kings beginning with Navaghana I. extend over 151 years, and then a blank occurs of 22 years between Navaghana II. and his successor Maṇḍalika I. Otherwise the list is pretty consistent, and gains support from the inscription on Mount Girnâr. I give it, corrected by the inscription, for what it is worth, inserting such additions from other sources, and conjectural corrections in the dates, as seem required. These corrections are applied only to the dates when converted into A.D., and where doubtful are marked with a (?).

MS. dates, Saṁvat.	Probable date, A.D.	
—	904 ?	Râ Dyâs or Dyâchh, the third in descent from Râ Gâriyo, the grandson of Râ Chuḍâchand, and first of the Chuḍâsamâs of Junâgaḍh. Râ Dyâs was defeated and slain by the king of Paṭṭan, S. 874 (? 917 A.D.) (*Ind. Ant.* vol. II. pp. 312ff.) Some copies give S. 874 as the date of Naughan's accession, and allow 42 years for his reign. Tod (*Travels,* p. 469), counting Chuḍâchand as the fortieth prince before his own time, and the eighth before Jâm Unaḍ, whom he places in S. 1110, assumes that Chuḍâchand must have lived about S. 960. Very little dependence, however, can be placed on such a computation. He says he was contemporary with Râm Kamâr, the fourteenth prince of Ghumli.
894	937 ?	Navaghana or Naughan, his son,

MS. dates, Samvat.	Probable date, A.D.	
		invaded Sindh and defeated "Hamir," the Sumarâ prince (S. 890).
916	959?	Khangâr, his son, killed at Bagasarâ by the Anhilvâḍâ Râja (possibly by Mularâja, who ruled from A.D. 942 to 996, and defeated "Graharipu the Ahir" of Vanthaḷi).
952	968?	Mularâja, "son of Khangâr" (perhaps of Anhilvâḍa).
1009	992?	Navaghana II., his son, "ruled for 38 (18 ?) years."*
1078	1021?	Maṇḍalika, son of Navaghana, joined Bhima Deva of Gujarât in pursuit of Maḥmûd of Ghazni, S. 1080, A.H. 414.
1095	1038	Hamir Deva, son of Maṇḍalika, 13 years.
1108	1051	Vijayapâla, son of Hamiradeva.
1162	1085?	Navaghana III., subdued the Râja of Umetâ.
—	1107?	Khangâra II., slain by Siddharâja

* Some copies give—

1047 A.D.	Jakhrâ as successor of Mularâja.
... „	Guṇarâja (? Kunarâja).
1076 „	Maṇḍalika.

Is it possible that these reigns should be arranged thus?—

S. 952,	A.D. 895	Mularâja,	36	years.
988	931	Jakhrâ,	21	„
1009	952	Naughan, II.	38	„
1047	990	Guṇarâja,	31	„
1078	1021	Maṇḍalika,	17	„

MS. dates, Saṁvat.	Probable date, A.D.	
		Jayasiṁha of Anhilvâḍa (*Râs Mâlâ*, vol. I. pp. 154ff. omitted by Amarji).
1184	1127	Maṇḍalika II., 11 years.
1195	1138	Alansiṁha, 14 years.
1209	1152	Gaṇeśa or Dhaneśa, 5 years.
1214	1157	Navaghana or Naughan IV., 9 years.
1224	1167	Khangâra III., 46 years.
1270	1213	Maṇḍalika III., son of Khangâra III. (mentioned in the Girnâr inscription, l. 9), 22 years.
—	1235?	Navaghana or Naughana V.*
1302	1245	Mahîpâladeva (Râ Kavât), 34 years, built a temple at Somanâth Paṭṭan.
1336	1279	Khangâra IV., his son, repaired the temple of Somanâth, conquered Div, &c. Shams Khân took Junâgaḍh.
1390	1333	Jayasiṁhadeva, son of Khangâra IV., 11¾ years, and subdued 84 petty chiefs.†

* Amarji omits Naughana after Maṇḍalika, to whom he assigns a reign of 22 years 3¾ months, beginning in S. 1270, and then makes Mahîpâla's reign begin in S. 1302, leaving 10 years unaccounted for, or about the same time as Navaghan IV. reigned.

† This Jayasiṁhadeva is mentioned in the Girnâr inscription in such a way as to suggest to Dr. Bühler and Kinloch Forbes that Siddharâja Jayasiṁha of Gujarât, who slew Râ Khangâra the son of Naughan, in the early

MS. dates, Samvat.	Probable date, A.D.	
1402	1345	Mugatsiṁha or Mokalasiṁha, son of Jayasiṁha, 14 years.
1416	1359	Melak Deva, son of Mugatsiṁha, saved Jhâlâ Kṛishṇâji, who sought his protection from the Yavana *Muslims*.
1421	1371	Mahîpâladeva II. or Madhupat, married Kuntâ, daughter of Arjuna the son of Bhimâji. Arjuna was succeeded by Dûdavanish (? Dûda of Sathî).
1439	1376*	Maṇḍalika IV., son of Mahîpâladeva, defeated Śangana of Okhâ.

part of the twelfth century, is meant. If this were the case, Amarji's chronology would be useless;—an interval of 200 years would occur between Siddharâja Jayasiṁha (d. 1142 A.D.) and his successor Mokalasiṁha or Magatsiṁha 1345 A.D.

* Amarji gives the three successors of Mugatsiṁha in the order—Madhupat, 5 years (S. 1416-1421); Maṇḍalika, 17½ years (S. 1421-1439); and Melakdeva, his illegitimate brother, 12 years (S. 1439-1450). This he probably derivedfrom an inscription (of S. 1473) at the Revatikuṇḍa, which gives the genealogy thus:—Maṇḍalika III.; his son Mahîpâla; his son Khangâra IV.; his son Jayasiṁha; his son Mugatsiṁha; his sons Maṇḍalika and Melak; and Jayasiṁha, son of Melak. The chronology in the text is confirmed by the *Maṇḍalika Kâvya*. I have allowed the dates S. 1421 and 1439 to stand, but probably they should be altered to 1428 and 1433.

MS. dates, Samvat.	Probable date, A.D.	
1450	1393	Jayasiṁhadeva II. (apparently "the Râî of Jehreṅd" or "Jiran" mentioned by Firishtah* as defeated by Muzaffar Khân of Gujarât in A.D. 1411). He is said to have taken Zanjirah (Jhinjhira?) from the Muhammadans.
1469	1412	Khangâra V.; war with Aḥmad Shâh.†
1489	1432	Maṇḍalika V. restored the Uparkoṭ in S. 1507; subdued by Maḥmûd Begarha in A.D. 1469-70.‡

After their subjugation to the Ahmadâbâd kings the dynasty seems to have been preserved as tributary Jâghirdârs for another century; the list of these princes stands thus :—

A.D. 1472, Bhupat, cousin of Maṇḍalika V., 32 years.
„ 1503, Khangâra VI., son of Bhupat, 22 years.
„ 1524, Naughana VI., son of Khangâra, 25 years.
„ 1551, Śrî Siṁha, 35 years; Gujarât subdued by Akbar.
„ 1585, Khangârà VII., till about 1609.

GOVERNORS ON BEHALF OF THE PÂDISHÂHS OF ÂHMADÂBÂD.

Naurang Khân ruled two years, Sayyid Kâsam three years, Bhaya Manḍar§ three years,

* Briggs's *Translation of Firishtah*, vol. IV. pp. 5, 6; conf. Forbes, *Râs Mâlâ*, vol. I. p. 328.

† Briggs, *ibid.* pp. 17, 20.

‡ *Ibid.* pp. 52-56; the inscription over the gate of the Uparkoṭ is dated S. 1507, but has been badly used by the Muhammadans.

§ Mandan or Mandal according to some editions.

Râja Ráisingh, Abdullah Khân one year, and Tâtâr Khân Lodi thirteen years. Isâ Tar Khân became in Saṁvat 1687 the *Mutasaddi* of this glorious country, Junâgaḍh, and built the town wall in 1690. The Sayyids, the Kâzîs, the Momans and Bohrâs were introduced by Sulṭân Maḥmûd. Isâ Tar Khân governed for ten years, and in his time the English established themselves in Hugli.

Mirza Khurram* ruled the first time for three years; Kutb-al-dîn Khân Kâkar one year; Bhovâldâs one year; Kamrân Bêg two years; Abu'l Kâsim one year; Sardâr Khân one year; Mirzâ Khurram for the second time one year; Sâdu'-llah Khân eight years, Bâgi Khân one year; Jahângir Kuli Khân one year; Behrâm Khân one year; Amir Khân one year; Sâleh Tar Khân two years; Shams Khân and Kutb-al-dîn Khân one year; the Shâhzâdah Murâd Bakhsh two years; Muḥammad Khân one year; Sardâr Khân fifteen years. He was of a noble disposition, and laid out the Sardârbâgh in the west of Junâgaḍh, which contains a harem, a tank, baths, a mosque, an *idgah*, and tombs; this garden is the mole of beauty on the countenance of the town. The garden was laid out by Ghori Pir, one of Sardâr Khân's companions, and for some time—that is, till Saṁvat 1732—Zâhid Khan was Nâib on the part of Sardâr Khân. The date of the Navâb

* Afterwards the emperor Shâh Jahân.

Sardâr Khân's demise [1732] is contained in the words

شد از باغ عالم گلی بی نظیر

"An unparalleled rose departed from the garden of the world."

If from the words باغ عالم, the sum of which is A.H. 1144, the numerical value of گل 50 be subtracted, we obtain A.H. 1094, in which the Sardârbâgh was made, *i.e.* Saṁvat 1740.

Abel Patan governed three years; Mukim Khân three years; Mirza Khurram for the third time four years; Sad'ullah for the second time four years; Kutb-al-dîn Khân five years; Divân Sakhânand with Muḥammad Beg five years; Ja'far Khân one year; Sardâr Khân two years; Sarbuland Khân one year in Saṁvat 1763; Sherafgan Khân two years; Pirsâheb and Divân Udyarâm one year. He became governor in Saṁvat 1764. Sangarâm Singh, the Nâib of the Mahârâja Ajitsingh and Divân Pratâpsingh, one year; Navâb Yâsin Khân and Kârbhâri Udyarâm one year; Dilâwar Khân and his Kârbhâri Jagatsingh nine months [*or* three years]; Pir Sâheb for the second time, and the Shâhzâdah's Divân, and Kâhandâs the Vâṇiâ for the second time, two years and three months; the Shâhzâdah and Divân Mukbil Khân four years Ma'sum Beg Khân three years and two months;* Jangli Khân one year; Kâzi A'bd-al Hamid two

* Other copies—"twice, but two years in all."

years; he required every night several women, and took forcible possession of the village of Mendardâ. In this manner during 106 years the governors who came from the Shâhs of Gujarât and Dehli spent their time dishonourably, like owls in a wilderness, and did nothing worthy of record.

Asad Kuli Khân was the *Mutasaddi* of Junâgaḍh in Saṁvat 1778, who plundered the country, and he kept also Salâbat Khân Bâbi and Sher Khân Bâbi as his Nâibs; and Sharfud'dîn was his treasurer. In his time Shujaat Khân arrived in this zillâ from Gujarât to collect the *peshkush*. His government lasted six years.

Ghulâm Mâhyau'd-din Khân, after the demise of his father, was appointed by the cabinet of Sulṭân Muḥammad Shâh to be Foujdâr of Junâgaḍh, in Saṁvat 1784; he on his part also made the above-mentioned Salâbat Muḥammad Bâbi his Nâib, who governed personally for a while, and then left his son Sher Khân, surnamed Bahâdur Khân, as his deputy, and went to Ahmadâbâd. Sher Khán obtained the *ijârah* or farm of the revenues of Junâgaḍh, for the sum of eighty thousand rupees, from Ghulâm Mâhyau'd-dîn.

In Saṁvat 1785 [1789] Mubâriz-al-mulk, surnamed Sarbuland Khân, accompanied by Sher Khân, arrived with an army and took the fort of Mâdhavpur; in this fight Ranchoḍdâs Nâgar, the Thânahdâr of the Râṇâ Vikamátji, was slain after a brave resistance, and the idol of Pârasnâth taken away, but afterwards ransomed for 40,000 Jâmîs [*koḍîs*]. In Saṁvat 1787 Salâbat Muḥammad Bâbi departed this life, and in the same year Sher Khân, surnamed Bahâdur Khân, was removed, and Mir Ismâil was appointed in his stead by Ghulâm Mâhyau'd-dîn; Pilâji Gaikvâḍ also came the same year with an army to Soraṭh. In Saṁvat 1789 Mir Fakhr-al-dîn came with an army to take charge of Junâgaḍh as its Foujdâr, but when he arrived in the plain of Amreli he was met and opposed by Mir Ismâil and his Divân Bhavânidâs, a Vaishṇava Nâgar; and in that same zillâ a battle was fought in which Mir Fakhr-al-dîn and Sayyid A'kali Khân were slain after a heroic battle; their camp was plundered, and Mir Ismâil returned victorious. In the same year Ghulâm Mâhyau'd-din died; his government lasted four years.

Nahr Khân, known as Hazabar Khân, son of Asad Kuli Khân, after the demise of his brother Ghulâm Mâhyau'd-dîn, obtained the *sanad* of Junâgaḍh from Muḥammad Shâh, and left Mir Ismâil in his former position. One year after this, the Navâb Sohrâb Khân, at the behest of Mahârâja Ajitsingh, the Subâh of Ahmadâbâd, ousted Sher Zemân Khân and Diler Khân from their *jâgir* of the port Goghâ, and Mir Ismâil Khân from his post in Junâgaḍh, where, however, he still remained as a private person; but when the Navâb Sohrâb Khân took possession of the city he departed by sea to Thâthâ. Junâgaḍh was taken in the year 1790 of the era of Vikrama.

In Saṁvat 1792 Sohrâb Khân, through Burhânu'l-mulk, obtained a *sanad* for Viramgâm from the cabinet of the Shâh, and went there with an army, leaving Sâdak 'Ali Khân in Junâgaḍh; but the latter was of so weak a disposition that he allowed robbers to plunder the shops of the bâzâr in broad daylight, and to carry off the people as captives. When Sohrâb Khân went from this place, he was prevented from entering Viramgâm by Ratan Sing Bhâṇḍâri, and by the commander of the troops, Safdar Khân Bâbi, against whom he fought for three days and then lost his life, but his maternal uncle lived in Junâgaḍh for some time longer, in poor circumstances.

In Saṁvat 1793 Hazabar Khân again arrived with a *sanad*, and Sâdak 'Ali Khân, being degraded from his position in Junâgaḍh, entered the service of the Navâb Momin Khân, whom he aided in besieging Ahmadâbâd; and, as a blood-ransom for Ânupsing, who was slain fighting with Sohrâb Khân, his son Bhairavasing obtained the parganah of Upletâ in *inâm* from Ahmadâbâd. In this year Nâdir Shâh of Irân conquered Muḥammad Shâh and plundered Dehli.

When Hazabar Khân arrived for the second time, he left Mir Dost A'li as his Nâib in Junâgaḍh; and the latter, being perplexed how to pay the *sipâhis*, sent for Bahâdur Khân Bâbi, who was ruling the port of Goghâ on behalf of the

Navâb Momin Khân, and surrendered to him the Subâh of Junâgaḍh without any further ado in Saṁvat 1794.

Distich :—

Whatever is decreed must you befall;
Unwilling though you be, force you it will!

As good luck would have it, Hazabar Khân in that very year disappeared like a fox into the obscurity of destruction at Dehli.

Navâb Sâheb Bahâdur Khân Bâbi

Was the son of Salâbat Khân, who was the son of Safdar Khân, who was the son of Jâfar Khân,* who was the son of Sher Khân, the son of Bahâdur Khân Bâbi. As the author was in the service of this family, he conceived it incumbent upon himself to give some account of it.

Bahâdur Khân Bâbi the Afghân was for a long time at the court of the emperor Shâh Jahân, and became a favourite on account of his affable manners, his bravery, and his good family. He was presented with a *jâgir* in Gujarât, and when the star of his prosperity began to rise he obtained advancement from the governors and high officials of Ahmadâbâd. He farmed the revenues of the parganahs of Karḍi, Viramgâm, Bijâpur, and other mahâls several times, sometimes from the Shâhi or imperial Subâdârs, and sometimes from the Sarkârs of the Śrimant Peshvâ and the Gaikvâḍ on his own responsibility; he used also

* This is an error of Divân Ranchoḍji's, as Safdar Khân and Jâfar Khân are the same person.

to precede the army which came from Ahmadâbâd to receive the *peshkash* or tribute, and to stand security for the payments which the zamindârs of Gujarât and Soraṭha had to make; and some time afterwards the Mahârâja Ajitsingh, who was appointed to the Subâhdâri of Ahmadâbâd, bestowed upon him the tbe title of Bahâdur, and Sarbuland Khân bestowed on him the title of Khân. In Saṁvat 1799 Kumâl-al-din Khân Bâbi was appointed Nâib of Ahmadâbâd, first on behalf of Makbûl A'âlam, and afterwards on the part of Fakhr-al-daulah ('Boast of the monarchy'), who was in reality Kharr-al-daula ('Ass of the monarchy'); he governed ten years at Ahmadâbâd, and in Saṁvat 1810 received the *jâgirs* of Kheḍâ, Wâḍâsinor,* and Goghâ from the Śrimant Sâheb Peshvâ and from the Gaikvâḍ. From the Sarkâr of the Śrimant Peshvâ and from the Huzûr of Bâlâji Râo and Dâmâji Gaikvâḍ, when they took possession of Ahmadâbâd, he also obtained the following nine places:—Pirânpaṭṭan, Vaḍnagar, Visalnagar, Munjpur, Tharâd, Kherâlu, Bijâpûr, Sami. In course of time Paṭṭan, Vaḍnagar, Visalnagar, and Bijâpûr were again taken, and Dâmâji Gaikvâḍ Shamsher Bahâdur besieged Visalnagar for a year and a half till he was able to retake it, at which time Zorâvar Khân was slain, in Saṁvat 1819.

Salâbat Muḥammad Khân Bâbi died

* Bâlâsinor, in the Rewâ Kâṇṭha.

in Saṁvat 1787, and in the same year Bahâdur Khân was dismissed from Junâgaḍh ; in that year also Pilâji Gaikvâḍ came with his troops to collect the *jama' bandi* or tribute of Soraṭha, but they remained for two years in Junâgaḍh waiting for the payment of the *chauth* (fourth part of the revenue). By means of the intervention of Râja Vakhatsingh, the brother of the Mahârâja, Sher Khân, surnamed B a h â d u r K h â n, was admitted to pay his respects to the Mahârâja Ajitsingh, and presented him with an elephant, several horses, money, and dresses of honour, as a *nazar*, and was confirmed in his hereditary *jâgir*, and obtained a *sanad* for the *jâgirdâri* of Morbi, the title of Bahâdur, earrings, and a yellow flag. In the second year he obtained from the Mahârâja Ajitsing the Foujdârship of the country of Baroda in partnership with S a r b u l a n d K h â n ; but in course of time he was lucky enough to obtain, without the least trouble, the government of Junâgaḍh from Mir Dost 'Ali, and then Bahâdur Khân afterwards again returned to the country of Gujarât, where he was duly honoured by the authorities of the period ; but, as this recital chiefly concerns the history of Junâgaḍh, it is not expedient to give more details about Gujarât.

In former times Mir Dost 'Ali Khân and Sâdak 'Ali Khân were joint rulers of Junâgaḍh, but could not manage the affairs of the State ; for this reason the ryats and Desâis sent Dalpatrâm, a Gujarâti Nâgar, whom the Navâb Bahâdur

Khân had formerly brought from Vâḍâsinor to Junâgaḍh, for the purpose of recalling the abovenamed Navâb from Baroda, which had fallen into the hands of the Gaikvâd; accordingly the said Navâb left his son Sardâr Khân at Vâḍâsinor (*i.e.* Bâlâsinor) and came to Junâgaḍh. In the same year the adopted son of Umâbâî, wife of the Senapati Khaṇḍerâo, arrived with an army of twenty thousand men in Soraṭha for the purpose of collecting the tribute. The Navâb Bahâdur Khân brought with him from Baroda Muḥammad 'Ali Khân, 'Abdullah Khân Paṭani, Farid Khân Karâni, and Buli Khân Yusufzai, Kâmeśvara Pant, Karsanchand Bakhshi, Pitâmbar Modi, and Gulâbrâî Nâgar.

In Saṁvat 1802 the army of Pilâji Gaikvâḍ arrived with the intention of conquering Junâgaḍh, and encamped near the town in a garden called the Târvâḍi. Navâb Bahâdur Khân, seeing no other expedient but to make peace, managed by the stratagems of Mohanlâl Jikâr, a Nâgar, who was the Aristotle of the period, and whom he appointed his *vakil* for the occasion, to get the army sent off by flattery, and by presenting a *nazarûnah* of gold and a dress of honour of small value.

In Saṁvat 1803 Kânoji, taking with him Fakhr-al-daulâ for a make-believe, besieged the fort of Vanthali, under Junâgaḍh, but departed without having been able to take it; nevertheless Fakhr-al-daulah, by way of boast (*fakhr*), got golden keys prepared, and sent them with a *nazarânah* of twenty-one *ashrafîs* to the exalted court of the Shâh of Dehli, with the message that they were the keys of the fort, and after this confusion had been quelled the Navâb went to Gujarât.

On the 3rd Chaitra Vad of Saṁvat 1804 the Divân Dalpatrâm succeeded in expelling from the town Vasantrai Purbhiâ, who was a foreigner but had obtained a footing in the town by employing a number of Arabs who plundered right and left. After his expulsion he became the companion of the robber Mânsiâ Khânt, and with him and a number of others made a night attack on and captured the fort of Uparkoṭ, which had at that time no *chaukî*, and thence these people used to sally out and plunder the whole neighbourhood; these depredations they carried on for thirteen months, but at last departed after a great deal of fighting. About this time also the Navâb Sâheb Bahâdur Khân arrived in Junâgaḍh, and two years afterwards Divân Dalpatrâm departed this life. Because his sons were ignorant, Jagannâtha Jhâlâ, a Nâgar who was at first the Peshkâr or manager for Dalpatrâm, and also the Vakil of the Arabs, carried on his government business also after his demise, with the aid of Sheikh 'Abdulla, who kept possession of the fort of Uparkoṭ. When the latter demanded his arrears of pay, the Navâb Sâheb came to the determination of crushing him;

accordingly he allured Jagannâtha to his party by prospects of gain, and by the promise to appoint him Divân in case he defeated the Arabs. Accordingly, when the Navâb and Jagannâtha proceeded with the army to Kâṭhiâvâḍ to collect the *jama'bandi* tax, Rudráji, the brother of Jagannâtha, managed to carry away from the fort of Uparkoṭ the gunpowder and ammunition the Arabs trusted to in case of war, on pretence that it was old and useless for that purpose, and that therefore it ought to be sold and a fresh store bought in lieu of it; then he sent information to the army, and when the whole world was lulled to sleep in the citadel of darkness the Navâb Sâheb left the camp with Jagannâtha, entered the town, approached the Uparkoṭ, laid siege to it, and caused the Arabs outside [of the Navâb's party] to place ladders against the wall, dig a mine, and attack the Arabs who were within the fort, and after some fighting a compromise was made with Sheikh A'bdulla Zubaidi and others by pledging the village of Dhorâji to Jâḍejâ Kumbhâji of Gondal and obtaining money from him, which being paid to the Arabs they departed from the town in Saṁvat 1810, but the Navâb Bahâdur Khân died on the 25th of the month Bhâdaravâ in Saṁvat 1814, after having reigned thirty-six years in Junâgaḍh, reckoning from the beginning of his appointment as the Naib of Asad ('Ali) Kuli Khân and of Ghulâm Mâhyau'd-dîn Khân.

When the Navâb Sâheb Mahâbat Khân, after the demise of his father, perceived that the Divân Jagannâtha Jhâlâ, who had accumulated some property, and acted according to his own will in everything, he was displeased, and had him assassinated in the night by a negro slave of the name of Ballâl, near the Manjavaḍi gate, where the Gaikvâḍ's army was encamped, and where Jagannâtha was staying in a tent to keep an eye on the *chaukî*. After that, his house was attacked, and at the instance of Jâḍejâ Kumbhâji, Jamadâr Radvi Khân Rehên Dholkiyah, and of Sayyid Khalafshâh, who offered themselves as bail, his brother Rudrâji was allowed to depart safely to Purbandar with the family and property, and did not return to his country until a long time afterwards, through the intervention of the Divânji Sáheb Amarji, and on paying a small amount of money as *nazarânah*. After that Somji Jikâr became Divân, and after him Dayâl the Vâṇiâ, and again Somji Jikâr; but they were not liked, and obtained no firm footing.

In Saṁvat 1810 the news arrived that the fort of the *bandar* of Surat had been taken from Aḥmad Khân and Sidi Masu'd by Captain Austin Shore under the command of General Butcher, and also that the English had by force occupied and taken from Surâju'd-daulâ a portion of Orissâ, the Subâh of Bihâr, and the Subâh of Bengal; and from Asafu'd-daulâ, governor of Oudh, the zillâ of Banâras or Kâśî; lastly, that Shâh A'âlam had bestowed the title of Divân on the English Sarkâr.

In Saṁvat 1818 Aḥmad Shâh Abd'ali fought with an innumerable army of Marâṭhâs and defeated it.* The total amount slain was nearly two lâkhs, and among the killed were many Sardârs of Holkar, Sindhiâ, the Bhonslâ, and of the Gaikvâḍ. Some fled and some were made prisoners; the latter met their death by being blown from cannon, and consisted not only of men, but also of females and children.

Captivity of the Navâb Sâheb Mahâbat Khân.

In Saṁvat 1818 the Jamadâr of the Arabs, Bâsalmân by name, imprisoned the Navâb Sâheb Mahâbat Khân in the Uparkoṭ, with the consent of the Bibî Sâhebah Sulṭân (the wife of the Navâb Bahâdur Khânji), and made Muzaffar Khân bin Jâfar Khân Navâb of Junâgaḍh. When the Navâb Kamâlu'd-dîn Khân, who was the uncle of Mahâbat Khan, heard of this, he brought an army from Pirân Pâṭan under the pretence of liberating him, but in reality to give Junâgaḍh, in case he should be able to get it, to his own son Ghâzi-al-dîn Khân, and to convey Mahâbat Khân to Râdhanpur. Accordingly he brought his troops during the night under the fort walls, which they attempted to scale by means of ladders; but by the watchfulness of the *chaukidârs*, and the good fortune of

* The great battle of Panipat.

the Navâb Sâheb Mahâbat Khân, being unable to effect an entrance, and when the sun at dawn, the world's illuminating commander-in-chief, popped out his head from the citadel of the azure sky, the soldiers were put to flight and retired with shame. When Sadâśiv Pâṇḍâ Nâgar, uncle of the author, was made aware of this futile attempt of Kamâlu'd-din Khân, he became cooler in his partizanship, and the Navâb Kamâlu'd-din, seeing himself discomfited, beat the drum of departure in his disappointment.

After the army had marched about two stages from Junâgaḍh, Kumbhâji Jâḍejâ and other Zamindârs, through the intervention of Śivadâs Pâṇḍâ, made an arrangement with Sulimân the Jama'dâr, so that he released the Navâb Sâheb Mahâbat Khân from captivity, and the following arrangements were made:—The two brothers Muzaffar Khân and Fathyâb Khân obtained the *jâgir* of Râṇpur and Dhandhusar with eighty-four villages as an *inâm* on their abandonment of all claims to participate in the *râj*. The parganah Upleṭâ was [for the sum of 35,000 Jâmîs (*koḍîs*) given as a bribe to the agents] bestowed upon Kumbhâji for a yearly *peshkash* of 5000 Jâmîs (*koḍîs*). During two years Dayâl the Vâṇiâ became Kârbhâri twice, and was also removed twice.

The Navâb Sâheb Mahâbat Khânji used to plunder the surrounding country of Kâṭhiâvâḍ in order to maintain himself and to pay his troops;

in several tâlukâs he collected a variable *jama'bandi* illegally. When he was pressed to pay his army, he used to flee with a select party of friends to the town under the shelter of night, to which he was tracked by the helpless *sipâhis*, who were in a destitute condition from not having received any pay; but he generally expelled them with threats and by force from the town, in order to relieve them from the trouble of wandering about and from the misery of service, and to compel them to return to their homes, where they might take rest with their children; this went on until Mevalâl bin Jagjivandâs bin Sadânand, a Kâyath from Gujarât, became Divân, who, like his brother Śivalâl, used to make a living as a *munshi*. He was a man who wrote a pleasing hand, had agreeable manners, and dressed well; and about this time Sher-zamân Khân Bâbi, the uncle of the Navâb Sâheb, who had formerly been expelled by Sohrâb Khân from Goghâ, and who had been reinstalled there and had come to Junâgaḍh and received in *jâgir* from the Navâb Sâheb the eighty-four villages of the Bâṇṭvâ parganah, carried on the business of Kârbhâri for about two years.

Shekh Miyân takes Verâval.

Sulṭân Bibî, sister of Navâb Bahâdur Khân, and spouse of Shahâmat Khân Bâbi, who had taken possession of Verâval, was forcibly deprived thereof by Kâzi Sheikh Miyân and by Mâlik Shahâb-al-din, and Sheikh Miyân ruled there with entire authority, and concluded a covenant of peace and friendship with Desâi Sundarji and other Nâgars.

The Divânship of Divânji Sâheb Amarji.

At the age of eighteen years Amarji left Mângrol and went in search of service to the court of the Navâb Sâheb Mahâbat Khânji, who was at that time besieging the fort of Uparkoṭ, where the Arabs had taken refuge. The Navâb Sâheb said to Amarji, "If you could obtain possession of the Vâgeśvari gate, which is in the possession of the Arabs of the fort, and could surrender it to the officials of the Sarkâr, you would establish a claim to enter my service." Accordingly he went to Purbandar, whence he brought an Arab Jamadâr named Sâlmân with a number of other Arabs, but as the Navâb Sâheb would not allow them to enter the town they remained outside, but assaulted the Vâgeśvari gate in the night, slew some of its defenders, and finally handed it over to the servants of the Navâb Sâheb, whereupon the entire party was engaged to remain at the court, and they discharged well and ably whatever service was entrusted to them. Two years had not yet elapsed when the Divânji Sâheb conceived the idea of subjugating Verâval. Keeping a portion of the army with the Navâb Sâheb at Âdri, two *kos* from Verâval, Amarji, when the moon with her army of stars was ascending by means of the scaling ladders of degrees to the citadel of the firmament, proceeded to Verâval in the company of the Jamadâr, 'Abdu'lla Khân, and others, and planted their standard on the wall on the west of the town, and fell on the garrison suddenly like a calamity from heaven, and made them food for the sword. After that they attacked four or five hundred Arabs who were in the *thânah*, whom they put to flight; then Jamadâr Wâhdîu'd-dîn entered the town with a detachment of Sindhîs from the seaside, and great bloodshed took place, so that the conquered party lost heart, and, not caring for their honour, fled with Shekh Jahângir and Shekh Miân, and arrived safely at Paṭṭan Div, but Sundarji Desâî with his adherents was captured. In the morning the news of the conquest of the fort was conveyed to the Navâb Sâheb, who entered it with the joyful sounds of the kettle-drum, and the populace came out to welcome him. On this occasion Divânji Sâheb, the deceased Amarji, father of the author, succeeded in preserving the honour of the ladies of Sundarji Desâî from the Navâb Sâheb, who was addicted to pleasure. The Divânji Sâheb was not employed in the (*muḷaki*) revenue and judicial branch, but merely superintended the (*faujdâri*) army administration of the state. According to the freaks of the times, Popaṭ Pârikh was Divâṇ for three days, Jhavarchand for twenty days, and Mulchand Pârikh for one month, and their management was so confused and ruinous that they abandoned it in disgrace.

Sher Zamân Khân attacks Junâgaḍh.

In Saṁvat 1825 Sher Zamân Khân arrived from Bântwâ, with the vague intention of effecting a night surprise, with a company of vagabonds from the wilderness of misfortune, and took up a position in the Basârat Bâgh (a garden near the Majhâvaḍi gate). In the morning, when the portal of light was opened, and also the town gate was to be unlocked, these vagabonds quickly approached it, and suddenly met the woodcutters and other inhabitants of the country, who were arriving on a pilgrimage to Pir Dâvalshâh, who is called Maidani; and when they reached the gate, it was shut upon them from within, and the people commenced to fight with them, whereupon Sher Zamân Khân fled like a gazelle and leaped like a hare, from terror and fright, in the direction of his own abode.

Demolition of Dilkhâniâ.

In the same year the Kâṭhi Kumpâ Wâlâ asked for the Divânji's assistance and induced him to demolish Dilkhâniâ; and the said place, which was an asylum of highway robbers, was razed to the ground by the Divânji Sâheb Amarji, accompanied by the above-named Kâṭhi Kuṁpâ Wâlâ, who was a Grâsia of Chitalgâm.

Acquisition of Kutiânâ fort.

The troops of the Divân Sâheb were still in the zillâ of Dilkhâniâ when Pir Khân Shirvâni, Bhâvata, Khokhar, and other Kasbatis represented to him that they had made over the fort of Kutiânâ to Hâshim Khân Bâbi, a young son of the Navâb Sâheb Bahâdur Khân, and that he was severely oppressing the inhabitants of the country; and that if he should perchance be wheedled into parting with the fort to Râṇâ Sulṭânji, whose Kâmdâr, Premaji Lohânâ [Ṭhakar] would be ready enough to buy strange property, it would be a difficult matter [to retake it].

Distich:—A pin can stop the water at its source;
When full, no elephants can pass it then.

As soon as he obtained this information the Divân immediately marched to Kutiânâ, where he began to carry on all the operations proper in a siege, and soon made use of mines, by which he blew a bastion into the air, which destroyed likewise all the *chaukidârs* of the garrison. Hâshim Khân, being thus rendered helpless, sued for peace, which was soon concluded; he lost the fort, but obtained in lieu thereof the village of Majhávadi as a *jâghir*. When the Diván conquered the fort he installed therein his younger brother Govindji [in behalf of the Navâb], who remained there till his death in Saṁvat 1846, after which his son Mangalji kept it till Saṁvat 1849. Having terminated this affair, the Divân again unfurled his banners, to proceed on the Mulukgiri expedition.

Conquest of the fort of Talâja.

Vakhat Sing Râval, Râja of Bhâunagar, called to his aid the Divan, who being aware that it is the duty of governors to cherish their subjects, responded to the call, and when he arrived at Goghâ, Vakhat Sing requested him to reduce the fort of Talâjâ. Accordingly he marched in person with his soldiers, who succeeded in scaling the wall of the fort; their antagonists, the Kolis, however, met them bravely, and severe fighting continued for some time, during which there was much bloodshed, and the Divânji himself was wounded in the leg by a musket-ball; but fortune favoured his party, their opponents were unable longer to resist, and were compelled to pay a large nazaránah. In course of time the fort came into the hands of the English, who gave it to Naváb Nur-al-dîn, the governor of Khambhât, who in his turn sold it to Râval Vakhat Sing, ruler of Bhavnagar, for 80,000 rupees. The Divânji Sâheb then returned to Junâgaḍh, but, in spite of the station he had attained, he did not desire to be addressed by the title of Divân; on this occasion, however, on the day of his bathing on recovery he was presented with the presents bestowed on a Diván, viz., a palanquin, a big drum, sword, dagger with golden hilt, chobdâr, torches, and the other insignia.

Conquest of four forts of Mângrol.

As Shekh Miyân of Mângrol excited a rebellion and would not submit, the victorious standards of the Divânji proceeded against him in Saṁvat 1827, and the forts of Sil, Divâsâ,

Mahiâri, and Bagasrâ were forcibly taken from him. In the battle which was fought under the fort of S i l the horse ridden by the Divanji received no less than eleven wounds; but he himself, by the hand of the true Preserver, was kept from all harm. After chastising the Thânahdârs, the Divânji besieged Mângrol, but when the firing of his cannon began to take effect, Shekh Miyân lost heart, and despatched Jibhâi, the paternal uncle of the Divânji Sâheb, to intercede for him; thus he obtained pardon after surrendering the moiety of his parganah [to the Naváb]. During the same year that mine of virtues K u v a r j i,—mercy be upon him,—the father of the Divânji Sâheb Âmarji, after becoming a Sanyâsi (or Brâhmaṇ ascetic) became an inmate of Paradise.

Liberation of the Mutasadis of Kachh Bhuj.

The R â o S â h e b G o ḍ j i had surrendered his Mutasadis (darbâr officials) as securities to the custody of the Arab and other Jamâdârs, whose salaries he was unable to pay; but, as the delay was long, the Arabs, after exposing them to innumerable calamities, brought them to the district of Hâlâr. Their Jamâdâr, who was an honourable man, was so greatly distressed at their insubordination that he put on his coat of mail and threw himself into the river Aji. When the Divânji Sâheb, who was at that time collecting *peshkash* (tribute) in this zillah heard of it, he, for the sake of the honour of the Râo Sâheb, paid the debt, and released the Mutasadis. In return for this handsome act the Râo Sâheb for some time used to send the Divânji Sâheb all sorts of presents and gifts.

Punishment of the Vâghars and Mâliâs.

Crowds of Vâghars were in the frequent habit of attacking the troops of the Śrimant Peshvâ, of the Gâekvâḍ, and of the Jâm, of spiking the cannon with iron nails, and of plundering the regions of Hâllâr, Jhâlâvâḍ [and Kachh]; accordingly the Divânji reduced them to obedience after some fighting, and caused them to pay a fine.

Punishment of the Bâbriâs and of the Unâ Qasbâtis.

The Bâbriâs, who subsist on impure food, were sallying forth from the shelter of their thorn-bushes and hills to commit depredations in the villages of Nâgher, Kâṭhiâvâḍ, and Wâlâk. The army was sent against them; they stood the first shock, but

Distich:—An antelope which with a lion plays
Will soon the earth touch with its face.

They were soon ground to powder by the hoofs of the steeds of the victorious army, and compelled to cease from their deeds of rapine, and obliged to restore the plunder they had taken, and they moreover agreed to pay a yearly tribute. When the troops marched back, they passed through the town of Unâ, and the Qasbâtis of the place, confiding in the strength of their foot and the bravery of their men, attacked the artillery train, and Poi, the nephew of the author, who was in charge thereof, honourably sacrificed his life to preserve the train; and after hard fighting the people consented to pay a fine, and, as a security for the disbursement of it, the Divânji Sâheb carried off the son of Qasbâti Shekh Tâhir to Junâgaḍh.

Kumbhâji attacks the Divânji Sâheb.

Jâḍejâ Kumbhâji of Gondal trusted much in his wealth and his Râjputs, and entertained for some time evil designs against Junâgaḍh. Accordingly when the Divânji Sâheb had left the troops to guard the frontiers and had himself returned to Junâgaḍh, Kumbhâji called the Marâṭhâ army of the Gâekvâḍ to his aid, and also privately consulted the Navâb Sâheb of Junâgaḍh, who entertained at that time a little spite against the authority of the Divânji, the breaking down of which, he conceived, would increase his own; wherefore he considered this a good opportunity, and connived with Kumbhâji, who was now encamped at Mâlâshamḍi, a village four miles from Junâgaḍh, and was only waiting for any encouragement (from the Navâb) as an excuse for ruining the Divân, attacked the army, which fled; but Jamadâr Salmin, not being able to mount a horse, was captured by the Maraṭhâs, who, however, released him without injury. When the fugitives arrived in Junâgaḍh the Navâb Sâheb loaded them with reproaches, but the Divânji Sâheb marched with an army numerous as locusts, and pitched his camp opposite to that of the confederates. Kumbhâji now repented, separated from Bâmanioji, who was the instigator of this evil action, and agreed to pay a fine and to restore all the plunder he had taken. When peace was restored, the Divânji Sâheb, on his return, besieged the fort of Chatrâsah; and Bâmanioji, its proprietor, after paying a large fine in cash and in kind, again took the ring of obedience to Junâgaḍh into his ear.

Imprisonment of the Divânji Sâheb with his brothers, and murder of Jamadâr Sâlmin the Arab.

Certain conspirators, such as Bhim Khojah the vegetable seller, Gulâbrâî Mehta, Khushâl Râi, Magatrâm Bhagat, Jagjivan Kikani, and other Nagars, caused the Divânji Sâheb Amarji, with his brothers Dulabji and Govindji, to be cast into prison. The Navâb Sâheb Mahâbat Khân, owing to the statements of those calumniators, was displeased; nevertheless he secretly honoured the prisoners by his visits and consoled them. On the fourth day of Phâlgun in Saṁvat 1829 the three persons just mentioned were imprisoned, and on the same day Sâlmin the Jamâdâr, their adherent, was summoned to the

Rang Mahâl (court), under the pretence that as Sheik Miyân of Mângrol had taken possession of the fort of N a v î, in the parganah of Porbandar, and was plundering the parganahs Chorvâḍ and Kesoji, his services were required to repel these attacks. When he entered the door, slaves jumped from an ambush and slew him, but his follower Sayyid 'Ali Châvush was quick enough to save his own life by striking out right and left at the slaves of the Sarkâr, and escaped. This same Châvush rose in course of time at Baroda to the dignity of a "sitter on an elephant," but was at last trampled to death by being tied to the feet of one. The Divânji Sâheb was set at liberty on the 7th of Śrâvaṇa Vad, after a captivity of five months and three days, on the condition of paying a *nazaránah* of 40,000 Jámi *koḍîs*, and until the payment thereof his eldest son, Raghunâthji, then ten years old, remained as a hostage; the Divânji himself, however, with his family, relatives, and followers, departed to the town of Jetpur.

The Navâb Sâheb marches against Mângrol, and recalls the Divânji Sâheb.

As Sheik Miyân was ravaging the country with a numerous army, and carrying off men and beasts, the Navâb Sâheb Mahâbat Khân marched against him, but, being unable to cope with his foe, he encamped at a distance of seven *kos* from the town and spent his time in reconnoitring. He kept the Divân Raghunâthji at his court, and entrusted his education to Bibî Sardâr Bakhtâ (his favourite wife), the daughter of Kumah-al-dîn Khân, who treated the boy like a mother, and who likewise accompanied the Navâb. In course of time Sheik Miyân became so bold that he not only stole horses and camels, but also harassed the army itself, so that no one dared to go out of the camp; and the Navâb, being thus greatly pressed, called Bhim Khojah and the other calumniators into his presence, and addressed them as follows :—" The Divân Amarji, the like of whom no potentate ever had in his service, and who augmented the honour of the Darbâr of Junâgaḍh, was by you removed from office without any fault of his own, and is at present living at Jetpur. He has received invitations from Kumbhâji of Gondal, from Râval Vakhtsinghji of Bhâvnagar, from Kâṭhis Bhoka and Kânthaḍ of Jetpur, from Rāṇá Sulṭânji of Porbandar, from Meroji of Râjpurâ, from Lâkhâji of Râjkoṭ, from Hothiji of Kotrâ, from Jâm Jasâji of Navânagar, from Bhârâji Jhâlâ of Wânkâner, from Wâghji of Moṛbi, from Śeshâji of Sâelâ, from Râj Gajsinghji of Dhrângdhrâ, from Jhâlâ Harbhamji of Limbḍi, from Jasâ Koli of Mahuwâ, from Sheikh Miyân of Mângrol, from Râizâdah Singhji of Chorvâḍ, from Daghoji Raizâdáh of Kesoj, from Mukhtâr Khân and Âdil Khân of Bânṭwâ, from Muzaffar Khân Bâbi and Fathyab Khân of Rânpûr, from Sheikh Tahir of Unâ, from Sayyid

Latif of Delvâḍâ, from the Faranghi Lewis Jhujhu of Divbandar, from Sidi Yaqub of Muzaffarâbâd, from Râo Sâheb Goḍji of Bhuj, from Lalubhâi of Bharuch, from the Navâb of Bandar Surat, and from Momin Khân of Khambhât, all of whom have sent him letters upon letters, presents in money, and kind messages with many compliments, and though he has no need of me, yet without him the state of Junâgaḍh is daily getting worse; if, therefore, you love your lives, you must obey the Divânji Sâheb and immediately recall him." Having obtained the orders of the Navâb Sâheb, those ill-natured men feigned repentance for what they had done, and gladly went to Jetpur, where they fell down at the blessed feet of the Divân Sâheb.

On the same occasion it happened that agents of the Râo Sâheb Goḍji had arrived with rich dresses of honour and splendid gifts and an invitation to the Divânji Sâheb to become the Divân of Kachh; they had been there for several days, but he gave them leave to depart, and thought proper to remember his old service and his duty of assisting the Navâb in this emergency. Accordingly he immediately joined the Navâb Sâheb, who restored to him the Divân Raghunâthji hitherto kept as a hostage, with a handsome present, and assigned to him the revenues of two villages for his private expenses. As soon as Sheikh Miyân heard of the arrival of the Divânji Sâheb, in spite of his bravery his heart failed him and he made his appearance with hands bound returned the property he had taken, paid a fine, and again became a vassal of Junâgaḍh.

Conquest of Sutrâpâḍâ.

When the army departed from Mângrol, the rayats of the parganah of Pâtan complained that Chând Pâtani, the Zamindâr of Sutrâpâḍâ, had reduced them to the last extremity of destitution. After hearing this complaint, the world-conquering banners of the Divânji Sâheb were unfurled; he besieged the fort, and the gunners kept up continual firing during a month, whereupon Chand came out with a grieved heart and a yellow face, suing for pardon, and having obtained a guarantee of his life and honour from the Divânji Sâheb, surrendered the fort to Mehta Gangârâm Lâlâbhâi, son of the Divânji's aunt.

Chând Pâtani had a virgin daughter, handsome like the brilliant moon, and as the Navâb Sâheb heard of her beauty, he dropped the reins of patience from his hands and desired to procure an interview with her; but as Chand refused to comply, he sent some persons to bring her by force. But the Divânji Sâheb kept his word, by which the honour and life of Chand were guaranteed, and accordingly he and his beautiful daughter were allowed to depart to Gorakhmaḍi, which is a sacred place of the Jogis.

Conquest of the Fort of Positrâ.

Merâman Khavâs, the Kârbhâri of the Jám Sâheb Jesâji, was greatly distressed by the depredations of Wâghars of Okhâmandal, accordingly he invited the Divânji Sâheb in Saṃvat 1830 to reduce the fort of Positrâ. The noble-minded Divânji Sâheb, who was constantly on the outlook for similar events, arrived in a short time in Okhâ and engaged in the siege of Positrâ, a fort never conquered by any one, but taken by the good fortune of the Divânji Sâheb in a single assault after exploding a gunpowder mine, and then mounting the breach. An amount of plunder considerable beyond all expectation was found, which those pirates had collected in the ports of the Dakhaṉ, of Arabia, the Soahili coast, Maskât, Abyssinia, Sindh, and the Farang (Portuguese) settlements. On that occasion the doleful news arrived of the demise of the Navâb Sâḥeb Mahâbat Khân on the 14th Kartak Vad in Saṃvat 1831 [A. H. 1177]. The duration of his reign was 16 years 2 months and 2 days.

Navab Sâheb Hâmed Khan, son of Mahâbat Khân Bahâdur Bâbi.

After receiving this terrible news the Divânji Sâheb immediately left Okhâ, marched quickly to Junâgaḍh, and placed the Sâhib Zâdah of exalted fortune Hamid Khân, who was born of Sujân Kuṅvar, upon the *masnad* of his father, and started the army to collect the *jamâbandi*. In that year also the *peshkash* (tribute) for Jhâlâvâḍ was for the first time fixed. Whilst the army was at a distance, collecting *peshkash*, Bâbis Adil Khân and Mukhtâr Khân, the Jâgirdârs of Bâṇṭwâ, formed an alliance with the Nágoris and other Kasbâtis of the town of V a n t h a l i, and without difficulty took that fort. When this disastrous news reached the Divânji Sâheb, he quickly marched to Vanthali and beleaguered the fort on all sides. Most of the instigators of this rebellion now tried to divert the Bâi Sâhibah Sujânbâi from the path of her duty, and to bias her towards Mukhtâr Khân and Âdil Khân; and at this time, Âburâi Mahipâtrâo, the Subâh of A'hmadâbâd, happened to bring an army into the country to collect *peshkash*, and the malcontents bought his aid, but, owing to their fear of the Divânji Sâheb, they were unable to effect anything, and he kept up the siege and skirmished with the troops who approached his army. And when the Dakhaṇis perceived that they were unable to effect anything, they made peace with the Divânji and presented him with a dress of honour, and abstained from fighting, and entrusted to him the collection of the rest of their *jamâbandi* and returned. After getting rid of this interference the Divânji Sâheb pressed the fort more closely, so that Mukhtâr Khân sued for mercy, and was allowed to depart to Bâṇṭwâ, and the fort was occupied by the servants of the Naváb of Junâgaḍh.

VICTORY OVER THE SUBAHDARS OF THE PESHVÂ AND GÂEKVÂḌ.

Amrat Râo and Thoban, Subahdârs of the Peshvâ and the Gâekvâḍ, arrived together whilst the army of the Divânji Sâheb was in the Panchâl district. These troops advanced with the intention of fighting under their valiant officers. The Divânji Sâheb, as then seemed best to him, and remembering his position as a Zamindâr, suffered them to be without molestation, but both the antagonistic armies were close to each other at Jetpur, and the warriors were anxious to fight. Accordingly at dawn, when the sovereign of day drew forth the scimitar of light from the scabbard of darkness, the command to attack was sounded on both sides by beating drums and blowing clarions noisy enough to cause an earthquake. The Dakhaṇis rushed forth with great ardour in large masses, carrying swords, guns, and lances, compelling the Divânji, who put his trust in the Lord of Girnâr, to defend himself with his infantry and cavalry and to open fire with his artillery. At last the fight became general, and in it a trooper wearing a coat of mail inflicted a blow with his sword on the shoulder of the Divânji Sâheb, which would have killed him had it not been rendered harmless by the armour he wore, and, turning swiftly round, at one spear-thrust he slew the trooper. The enemy left their dead on the battle-field and carried off their wounded; and, the Divânji Sâheb being victorious, the Marâṭhâs began the second day to treat for peace, and a meeting having been held, through the mediation of Jâḍejâ Kumbhoji and Wâlâ Kânthar, peace was finally concluded, with many compliments on both sides; when, however, Amrat Râo arrived in Ahmadâbâd, he was treacherously killed in the bazar by an Arab.

March to Pâlanswâ, in the country of Vâgad.

At the request of Vâghji Râjâ of Morbi, the Divânji marched to Vâgaḍ, but some of his men died for want of water whilst crossing the Salt Ran; but the fort of Pâlanswâ and the town of Keriânagar were taken after considerable trouble, and countless booty fell into the Divânji's hands, and he returned to Junâgaḍh after receiving a large sum of money sent by the Râo Sâheb of Kachh to avert further misfortunes.

As the Jâm Sâheb Jasáji was besieging the fort of Bethâli, in the parganah of Porbandar, Râṇâ Sulṭânji sued for assistance, as narrated in the account of that parganah, and it was granted. Peace was concluded, on condition that the fort of Bethâli should be demolished. On this occasion an attempt was made by Merâman Khawâs secretly to poison the Divânji Sâheb at an entertainment to which he was invited. But, as he was destined to live, he excused himself from accepting the invitation, on the pretext that Daftari Khushâlrâi had died at Junâgaḍh; and he ordered his army to march in that direction. Jivâji Sâmraj, Subah of the Gaikvâḍ, had come to collect the *peshkash* (tribute) of Kâṭhiâvâḍ, and, having stationed his army at Amreli, aimed at independence and the conquest of territory and caused much disturbance in the country. Accordingly the victorious army marched to coerce him, and after he was defeated in open battle he took shelter in Amreli, which place he was also forced to quit; the Divân Sâheb granted him pardon, and allowed him to depart to Gujarât, and razed the fort to the ground. At this time Sheikh Miyân caused a disturbance in Mângrol, and the Divân Sâheb Amarji sent his younger brother Divân Dulabhji, who was a pillar of the government and wise like Aristotle, to punish him, and he took up his station at Sil, where hostilities were being carried on with equal results, when, by the will of God, Khushâlbâi, mother of the author, and daughter of Dosâ Mehta Mânkaḍ, expired on the 13th of Jeshṭa Vad in Saṁvat 1834 (A.D. 1777). She had given birth to three sons, the eldest of whom, Raghunâth, was born on the 11th of Asâḍ Shud Saṁvat 1819 [A.D. 1762]; the second, Ranchoḍji, was born on the 10th Aso Shud in Saṁvat 1824 [A.D. 1767]; and the third, Dalpatrâm, on the 2nd Bhâdarvâ Vad in Saṁvât 1829 [A.D. 1772]; her fourth child was a daughter Âmâbâi, who was born in Saṁvat 1832 (A.D. 1775). Sheikh Miyân thought this a good opportunity, and came on the pretence of condolence to Junâgaḍh, and sat down with some of his companions in the large tent where the mourners were assembled, and sued for pardon, which the Divân Sâheb was thus obliged to grant.

At the close of Saṁvat 1834 the Râo Sâheb Fatehsing Gaikvâḍ, who reigned at Baroda, and who had heard of the expulsion of Jiwâji Sâmraj from the fort of Amreli, entered Sorаṭh with a large army; when he arrived at Jetpur and encamped there, he heard how well the Divân Sâheb stood with his army, how liberal and how brave he was, and he saw that it would be a difficult matter to subdue him: accordingly through the mediation of some of the Zamindârs, he overlooked his injury, and presented the Divânji Sâheb with a dress of honour, and also bestowed on him the tribute which was in arrears, and returned. In Saṁvat 1835 the Gâekvâḍ went again on *mulkgiri* expedition to Kâṭhiâvâḍ, though it had been his intention to avenge the disaster of Jivâji Sâmrâj, and to boast of his success; but his object was not accomplished.

By the advice and boldness of Premji Lohânâ, his Kâmdâr, the Râṇâ Sulṭânji had employed all the Arabs he could enlist in his service on a higher monthly salary, and had thus become the source of disturbances. Accordingly the army was got ready to punish him, and when Premji saw his inability to resist in the field he began to tremble like a willow-leaf, and sent tribute in excess of the usual amount, as well as all the booty he had taken, and, in addition to this, costly presents obtained from the cargo of a ship sent by

Navâb Haidar 'Ali as presents to the Khalifah of Baghdâd, and which vessel had been wrecked on his coast, and sought forgiveness of his transgressions.

In the year Saṁvat 1836 [A.D. 1780] there was a slight famine, during which the Sindhis of Devrâ and Khâgasri, under the leadership of Malik Muhammad and other Sindhis, had collected their people from all quarters, and commenced to plunder the country of Kumbhâji, who complained to the Divân Sâheb. Accordingly the army marched, and was joined also by Divân Govindji with his forces from Kutiânâ; both forts were besieged and cannonaded, the garrisons fled, and they were taken possession of by the servants of the Junâgaḍh government.

The Thânadâr of Kandornâ, Jivâ Seṭh by name, an Amir of the Jâm Sâheb's darbâr, was a brave man who constantly kept his army fighting, and supported it by plunder. In Saṁvat 1837 he ravaged Gadhâli, in the parganah of Bhâvnagar, in Gohelvâḍ, and captured Motibhâi, a Râjput Zamindâr who was the adopted uncle of the author, and imprisoned him in the fort of Mewâsá [under Kandornâ]. When this news reached the Divânji he quickly marched to Mewâsá; on the road, however, he met certain men coming from Dhrol with the intention of aiding Jivâ Seṭh; most of these he killed, and then besieged the fort. When Jivâ Seṭh saw death staring him in the face and fortune abandoning him, he sent out Motibhâi with valuable presents, and thus escaped from the whirlpool of destruction. Meru Khavâs, although he had arrived with an army at Kandornâ to aid Jivâ Seṭh, had not the courage to do so, and halted there without engaging. Shekh Tâhir had formerly killed the half-brother of the Divân Sâheb Raghunâthji, by name Pipi, who was in charge of the artillery. To avenge this murder the Divânji marched against him in Saṁvat 1838, and obtained the place without fighting, and bestowed on him one or two villages in *inâm*. Gangâdâs, half-brother of the Divânji, and who formerly was Thânahdâr of Delvâḍâ, owing to disputes with Sayyid Latif and others came to Unâ and thence attacked Delvâḍâ, but was killed by a musket-ball in the last-mentioned place; after that, Tuljârâm, the Divânji's own brother, was slain in a fight, and in his place Parbhâshankar Nânâbhâi, a Bânsvâḍâ Nâgar, who was a good soldier and a brave man, was made Thânadâr of Unâ and Delvâḍâ, and after great trouble he succeeded in subjugating the Bâbriâs, and the Habshi of Muzaffarâbád and the Portuguese of Div feared him greatly.

On this joyful season of the Huli the Divânji Sâheb was desirous that the young Navâb Hamid Khân should preside over the festivities; accordingly within the camp many tents were pitched, and a spacious *shâmianâh* was erected, adorned with garlands, in which he was installed on a gorgeous throne of many hues, and numerous dancing girls were engaged for the occasion, and carried on their diversions with music and singing for a whole month.

Victory over the Jâm Sâheb Jasâji, the Râṇâ Sulṭânji, and Kumbhoji.

The Jâm Jasâji was Jâm in name only, as he was kept by Merâman and Bhowân Khavâs, the Karbhâris, under surveillance, like a parrot in a cage, whilst they reigned in Nagar according to their pleasure, and collected much gold and silver. To free her husband from this tutelage, Achubâ Râṇî, wife of the Jâm, the daughter of Râja Gajsingh of Halwâd-Dhrângadhra, planned various stratagems. The Râja of Porbandar, Râṇâ Sulṭânji, Kumbhoji the Râjâ of Gondal, and all the Zamindârs of those parts entered into an alliance, and after fighting some battles in the parganah of Kutiânâ in the month Maghsar Saṁvat 1838, encamped with their armies, which exceeded ants and locusts in numbers, on the banks of the river Bhâdar. To meet these foes the Divânji Sâheb marched with his glorious army, and pitched his tents near Jetpur. Merâman Khavâs discovered that he could not cross the river save by stratagem, and accordingly despatched Jagu Râval, a man whom he greatly trusted, with a humble message to the Divânji Sâheb to send over Rudrâji Chânya and Punjmal, a Bânsvâḍâ Nâgar, that he might treat with them; when, however, these two men arrived in his tent, he addressed them in so overbearing a manner that they could scarcely endure it, and replied in their turn that he was wrong in placing too much confidence in the multitude of his troops, and to consider the Divânji Sâheb as a weak man, but rather to liken him unto a valiant lion who can put to flight a flock of goats, or a hungry wolf who would disperse them like a herd of antelopes. At these words Merâman became afraid, and in the dead of night, when both these Vakils were fast asleep, he crossed the river with all his troops. As soon as the Divânji Sâheb was apprised of this, he beat the drum to pursue the enemy, whom he overtook in the plain of Pânchpiplâ, where Meru had drawn up his army in battle array, and surrounded his camp with large and small artillery. When the two armies encountered each other, the cannonade began immediately.

Verses: —

Troops numerous were here assembled all,
No one had ever seen the like before—
Combatants more than locusts or large ants,
All wielding dirks and fiery scimitars,
And furious like to raging elephants,
With poniards, spears, and arrows in their hands.
The rush of troops so blocked the roads
That earth's surface seemed too small for them.
The din of war arose from all the troops,
Black smoke confused the earth and sky in one.
The yells produced anxiety of heart,
They chased the sense from heads, and hues from cheeks.

The noise of kettle-drums, and laments of trumps,
Made lions lose their way in deserts wide.
The brazen roar, enough to split the stones,
Distressed the Simurgh on Mount Qâf.
The lamentation of the Trumpet sounds
Produced quaking fear in hands and feet.
The noise which the chiefs heard was such
That you have said the resurrection trump had sounded.

The antagonists fell upon each other like the waves of the ocean, the Divânji Sâheb's army began to give way a little, but order was soon restored by the exertions of Muzafar Khân, Fatehyâb Khân Bâbi, 'Abdu'llah Khân, Abdul Rahim Khân (Karâni), Haiyât Khân Baloch, Harising Solankhi, Syad Karam 'Ali, Sayyid Gul Muhammad, Mulvi Ahmadu'llah, Omar Khân Khokhar, Himatlâl, Jitârâm, and Sampatrâm Nâgar and others, who restored the battle. Shekh Miân also arrived after the battle had commenced, and joined in it, and flashed like lightning on the threshing-floor of the enemies.

Verses :—

What battle lines did they arrange !
Each champion looking for his rival foe.
Both armies were amazingly confused,
It seemed the sun and moon commingled were.
On both sides streams of blood did flow ;
The fathers for their sons did look,
And all were waiting for the turn of fate.

At last the enemies were scattered like the stars of the Great Bear. Bhavân Khawâs, brother of Meru Khawâs, was wounded by a musket ball.

Meru, the commander-in-chief of Hâllâr, fled with all the troops, which would have found no resting-place, had not the mantle of night screened them, and the Divânji Sâheb with much joy took possession of the enemy's camp, beating the *shâdiânah* drum of delight, and was applauded by everybody.

Merâman Khawâs, being thus foiled by this ill-luck, called to his aid the army of Sena Khâs Khel Shamsher Bahâdur Mânâji Gaikvâḍ, and the Divânji Sâheb, wishing to remain on good terms with the latter, returned to Junâgaḍh and encamped near the town. The Zamindârs and the army of the Gaikvâḍ dared not follow him, but beleaguered Devrá, which has four towers, and by cannonading it on all sides they demolished it after a week's siege; but the garrison, under Fakirchand Purbiah, Balkhair, an Arab Jamâdâr, and Abherâm the Nâgar, were allowed to depart with their arms and ammunition, and after this affair the army of the Gaikvâḍ returned to Baroda. Hereupon the Divânji Sâheb proceeded with his victorious army to punish the Zamindârs for their rebellious spirit, and invaded the country of the Râṇâ Sulṭânji, with whom Merâman Khawâs had made an alliance, but, time-server as he was, he broke it and supplicated the Divânji Sâheb to pardon his transgressions.

Accordingly he joined the army; and after devastating the country of the Râṇâ the Divânji Sâheb left a detachment to besiege the fort of

Khirasrâ, and proceeded with the army to collect the jamâbandi (revenue) from the Khambhât, Dhandhukâ, and Limbḍi frontier. The Rânâ, who was now helpless, agreed to pay a fine and heavy tribute, and to repair the fort of Devrâ, whereon he again obtained peace. During this year the parganah of Dâthâ came into the possession of the government of Junâgaḍh.

Verses :—

The night is dark, the storm so terrible,
What know the happy people on the shore?

Murder of the Divân Sâheb Amarji.

The Navâb Sâheb Hâmed Khân left the army, which was on a *mulukgiri* expedition, in Saṁvat 1840 [A.D. 1784], on pretence of sickness, and made a night's halt at Gondal on his journey; on this occasion Kumbhâji, who was always apprehensive that the Divân Sâheb might retake Dhorâji and Upletâ, spoke as follows to the Navâb :—"I will give you three lâkhs of Jami *koḍis* if you will get rid of your Divân, who is an ambitious man and carries on the affairs of your state with a high hand, and if you effect this you will acquire independence and freedom from control, as well as full authority in your government." When the Navâb Sâheb entered Junâgaḍh he set about the execution of his plan, by alluring with abundant gifts and promises of high offices Manohardâs, son of Trikamdâs, a Nâgar of the Vaishṇava sect who was in the confidence of the Divân Sâheb, and Mehta Khân and Jubah Khân Gujarâti and Jivan Khân Afghân, all of whom were companions and guards of the Navâb, to aid him in the execution thereof. Accordingly, when the Divân Sâheb had returned from the collection of the *peshkash* [tribute] to Junâgaḍh during the Huli festival, and B i b î S a r d â r B a k h t â, widow of the deceased Navâb Mahâbat Khân, invited him to the palace on the pretence of showing him the *trousseau* she had prepared for the marriage of Bibî Kamâl Bakhtâ, daughter of Ghâzi-al-dîn Khân to the Navâb Hâmid Khân, and which consisted of garments, jewellery, with gold and silver ornaments, &c., they there put him to death. They who committed the deed acquired thereby eternal infamy. The murder was committed on the 11th Rabi II. A.H. 1198 (March 6th, A.D. 1784). On this occasion the author and Divân Dulabhji, with Desâi Sâmaldâs, and Rudraji the Gomashtah, were thrown into prison, in spite of the aid of the Arab Jamadârs Sheikh Muhammad Zubaidi, and Mâsud, and Sâleh Abdullâ, and Hâdi, and the Sindhi Jamadârs Sharfud-dîn and Malhâr, and other Gujarâtis and Afghâns, but it availed nothing.

At this time the army of the Gaikvâḍ Morâr Râo Senâ Khâs Khel Shamsher Bahâdur was camped in the zillah of Gohelvâḍ, levying tribute. Rupaji Sindhia, who was a cousin of Mâdhavji Sindhia, the intimate friend of the murdered

Divân Sâheb, accompanied the Gaikvâḍ army. On hearing the melancholy news, he advanced by forced marches and encamped in the plain of Dhandusar, at a distance of four *kos* from Junâgaḍh, where he pitched his victorious tents. Thence he demanded from the Navâb Sâheb satisfaction for this wanton murder, and enjoined him to release the men whom he had imprisoned, as the Arabs had confined the Navâb to the Rang Mahâl until he should give proper securities ; he therefore, perceiving the altered circumstances of the time, released the prisoners after one month.

Râval Vakhatsingh, observing his opportunity, expelled the thânah of Junâgaḍh which had been recently placed at the port of Mâhuwâ, and gradually acquired possession of Loliânâ, Pâtṇâ, Salḍi, and other places. The Navâb Sâheb, when he saw there was no other remedy, invested Raghunâthji, the excellent son of the late Divânji Sâheb Amarji, with the garb of minister. The date of this event has been found by Pânti Miân Chisti as follows :—

Verses :—

"When Raghunáthji received the robe of the ministry
Venus came dancing with joy at the sight,
And a joyful voice issued from the sky
'The good fortune which has departed has again returned.'"*

* The numerical values of the letters amount to............the year A. H. in which the event happened.

And the demands of the late Divânji Sâheb, which amounted to sixty lâkhs of Jâmi *koḍis*, were thus settled in the presence of the Gâekvâḍ, the ruler of the age.

The parganahs of Unâ, of Delvâḍâ, of Mângrol, of Sil, and of Divâsâ were mortgaged until the liquidation of the debt with interest was effected. This was arranged in Saṁvat 1840. The second agreement was that the four villages of Halyâd, Bhensân, Antaroli, and Akhodar, bestowed as a reward for the conquest of the forts of Verâval and Kutiânâ, should be considered as a ransom for the murder of the Divân Sâheb, and his children should also receive five villages from the parganahs of Mângrol and Sutrâpâḍâ respectively. To this agreement Sayyid Ghulâm Mahi-al-dîn and Sayyid Ahmad Qâdari, with the Arab and Sindhi Jamadârs Haiyât Khân Baluch and Hari Sing Qasbâti, stood security. As, however, the army of the Gaikvâḍ would not move without the consent of the sons of the murdered Divân, the Divân Dulabhji despatched the author to that chief of exalted fortune Morâr Râo Gaikvâḍ to plead for the pardon of the Navâb Sâheb. When the author arrived at the tents, the Gaikvâḍ himself, with Râja Nârâyaṇ Râo Pândre, Jivâji Sâmrâj, Rupâji Sindhia, and the Nimbâlkar, the Sardârs of Baroda and the Deshmukhs, and Jamadâr Hamid, and the Yemani Amirs Obayd, Qâsam, Hâra, &c. came to condole with him one by one, and each noble presented him with two shawls and an embroidered scarf and turban. In all they amounted to about a hundred. The Râo Sâheb advanced a hundred paces from his private tent and presented me with a palanquin and with the turban from his own blessed head, and directed that I should be appointed his Divân, and Superintendent of a *pâgah* of 1500 horsemen according to the rules of Pândre; and the annual pay of all these men amounted to six lâkhs and forty thousand rupees, and to defray this he assigned the revenues of the parganahs Mahudha, Amreli, Dâmnagar and Koḍinâr, but, as I was brought up in this country, and had my relatives here, I could not accept of this bounty.

Finally the fort of Kutiânâ was given to the Divân Govindji, and Unâ and the Mângrol parganah to the Divân Dulabhji, Verâval to the Divân Raghunâthji, and Sutrâpâdâ to Sâmalji Mânkaḍ, the maternal uncle of the author. In spite of his favours the Srimant Gaikvâḍ made a demand for these parganahs, but Divân Dulabhji, being faithful to his salt, refused to consent.

When the army of the Gaikvâḍ had marched away, Sayyid Sâlim, Abdu'llah bin Hamid, Omar bin Hamid, Ahmed Umar, Sheikh Muhammad Zubeid, and other Arabs kept the Navâb Sâheb Hâmed Khân for four months confined to his tents near the Vanthali Gate, to enforce payment of their arrears of salary. The Navâb, however, who was as cunning as Lokmân, sent for a covered carriage from the darbâr, and spread a rumour that his mother, the Bibî Sâhebah Sardâr Bakhtâ, whom he had not seen for several months, was coming to pay him a visit; the simple Arabs kept their guard without the tents, whilst the Navâb Sâheb made his servant Rahmat Khân lie down on his bed and represent him, whilst he left in the carriage in the assumed garb of a woman. As soon as he entered the Rang Mahal, he began to fire muskets and cannon upon the Arabs; when the Arabs saw that their scheme had failed, they took refuge in the Uparkoṭ; this, however, he also attacked, and after some more fighting peace was concluded on the condition that the Arabs should receive one-half of the wages due to them. The Divân Dulabhji and others, being tired of the perpetual fightings, emigrated to Jetpur with their families.

THE FORT OF VERÂVAL IS TAKEN FROM THE DIVÂN RAGHUNÂTHJI BY TREACHERY.

Since Saṁvat 1836 the fort of Verâval had belonged to the Divân Raghunâthji, but three confidential leaders of *sibandi*, namely, the Jamadârs Rabyâ, Rakhyah, and Nebhor, and Tâj Muhammad Qamar, were decoyed by the Navâb to his own side from motives of gain, and they, forgetting the obligations under which they were to the Divân Sâheb Raghunâthji, expelled him from the fort; accordingly he went by the way of Gorakhmadi first to Jetpur, and then after a lapse of several months to Junâgaḍh, during which interval Tâpidâs Vaishṇava and Manohardâs Jikâr, like reptiles of the earth, endeavoured to carry on the office of Divân, but were not tolerated longer than a week.

The Navâb Sâheb instigates the Arabs against the Divânji.

In this year there happened to be a partial famine; and Ibrâhim Khân, with Hânsoji and Atâji and Khânji, having obtained a favourable opportunity, expelled Sâmalji (Mânkaḍ) from Sutrâpâḍâ, and took possession of the fort; accordingly the Divân Dulabhji sent Parbhâshankar Faujdâr from Unâ with troops to besiege it, whereupon the garrison, being helpless, accepted the author as their governor. The Divân Dulabhji had gone on a progress through the country, and leaving Junâgaḍh had reached Unâ when the Navâb Sâheb issued orders to have him killed, but was unsuccessful. Afterwards the Navâb instigated the Arab Jamadârs in Junâgaḍh who were in the employ of the Divân to abandon him; and Divân Govindji, with the Jamadâr Shekh Muhammad Zubeidi, Sâleh A'bdullah, and other Arabs, was besieged in the Uparkôṭ, but after some fighting an arrangement was made that the moiety of their wages should be paid to them. Then the Divân Govindji went to Jetpur; and the Divân Dulabhji, who was at Unâ, was joined by the Divân Ranchoḍji from Sutrâpâḍâ, whence he had been expelled by Ibrâhim Khân Hansoji Paṭhân and others who were in expectation of such work. The Navâb Sâheb appointed his servant Shekh Mahmûd Mângroli to conquer Unâ, and he took up a position at Gupt Prâg; and it happened that Mehtâ Parbhâshankar—a Bânsvâḍâ Nâgar who had been a confidential servant of Divân Dulabhji, and had been employed by him for years, and who had been the Thânadâr of Unâ and Koḍinâr, and who had subjugated the whole of Bâbriâvâḍ and Kâṭhiâvâḍ by his prowess, and whom the Governor of Muzaffarâbâd, (Jâfarâbâd) as well as the Portuguese of Diu feared—swerved from his loyalty in consequence of the events of the times, and instigated the Jamadârs of the Sirbandi, namely, Rayah (Rabi) and Punah, and Jesâ and Rahim, and Avud'Ali, to expel Dulabhji, which they did at the beginning of the rainy season. He now went to Delvâḍâ, where also he was not allowed to remain, but the people there kept his son Morârji as their nominal Sardâr. The said Divân then stayed for a month at Dhorâji, where he paid off the Arabs who had been in his service, and went to Jetpur, and was hospitably entertained all this time by Jâḍejâ Kumbhâji.

Gul Khân is slain. Marriage of the Bibi Sâhebah Kamâl Bakhta, and events of year 1842.

The Sindhi Jamadârs kept forcible possession of the fort of Vanthali to enforce payment of their arrears, whilst Jamadârs Karamshâh and Othmân and others had established themselves firmly in the Rang Mahâl at Junâgaḍh; but the Navâb Sâheb, who in deceit and artifice excelled Kalilah and Dimnah, induced the Arabs to slay the Jamadâr Gul Khân in the middle of the bâzâr during the celebration of the Îd, and to expel the other Jamadârs from the city by force. These men, however, took refuge in Vanthali, whither the Navâb himself went to oust them, and called to his assistance also Premji Lohânâ from Porbandar, but after his arrival they could not agree, and he was obliged to return in disgrace. Now, since no one could carry on the work of Divân or subjugate the Sindhis, the Navâb found himself forced to go to Jetpur, where he remained fifteen days, and after a thousand supplications invested the Divân Raghunâthji with the official dress of Divân, and finally brought him to Junâgaḍh; during the same year he contracted a marriage with the daughter of Navâb Ghâzial-din Khân, the Jâgirdâr of Sami, and Munjpur; the lady's name was Kamâl Bakhtâ, and the wedding was celebrated in the town of Morbi, on which occasion the Divân Sâheb Raghunâthji and Dulabhji gave large sums to Chârans and singers.

Conquest of the Fort of Sutrâpâḍâ.

After Ibrâhim and Hânsoji Pattani had expelled the author, they took possession of the whole parganah of Sutrâpâḍâ; the Divânji therefore gave orders to Parbhâshankar to come from Unâ and chastise them; and he issuing from

Unâ punished them and expelled them from the fort after a month's siege, and the author was installed there as Mutasaddi, and held the office for eight years.

Meanwhile the Navâb Sâheb carried on the government of Junâgaḍh in a wavering manner, various factions intrigued against each other, and the Divân Sâheb Raghunâthji again resigned his office; but as the Navâb Sâheb was unable alone to conduct affairs, he found himself under the necessity for six months of paying visits to the house of Raghunâthji to consult him, and finally he again persuaded him, whether he would or not, to accept the office of Divân.

Jâḍejâ Kumbhâji, who was a shrewd man, at the time when a disagreement had taken place between the master and the servant, obtained a deed writing over permanently the *jamâ* of Gondal and of Jetalsar, Meli, Majethi, Lath, Bhimorâ, and the parganah of Sarsâi-Châmpardâ, on account of the three lákhs of Jâmis which he had advanced in Saṁvat 1840.

Conquest of Kesoj.

The Râizâdah Dagoji, the Zamindâr of Kesoj, kept in his pay Arab Jamadârs and Masu'd, Omar, Salomi and others, as well as Bayi Khân the Makrâni, and plundered the villages of Bâṇṭvâ; accordingly Edal Khân and Mukhtâr Khân implored the aid of the Divân Raghunâthji. Divân Dulabhji, who considered himself as the

Nâib of the Divân Sâheb Raghunâthji, sent the author with a force and artillery to the theatre of war. The first place sacked and burnt by the enemy was Agatrâi; and at the instance of the injured people I started, and fought a severe battle in the plain of the locality just mentioned, in which the Jamadâr Omar Salomi was killed, and on our side Mukhtâr Khân was wounded by a dagger-thrust, but slightly, as he wore a coat of mail. The second battle, in which about one hundred and fifty men on both sides were wounded, was fought near the village of Mavânâ; it lasted long, as the Arabs, under the protection of date-trees, firmly held their ground.

In this fight a personal attendant of the Divân Ranchoḍji, with Jamadâr Jân Muhammad and the Risâlâh of Omar, made great exertions, so that Dagoji agreed to pay a fine, as well as restore the plunder he had taken in the Bâṇṭvâ parganah. A few months afterwards he became so embarrassed on account of the pay he owed his troops, that in Saṁvat 1844 he sold the fort of Kesoj to the Divân Dulabhji for a lâkh of Jâmi *koḍis*.

Divân Raghunâthji takes the forts of Chorvâḍ and Verâval, and chastises Rânâ Sultânji.

As Sanghji Râizâdah, Zamindâr of Chorvâḍ, had lost his life in the battle at Mâliâ, and his survivors were perplexed how to pay the troops, they made over the fort of Chorvâḍ to Râṇâ Sulṭânji of Porbandar, who took possession of it, and at the same time raised a quarrel with Mângrol, but the time blinded his eyes from seeing the future, and made his mind arrogant. Ibrahim Khân Pattani and other rebels from the Junâgaḍh government had joined him, and he had enlisted them in his service, and he took possession of the fort of Verâval by means of scaling-ladders during the night of the 13th Bhâdarvâ in Saṁvat 1844. Diler Khân and Thânahdâr Ghulâmi, the servants of the Navâb Sâheb, pulled off their shoes before they had even seen the water, and sued for quarter without having offered any resistance, and issued forth ; however, Ghulâmi was killed. On that occasion the author, who had been for four years employed as Mutasaddi of Sutrâpâḍâ, as soon as he heard what had taken place, marched at once to the fort, but before I arrived the cowardly Diler Khân had surrendered the fort. When this news reached Junâgaḍh, Divân Dulabhji, who considered news of this sort good tidings, exclaimed—

"Will dignity or gold avail a fool ?
A kick is all that he requires !"

Divân Raghunâthji and Govindji managed the army, whilst Dulabhji, who suffered much from dropsy, remained in Junâgaḍh and sent to them the war material they required, and took care that the Sibandis were paid. Meanwhile the army besieged Chorvâḍ, and troops having assembled from all parts, Kumbhaji Jadeja was fortunate enough to serve there, and the gardens of Chorvâḍ were so devastated that cows and donkeys grazed on the celebrated* pân leaves, whilst the people crawled under the shade of plantain trees.

Ibrahim Khân, who was the commander of the Rânâ's forces, one day led a sortie against the besiegers and was killed by a musket-ball, and finally on the day of Kârtak Sûd first, in Saṁvat 1845, the fort was assaulted on the side where it had been breached by the cannon on that occasion. The Navâb Sâheb and the Divân Sâheb Raghunâthji mounted the breach as a bridegroom goes to meet the bride, and thus entered the city, and after applying scaling ladders, scaled the walls. O'mars Khokher and several other brave warriors showed much gallantry. Another assaulting party was led by Sâmalji Mânkar, the maternal uncle of the Divân, which entered the fort after a few musketry discharges from their Arabs, and the garrison after a slight resistance pleading for quarter saved their lives, and the family and children of Mokâji Râizâdah, the Zamindâr of Chorvâḍ, by the intervention of Kumbhaji Jadeja, were allowed to depart honourably to Dhoraji; and from this date the government of the Râizâdahs ceased to exist in Chorvâḍ.

After this victory the Navâb Sâheb marched with his victorious army to Verâval and laid siege to it. The Jemadars Rakhiah Karamshâh

* Chorvâḍ is celebrated for its pân gardens.

Malik Sultân Yahia Ben Mansur and Atâji and Dâwudji Kunwar defended the fort with a large garrison provisioned from the sea by way of Porbandar, and placing cannon on boats they cannonaded the camp, and also made a sharp attack on the besieging batteries, but eventually were repulsed. In those times Budhanâth, the abbot of Gorakmadi, who was very liberal and hospitable, happened to die, and the Navâb Sâheb Hâmed Khân despatched the author with Sheikh Mahmûd and Parbhashankar to condole with the family. In the same year also Divân Dulabhji died suddenly of the dropsy on Mâgsar Wad 2nd, and although the Navâb Sâheb and the army were much distressed at the news, the Divân Raghunáthji and Govindji put their trust in the mercy of God, and continued the siege. At last on Posh Wad 6th they allured to their side Ali Khân Atâji and Hansoji, and the Pattani Jamadârs, who from desire of their jâgirs and former service, turning from their allegiance joined the Navâb, and the following arrangement was made, that at midnight they should open the wicket in the gate and admit the Navâb's men. The Divân Sâheb Raghunâthji in person and Divân Govindji, with the commanders of the forces Parbâshankar and Sâmalji Mânkar, with 200 Arabs, 100 Sindhis and the Jamadârs Jiâ Jânkhrâ, Syad Salim, Syad Ali, and others, entered the fort on the west side, which was as it were the rising east of the Navâb Sâheb's fortune. Immediately on their making their attack, the garrison stood to their arms, and fought with such constancy and unspeakable gallantry that the angels in heaven were compelled to applaud their prowess. And now that the sword play ceased, they still fought with knives and daggers and blows and pushes, till their coats of mail were all rent, and the grainyard of existence was in many cases entirely burned up. In this affair Dâwudji, who was one of the cousins of Rânâ Sultânji, was slain by a musket-ball, and the garrison losing courage, fled under the cover of night. Most of them however died either of exhaustion after they had escaped and became a prey to vultures and crows, or were reduced to the most destitute condition by thieves and plunderers. In the morning, which is the time of the rising of the sun of fortune, they sent the good news to the Navâb Sâheb, who at once entered the city with great pomp and bestowed much praise on the Divân Sâheb.

After the conquest of Verâval the Navâb Sâheb proceeded with his army to collect peshkash, and then advancing by forced marches, replundered and ravaged the Rânâ's country, who being distressed to see his country thus harried, and alarmed also at the siege of the fort of Kandornâ by the Divân Govindji, who was the governor of Kutiânâ, sued for peace, and agreed to pay a *nazaránah* and a fine, and on these terms peace was concluded in Saṁvat 1846.

The Arab Jamadârs Zobaidi, Sálih A'bdullah, Muhammad Abu Bakr, Hâmed Mohsin and Hâmed Nâsir with Naji had in various emergencies stood security to the troops for the payment of their wages by the Navâb, who was at present also unable to pay their own salaries. They accordingly kept him in close confinement at the Rang-Mahâl, and prevented him getting either food or water, nor would they listen to the intercession of the Divân Raghunâthji. One day, however, the Navâb Sâheb seeing his opportunity, took several of his guards into his counsel, and by a thousand artifices contrived to escape from his Arab guards. Like a flash of lightning he then collected the Khânts and Sindhis from the surrounding country, by whose aid he expelled the Arabs from the town with shame and ignominy, and in this fight Utamrâm Ghoḍâdra Nâgar, who was a peshkâr [agent] of mine, was slain. The Arab Jamadârs who had possessed the fort of Chorwâr for some little time now ravaged the country, and my maternal uncle Sâmalji encamped near Chorvâḍ with some sipahis to restrain their excesses. During this confusion [Divân] Govindji died, on the 10th of Mahasûd, in Saṁvat 1846.

In Saṁvat 1847 a great famine raged in the country, during which many persons of low caste became Musalmâns for the sake of bread, or emigrated, and Musalmâns became faithless. Grass became as precious as saffron, and grain was extremely dear; nevertheless the rayats of the parganahs of Mângrol, Verâval, and Pâtan, suffered during this heaven-sent calamity a great deal from the Arabs, but their depredations were put a stop to by the end of the year, and they surrendered the fort of Chorvâd, which was entrusted to the author, and I undertook myself to defray the pay of the soldiery. On this occasion Mehta Vâsanji Bin Vâsanji, a Nâgar, who was my maternal uncle, and Divân to the Jâm Jasâji, being on his way to Prabhâs and Prâchi, was present. The Divân Sâheb Raghunâthji having made an arrangement with his brother Morârji to divide the administration with him, took an army into the district to levy peshkash, of which however on account of the famine not much could be collected. Jamâdâr Hamid Sindhi now arrived in the Haweli parganah of Junâgaḍh on behalf of the Gâekwâr to collect peshkash, and when tribute was refused he commenced to ravage the country and laid waste many villages of the district of Verâval. On his return march, when he was at a distance of four kos from Junâgaḍh, the Arabs and horsemen who were loyal turned to attack him, and he himself was killed by a musket-ball in the conflict. This happened in Saṁvat 1848.

In the Saṁvat year 1849, on the 5th of Mâgsar, the Navâb Sâheb, with his usual faithlessness, at the advice of Kaliân Wânio and Mâdhurâibin

Khushálrainágar, imprisoned the Divân Raghunâthji, with Bhai Morârji and their adherents Prabhashankar, Dayalji, and other Nâgars, in return for their excellent service in conquering the country, and their houses were also plundered and their treasure confiscated. When this misfortune befel the family of the Divân Sâheb Amarji, the author happened to be at Chorvâḍ, and Antaji, the brother of Morarji, was at Unâ; they both made strenuous efforts to effect the liberation of the prisoners, and attacked the Navâb's men on several occasions, and under the protection of Shri Budhâ Bâvâ [the linga of Shiva in the possession of the Divân's family] in the year 1869 plundered the forts of Ghoghá, Sarasiâ, Mâliâ, Kâgwadar, and A'dri. On the 6th of Posh Wad I plundered the village of Shergaḍh, inhabited by the Maiyâs, and collected a great deal of booty. In the fight at Kodinâr, Bhai Antaji captured some of the Navâb Sâheb's jamâdars and dismissed them from thence, but a Sirdar of his army, and Wânio Mâdharji, the commander of their army, fell into a dry well and thus preserved the water of their lives.

In fine, on the 15th Posh Sud the Navâb Sâheb put to death Prabhashankar and Dayâlji, the chief agents of Divân Raghunâthji, whom he set at liberty on the 11th Mahâ Vad, and six months afterwards he released also Morârji without levying any fine, and by the decree of fate I happened on the same day to get possession of the fort of

Pâtana, held in behalf of Shekh Badar-ud-din by Kâzi Abd-ul Khâlik and Shekh Mâhmud. Now as we three brothers had been expelled from the country, we did not remain at Junâgaḍh in spite of the attention and courtesy of the Navâb Sâheb Hâmid Khân, nor would we accept the offers of Shekh Badar-ud-din to stay at Mângrol, nor those of Dâji of Dhorâji to stay there, but yielded to the sincere wish of Mehrâwan Khavâs, the minister of Jâm Sâheb Jasâji, who had sent Mehtâ Adâbhâi with one hundred sowârs, a kettle-drum, and banner as far as Chorvâḍ to meet me, and went to Nawânagar, where I was presented with the parganahs of Pardhari and Atkôt in jâgir. As I did not return quickly, the fort of Pâtan remained without a master, and the Pâtanis, who have an old grudge towards the family of Shâik Myân [Shekh Badar-ud-din] occupying it on behalf of the Navâb Sâheb, expelled my Thânadâr Kâzi Abd-ul Khâlik from thence.

Morârji, son of Divân Dulabhji, went to Bhâvnagar and obtained four villages in jâgir, and Mangalji, son of Divân Govindji, who was of tender age, had all his gold seized as a fine (by the Navâb); he remained for a short time in the service of Rânâ Sultânji and of the Jâm Sâheb Jasâji, with a pâga of horse. The Navâb now, whilst the office of Divân at Junâgaḍh was jointly held by Kalyân Seth and Madhurâi, son of Khushalrâi, exacted a fine of 10 lâkhs of jâinis from the Somparâ and Nâgar Brâhmans.

In Saṁvat 1850 Râwal Wakhtsingh began to harass the Kâthis, who lived under the special protection of Junâgaḍh. Accordingly an army was sent from thence to aid them; Râwal Wakhtsingh attacked Chital, which is the residence and habitation of the Kâthis, and the force sent in aid under Jamâdâr Abdullah and Chotamlâl Nâgar evacuated the place.

On their return from a mulukgiri expedition, the Navâb Sâheb and Kâlyân Seth happened to meet Mehrâman Khawâs at Kâlâwad, on which occasion the Navâb Sâheb said to the Divân Sâheb Raghunâthji with his own gracious mouth:—"I was wrong, I was wrong. Forgive what has passed; I give you the Divânship;" after that he placed the hand of the said Diyân in that of Mehrâman Khawâs, saying, "this is a pledge on my behalf."

Madhurâi, a Gujarâthi Nâgar, who gave vent to his high aspirations after the departure of the Divân Raghunâthji, although he was a duftur-writer, considered himself able to discharge the functions of a Divân, and actually did so conjointly with Kalyân Seth, sharing equally in the profits. In a short time, however, according to the proverb that "ten Darveshes find room under one coverlet, but not two sovereigns in one kingdom," Kalyân Seth and Madhurâi quarrelled with each other, the former took refuge in the house of Syad Ghulâm-Mâhya-ud-din, and the latter, abandoning all hopes of safety, departed at midnight under the protection of the Jamâdârs Ahmed Qor, Sheikh Sâyd, Nâsir Yamani, and Musa Muharriz Arab, through a passage dug under the western wall, and arrived on foot with his family in Vanthali, after suffering a thousand indignities. To punish him, the Navâb dispatched an invitation to the Divân Sâheb Raghunâthji, who sent the author from Nâgar with troops, whereon the Navâb Sâheb took his station beneath the fort, and Madhurâi, being alarmed, agreed to pay a ransom in cash and evacuated the fort. He went a few months afterwards from Gondal to Baroda with Bâbâji Saheb, who had come to this country to collect the jamâbandi, and in course of time his previous services were taken into consideration by the Navâb, who gave him the jâgir and office of daftari, and as he had no son, his son-in-law Keshavlâl received his appointment, which he still holds.

In Samvat 1851 Mâhâdâji Sindhia procured a vakil's appointment for Madhurâi by his influence to the Court of the Bâdshâh of Delhi, and obtained through his efforts a sanad prohibiting the slaughter of cows throughout Hindustan. On that occasion he received also a dress of honour, a turban plume of pearls, a bracelet studded with diamonds, and a necklace of the same kind; ear-rings, anklets, and inkstand and pentray, a seal, shield, sword, Arab horse, an elephant and howda, two elephants with drums and banners, and a palanquin. In the year St. 1851 also,

Prince Bahâdur Khân Bahâdur Bâbi, of exalted fortune, was born; of his mother Râjkunwarbâ on Jêth wad 12th, the date of his birth is embodied in the word بختاور May God grant him long life.

The Divânship of Kaļyân Seṭh.

When Madhurâi his rival disappeared, Kaļyân Sêṭh, considering that the rose was now without a thorn, carried on the administration on his own responsibility. In Saṁvat 1852 Fateh Muhammad Notyâr, minister of the Râo Sâheb, came from Bhuj with a numerous army and crossed the Raṇ with the intention of ravaging Hallâr. Accordingly Merâman Khawâs invited the aid of a band of Afghâns under Sher Jang Khân Alif Khâṇ, Zulfikâr Khân, Ánwar Khân, Karimdâd Khân, and Sâheb Dâd Khân, who in the service of Malhâr Râo Gâekwâṛ, zamindar of Kaḍi, had acquired much fame when warring against Śrimant Râo Sâheb Govind Râo Gâekwâṛ, and agreed to pay 2 lâkhs and 15,000 jâmis to them as remuneration for their services; he also obtained the alliance of the Navâb Sâheb, who marched with his Arab and Sindhi Regiments under Mukhtiâr Khân Bâbi, Jamâlkhân Balûch, Harising Solankhi the Grâsiâ of Bâlâgâm, the auxiliaries from Mangrol, the Qasbâtis of Kutiânâ, the Kâthis, and the pâgadârs Ázam Beg and Jamiat Khân, and joined the Nâgar army at the village of Dhensarâ, of the Âmbran parganah. Meanwhile the army of Bhuj encamped at a distance of about half a kos from us. I went with my brothers and a Risâlah of troops as a body-guard to the Navâb Sâheb; but after a while, Gajsing, the Râjah of Halwaḍ and Dhrâṅgadhrâ, who was a relative of the Râo, arrived, and by his mediation peace was concluded, the Divân Sâheb Raghunâthji representing Nagar in the negotiation, and Kalyân Seṭh Junâgaḍh; a battle being thus averted, the armies separated.

March of the Navâb Sâheb against Bhâvnagar, and the unsatisfactory result.

The Navâb Sâheb marched with his army from Dhensarâ against Râwal Wakhtsingh, be cause the Râwal had conquered the fort of Kuṇḍala, of which place Morârji, son of Divân Dulabhji, was thânadâr, and had also taken the fort of Râjulâ. The Navâb Sâheb captured Kanyâji Gohel in the Goghâbârah, and ravaged the country of Bhâvnagar; thence he came and encamped at Chital, and collected a great number of Kâṭhis and ordered a march with the intention of destroying Bhâvnagar. On the other hand Râwal Wakhtsingh also came to meet him, with a large and well equipped army, and encamped in the Dhasâ plain, opposite to the Navâb's camp. For one whole day both armies were engaged and kept up a constant cannonade. The Navâb Sâheb, considering the cowardly character of Kalyân Seṭh, perceived that peace was the only means to escape from this calamity, and therefore concluded it with the approbation of all his advisers, and agreed to receive one lakh and fifteen thousand Rupees, and wrote parwânahs for the forts of Kuṇḍalâ and Râjulâ, and pardoned Wakhtsingh his past transgressions. To make his return to Junâgaḍh glorious, the Navâb first took possession of the fort of Mâliyâ, which he conquered from the grâsiâ Pitháyat Hâthi, after a siege of three days.

The Jamâdâr Âmin cannonades Manjávaḍi.

In Saṁvat 1854 Âmin Sâheb, a son of Jamâdâr Hamid, became the Subah of Kâthiâwâr on behalf of the Gâekwâṛ; and to avenge the blood of his father [killed by the Navâb of Junâgaḍh] made his appearance at Manjâvaḍi, the battlements of which place he broke down with his cannon, and after taking treble the amount of the usual jamâbandi according to the rules of of Śivrám Gârdi, he departed.

Kalyân Seṭh, the Baniya who had formerly been the *modi* (purveyor) of the Divân Sâheb, not considering treachery unlawful, caused Parbâśankar and Dayâlji, confidential servants of the Divân, to be killed, and thus himself became Divân; afterwards however he was so much harassed by the soldiery, who clamoured for their pay which was in arrears, that he spent the whole rainy season under a thousand difficulties in the jungle of

Kantoliâ, and desired in some way or other to lessen the glory of Junâgaḍh. With this view he incited the Navâb Sâheb to conquer the fort of Dhândhalpur, the zamindar whereof was the Kâṭhi Godaḍ Khavaḍ, but after a siege of two months, he was forced to retire unsuccessful. When he arrived in Junâgaḍh, the Arabs assaulted his house for the payment of their wages.

The Divân Sâheb Raghunâthji is recalled from Nagar.

When the Navâb Sâheb perceived that not one of the pillars of the State was able to extricate him from this difficulty, in Saṁvat 1857 he despatched some of them, such as Jamiat Khân Shirvâni, Mûlchand, Hayât Khân Baluch, Amarji Jhâlâ, and others to Nagar with letters to the Jâm Sâhib Jasâji, declaring that he would confer a great obligation upon the Navâb by sending back the Divân Raghunâthji; accordingly the latter, although aware of his master's fickle temper, and of the envy of Wâniâ Karsandâs, of Nâgar Kâhandâs, Âzam Beg Chelâ, and others, he took into account that sincere excuses had been made, and that it was his duty, whether he liked it or not, to comply with the wishes of his old master, and went to Junâgaḍh, where he collected an army and took up a position at Vanthali, with the intention of subjugating both Kutiânâ and Bântwâ.

The author had been for two years at Porbandar, to which place Prabhudâs and Kamâl Chela were sent to recall him ; and on the occasion of his departure the Râṇâ presented him with a dress, a necklace of pearls, a palanquin, and a litter. When I arrived at Râṇâwâv, the cultivators of the Mahiâri parganah complained that Kalyân Sêṭh had plundered them and carried off much property. To break his power I accordingly engaged the services of the Jamadârs Muhammad Nâsir Boraq, Shâkar Khân, Sardâr Khân, Gulbâz Khân, Muhammad Rafia, Morâd Thôr, Murâd Khân Mekrâni, and many others, and encamped at Meth-Kotaḍâ. Hereupon Mukhtâr Khân Bâbi lost heart and came to my tent, repenting, separated from Kalyâṇ Seṭh, made peace, left his son's wife to the Navâb, and departed for Bântwâ after receiving a safe conduct.

Reduction of the Fort of Kutiânâ.

During the 14th night of the dark half of Asu of Saṁvat 1857, I placed ladders against the north wall and entered the fort of Kutiânâ with the Afghân and Arab Jamâdârs and the Sipâh Sâlâr Prabhudâs Nâgar. Kalyân Seṭh, however, came to meet us, was defeated and besieged in the Kâli-koṭah, Meanwhile the Divân Sâheb Raghunâthji, who was stationed at Wanthali and passed his time between fear and hope, heard of what had taken place and advanced. As I was harassing the foe with artillery from the towers and house tops in various directions, and was not expecting or needing any assistance, he encamped with his force near the Bhâdar river. Three days after the Jamâdârs Yahya and Nâsir Yamânî, with Gangasingh and Khândân and Ghiga, Hâmad Sindhi, and many others, sued for mercy and came out. The Divân Sâheb left the settlement of this affair to myself, and marched off with his force to collect the jamâbandi, accompanied by Kûṅwar Dewâji Jâdejâ, and levying *peshkash* as he proceeded, finally reached the Dhandhûkâ frontier, as his father had been in the habit of doing, and encamped in the Limbḍi pargaṇa, where he took up his quarters. Kalyân Seṭh, being distressed and reduced by the war, was taken prisoner with his wife and family on the 3rd of Mâgsar Śûd of Saṁvat 1858 and placed in confinement at Kandorṇa; but Muharriz, the Arab Jamâdâr, held out in the fort, and was suffered to depart on being paid the sum of 22,000 Jami koris, which was due to him as wages. Kalyân Seṭh, with his whole family, was conveyed to Patan Div, where the Navâb Sâheb was at that time residing. He honoured me by marching one kos to meet me, and made enquiries about the conquest of Kutiânâ, which I narrated to him in the following terms:—" We beleaguered the citadel during a whole month from four sides, and poured fire into it from cannon and muskets, but as it was extremely strongly built of hewn stone, the cannon balls took no effect. Accordingly I dug a mine on the east and another on the west, and it so happened that the latter was on the same spot where formerly the Divân Sâheb Amarji had dug one when he besieged Hâshim-Khân ; this mine I abandoned and filled the eastern mine with gunpowder, but got no chance to blow it up. For one night, Murâd Khân Makrâṇi set the gate of the fort on fire. Next day after battering down the battlements of the fort with my cannon, it was my intention to place ladders against the walls of the fort and to scale it. Kalyân Seṭh, however, being unable to hold out longer, hung out a flag of truce and surrendered himself with his whole family, whereon the fort came into the possession of this Sirkâr." On hearing this recited, the Navâb Sâheb was greatly pleased, and extolled my bravery and courage ; Kalyân Seṭh was again delivered into my custody, and dying by the decree of God in prison, was requited for his works. The forts of Chorwâḍ and Unâ, held by Lakhmiprasâd, the son of Kalyân Seṭh, were then taken possession of and surrendered by me to the officers of the Navâb Sâheb ; then I took leave, and proceeding by quick marches, and chastising Ânandpûr *en route,* I arrived at Limbḍi and there met the Divân Sâheb Raghunâthji. At that time (in Saṁvat 1858) the army of the Gaekwâṛ laid siege to Kaḍi, and by the intervention of Mir Sâheb Kamâl-ud-dîn Hûsain, he obtained the aid of the English Government. Accordingly a general arrived from Bombay with cannon of dragon-like aspect and landed at Khambhât. At this time vakils arrived on the part of both Malhâr Râo and the Śrimant Gaekwâṛ to ask for aid, but it so happened that in our doubt as to which would be successful, we ended by joining neither and marched back to Junâgaḍh. In a short time, after severe fighting, the army of the Gaekwâṛ conquered the fort of Kaḍi, Śivrâm, the commandant, and others who were in the service of Malhâr Râo, fled and dispersed in the surrounding districts, and when Malhâr Râo perceived that there was no way of escape for him, he went to the tent of the general and begged for quarter; his brother Hanmantrâo departed to the territories of Bhûj, and he himself received the parganah of Naḍiyâd from the Gaekwâṛ government. Nevertheless two years afterwards, in Saṁvat 1860, Malhâr Râo fled to Kâṭhiawâṛ, where he engaged the services of all the desperate characters out of employ, such as Jamâdâr Umar Ḥâmid Umar, with other Arabs and Sindhis, and became the centre of rebellion and raised disturbances. He plundered the country, but the zamindârs did nothing to defend the honour of the Gaekwâṛ, and at last the army of the latter marched against him under the command of the Divân Sâheb Viṭhal Râo, and pursuing him closely captured him on the plain of Bhâvnagar and surrendered him to the English, who carried him to Bombay, where he died.

In Saṁvat 1859 I was collecting tribute in the parganahs which did not regularly pay tribute, and levied double the usual amount, when I was met in the vicinity of Dhrângdrâ by the army of Commandant Śivrâm and of Hanmant Râo, but they were unable to hinder me in any way. Mukand Râo Gâekwâṛ rebelled and raised a disturbance in the fort of Amrêli, and excited a great sedition in the country. He captured the Nâgar Desâyas of Wânsâwaḍ and demanded from them a ransom. To punish him I marched by the command of the Navâb Sâheb with an army, and after a week's siege liberated the Dêsais and expelled Mukand Râo, who marched away in repentance and distress. In Saṁvat 1860 Bâbâji Sâheb, the Divân of the Gâekwâṛ, passed through this country with an army numerous as locusts, and levied thrice the amount of money Commandant Śivrâm had been in the habit of taking. Bâbâji also besieged the fort of Vanthali for two months ineffectually. Accordingly he marched off in great dudgeon and plundered the surrounding country as far as Patan Div, and hindered the pilgrims from visiting Śri Somnâtha; the author followed him everywhere with a numerous army, fighting with him continually; finally obtained from him all the deeds of agreement to pay tribute which he had extorted from the people, and taking tribute only according to the custom of the country, he returned. From the time of Bâbâji Sâheb the tribute of this country was raised to thrice its former amount.

During Saṁvat 1861, whilst the author

was away as far as Râjkoṭ and the Sarvaiya country to collect *peshkash*, Âzam Beg Chela, Karsandâs a Vaniyâ, and Kâhandâs induced the Navâb Sâheb to take part in carousals and drinking bouts, with music and dancing and singing, and administered the affairs of the state as they chose, and at their instigation the Navâb Sâheb mortgaged the parganah of Kutiânâ to the Divân Sâheb Raghunâthji, as security for the new debt of ten lakhs of jâmis which he owed him.

In the year 1862 Khima, Bhojâ, Karnâ, and other mehtâs, being disgusted with the tyranny of Karsandâs, took refuge at Kutiânâ, but afterwards took up a position at Drâphâ, from which they made predatory incursions. At last, after paying a fine, they were allowed to return to their former posts.

Mehtâ Revâshankar bin Trikamdâs, with Dâyârâm Nâgar, administered the office of Divân for three or four years, but only in name and under the dictation of Karsandâs, and Âzam Beg led out the army to levy jamâbandi but did not even annoy an ant. This fitful and unpromising administration lasted two or three years, and from that time the marching out of armies from Junâgaḍh for the mulukgiri expeditions was put a stop to, and giving up the right of collecting the jamâbandi, they received a fixed amount from the English Government. In the year 1864 Mehtâ Revâshankar and Madhurâi arrived on the part of the Nâvab Sâheb at Kandorṇâ, whilst I was likewise there paying my respects to Colonel Alexander Walker. The Divân Sâheb Vithal Râo, who bore a grudge towards the Divân Sâheb Raghunâthji, because he had hindered Bâbâji Sâheb from conquering the fort of Vanthali and from paying a visit to Somnâth, and because he himself aspired to obtain possession of Junâgaḍh and to turn out the said Divân, calumniated him to the Colonel Sâheb; the latter, however, being as it were the Nushirwân of the period, gave the following plain answer:—"An explanation will be asked about the sixty lakhs owing to the Divân by the Navâb as fixed by the Gâekwâṛ as a debt, as well as about the sixteen villages promised as blood ransom for the Divân Amarji's murder but treacherously taken away again from him in the year 1849. I will also attach all the country conquered by the efforts of the Divân Sâheb Amarji and will hand it over to his son Divân Raghunâthji; and by what *sanad* of the Sultân of Delhi is the Navâb in possession of the state of Junâgaḍh." When they had heard these words they became like flies in oil. On the festival (first) of January, Colonel Walker said to the Divânji Sâheb Vithal Râo and to the officers of the Navâb Sâheb in a public assembly—"You are the Divâns of the Gâekwâṛ Sarkâr and of the Navâb Sâheb, but this is the Divân and leader of our army, and whoever is his enemy is the enemy of the English Government." After that a fine was paid by the Junâgaḍh State for the goods the pirates of Nawâ Bandar had robbed from vessels bound to Surat and Bombay. Walker Sâheb Bahâdûr and Robertson Sâheb and Ballantyne Sâheb and others honoured the author by being present at nâches given by him. I have never seen a man so high and noble-minded as Alexander Walker, of little speech but great intelligence, acquainted with the affairs of government, versed in all political matters, and capable of appreciating men of worth. He conquered the fort of Kandorna in half an hour, and obtained a share in the Porbandar customs ; he demolished the fort of Châyya and also put the Gâekwâṛ under obligations to him. At last he went to Europe and left a good name behind him.

On the 10th of Kârtak Śud in Saṁvat 1862, Hallaji, on account of his rebellious and perverse disposition, made a treaty with Colonel Alexander Walker after his return from an expedition to Okha, in consequence of which he ceded the moiety of the customs of that port, as well as the east and north gate to the English. I paid my respects to the Colonel and was presented with a dress of honour.

On the 4th of Phâlgûn of the year 1807, corresponding to A.H. 1226, the Navâb Sâheb, the *qiblâh* of the inhabitants of the world, the angelic tempered Hâmed Khân Bâbi departed this life. The duration of his reign was 36 years 3 months and 5 days ; he was intelligent, sweet spoken, and faithful to his word, but apt to change with the times, ready to take offence, and slow in action. So excellent a sovereign is rarely seen in this world.

NAVÂB SÂHEB BAHÂDUR KHÂN BIN HÂMID KHÂN BAHÂDUR BÂBI.

This young prince with his mother Râjkûñwar was kept at Patan, because on returning home after a certain marriage procession which he attended on foot in the town, an Abyssinian boy in his service placed an earthen pot full of firewood close to the Navâb's palace and setting fire to it fled. As the Navâb Sâheb experienced much inconvenience by this fire, he considered that the boy had been instructed to act thus by his mother and therefore removed the prince to Patan. After his father's death, however, he was brought back to Junâgaḍh by the Jamâdâr Omar Mokhâsam, Ázam Beg Chelâh, Kahândâs Vaishnáv, Mugatrâm Bakshi, Jhinâ Mehta, and others, and ascended the throne in his 18th year, 9th of Phâgan Sud, Saṁvat 1867 (A.D. 1810).

The Divân Sâheb Raghunâthji had been living for seven years at Kûtiâna; he kept his family at Mângrol, and enjoyed the jâgir of Râṇpur from Nagar. But now Omar Mokhâsam, Hâmid Amru, Sâlim Bin Hamid, Hasan Abu Bakr, Karsandâs the Baniah, Kahândâs Vaishṇava, Mugatrâm Bakshi, Jhinâ Mehta, Vâghji Desai, and others, arrived in Kûtiâna, and with a hundred solicitations, promises, and oaths upon the Korân, and on Jamial Sháh Pir, carried him to Junâgaḍh to be Divân. On his arrival the Bâi Sâhibah Râjkûnwar, as well as the Navâb Sâheb Bahâdur Khán, received him with great kindness, but often repeated that in these times the power of the Gâekwaḍ and of the English Sarkâr was greatly on the increase, moreover that the State was encumbered with a debt of a karôr of jâmis due partly to the army and partly to the mutasaddis, and that no other man except himself, whose family had occupied the Divânship for fifty years, could carry on the administration of the Government properly. The Divân Sâheb Raghunâthji, true to his salt, accepted the office in perpetuity for himself and his descendants.

In Saṁvat 1868 Carnac Sâheb and Gangâdhar Śâstri, who were both in appearance and in reality distinguished men of the period, arrived with an army and brought also Śrimant Fatehsing Rao Gâekwar Sena Khás Khevl himself, with the Divân Sâheb Vithal Rao, the Jemadâr Amin Sâheb, Mir Sâheb Kamâlu'd-dìn Husain, &c., to attack Navânagar, because one of the Arab Chokidârs of the fort of Modpûr had unjustly killed one of the English Sâhebs; but the Jâm Sâheb of Nagar was so jealous of his own rights that he refused to give up the murderer in spite of the pressing demands of the English. When the army of the

English and of the Gâekwaḍ departed from Nagar, they marched to Lâlwaḍ, which is four kos distant from Junâgaḍh, and encamping there set forth their claim for a Nazarânah from Bahâdûr Khân on account of his succession to the throne. On that occasion the Divân Sâheb Raghunâthji took care of the defences of Junâgaḍh, and the obstruction of the roads, the erecting of thorn-thickets, and the destruction of the water-courses as dictated by foresight; but the sequel proved that all precautions of this kind were useless, for Mr. Carnac was of a kind disposition, and enmity was soon turned into friendship. Gangâdhar Śâstri took the Divân Raghûnathji and the author to see the wedding of the daughter of Divânji Sâheb Vithal Râo at Amreli, where they assisted at the festivities usual among Amirs, and received presents of dresses, ornaments and food—every guest being presented with cash and other articles according to his position in society; also the mutasaddis of the Navâb Sâheb's private household made their appearance, and came to exchange presents, not suspecting any harm to their master's affairs, they had set on foot thousands of intrigues against us, and considered that if a settlement with the Navâb were to take place by the mediation of the Divân Raghunâthji, his family would rise in importance, which would be a loss to them. Accordingly they had brought letters from the Navâb Sâheb Bahâdur Khan, addressed to the

Divân Sâheb, to Vithal Râo, to Râjuba, and to Gangâdhar Sâstri, to this effect: "Now leave off negotiations, as you cannot obtain what you wish from the Divân Sâheb. I will think over your demands and at a future time obey your wishes." The Divânji being thus helpless, asked for leave. Carnac Sâheb and Gangâdhar Sâstri gave us much consolation and comforted us; and if we had at that time accompanied them to Baroda, we should no doubt have attained to a very exalted rank.

When we returned to Junâgaḍh we consulted with Râjkuṅwarbâi whether we should agree or not to the Gâekwâr's order. She (at the instigation of her private advisers) said with a loud voice, "We will not give even a span's breadth of land, but have no objection to give a moderate nazarânah in money."

The Divânji Sâheb Vithal Râo, considering that the field was now clear, held out promises of presents to Jamâdâr Omar Mokhâsam and the private Kârbhâris, and obtained a deed in writing giving over the parganahs of Koḍinâr and Amreli to the Gâekwâr's government, and by degrees they also encroached and got several other tâlukâs also under their authority, and they completed the fortifications of Amreli, which had been commenced in the time of the late Navâb Hâmid Khân.

During Saṁvat 1869 (A.D. 1812-13) there was a severe famine; rain did not fall, and on account of the want of grass and grain many people died. During the preceding year, *i.e.* 1868, a comet was seen in the sky during four months ; its tail looked like a broom turned upside down, and its length was eight cubits. In astronomical books its description is as follows :—

त्रिभागसेवां कुरुते वसुंधरा.

Next year, that is to say in Saṁvat 1870, such a pestilence raged, that many who had survived the famine died of it. Sounds of wailing and lamentation issued from every house, and many corpses were left exposed in the midst of the bazar for two or three days, so that Hindus were unable to burn their dead, and Musalmans to shroud and bury theirs, and on the 6th of Mágsar Sudha, also my brother, of blessed memory, who was a pillar of the state, and a shining light in the family of Divân Sâheb Amarji, whose name was Dalpatrâm, departed this life, and we two surviving brothers suffered much grief at his loss, but there is no remedy for what is past.

Affairs of the Jamâdâr Omar, and his Expulsion by the aid of the British.

Aspirations to the office of Divân inflamed the head of the Jamâdâr Omar Makhâsam, and he became ambitious and desirous of obtaining this exalted post, and therefore he enrolled the Jamâdâr Hasan Abu Bakr ,Sàlih Bin Abud, Sâlim bin

Hamid, and others in his interests ; he obtained also aid and countenance from the Divânji Sâheb Vithal Râo, and carried on the administration of the Navâb Sâheb's government ; and got the control of all the thânahs into his own hands, but alienated the parganah of Amreli and Kodinâr to the Gâekwâr by way of securing his good graces, and with the aid and co-operation of the Divânji Sâheb Vithal Râo most ungratefully tried in every way he possibly could, to injure the Divân Sâheb Raghunâthji.

The taking of Kutiâna.

The Divân Sâheb Raghunâthji went for the purpose of performing ablutions in the Godâvar-Gangâ at Nâsik Trimbak, whilst the author went on pilgrimage to Bêcharaji Mâtâ, Sidhpur and Ambâji. The Navâb Bandah Ali Khân, zamindâr of Khambhât, at Sidapet Bharoch, Resident Romer Sâheb, Agent at the port of Surat, with Carew Sâheb, who were all men of noble disposition, and the râjas of every locality, received the Divân Sâheb Raghunâthji with honours, feasted him, and gave him escorts through their dominions. Carnac Sâheb, who had once been our guest at Kutiâna, said at the second interview :—"O Divân Sâheb, you are attached to the Honourable Company Sarkâr, and you, as long as you live, and your children afterwards, may expect favours for a long time." In fine this Jâtrâ cost forty thousand Rupees. Gangâdhar Śâstri, who had formerly at Amreli kissed the feet of the Divân Sâheb Raghunâthji, and who had now gone as Vakil to the Court of Śrimant Amratrâo at Pûṇa, sent him an invitation to come there, but no meeting could take place on account of the hot season, and Gangâdhar Śâstri himself was killed in that country. When we two brothers returned (from the pilgrimage) and arrived in Amrêli, we thanked the Divân Sâheb Vithalrâo for the hospitable treatment we had met with at Perân Pâtan from Nâgars Mûgatrâm and Motâbhâi, and Nânâbhai the Majmûdâr, and from Bandûji the Mukâssahdâr, and from Bahâdûr Singh the wine seller.

The Divân Sâheb, unwilling to practice treachery, and out of regard to Jamâdâr Omar Mokhâsam, entered into negotiations with Ballantyne Sâheb ; for we considered the English Government our protector. But he (Ballantyne Sâheb) did not act according to his own will, but his mind was entirely under the influence of Sûndarji Khatri, and he caused the parganahs which we held in mortgage for the sum of 10,000 jâmis and for the farm of which I had paid a sum of 70,000 jâmis, besides the *ghanim verâ*, to be restored to the Navâb. The Divân Sâheb, who relied on the favour of the English Government, when he saw Ballantyne Sâheb no longer showing kindness to him, became helpless, and was unable to offer any remonstrance.

Verse.

The fancied tyranny he did to us,
His neck it stuck to, over us it went.

And in exchange for those mahâls which the Navâb Sâheb had mortgaged to us, and on account of which 30 lâkhs of jâmis were due, he caused to be written over to us in jâgir, on the security of the English and Gâekwâr Governments, the four villages of Khâgasri, Iswariâ, Meswânah, and Wâḍâsârâ ; this was in Saṁvat 1871 (A.D. 1814-15).

Marriage of Śambhu Parsad.

When the light of my eyes Śambhuprasâd, son of Dulpatrâm's wedding with the daughter of Ávalram Ambâidâs was solemnized, the Navâb Sâheb Bahâdur Khân honoured it with his presence and came to see the spectacle in which various performances by male and female actors, musicians and singers were going on, and the place was decorated with various sorts of lamps made of glass, mica, coloured paper and ware, which transformed day into night and night into day. The marriage procession was escorted by a thousand soldiers on horseback and foot, and was accompanied by numerous chariots, carts and elephants; but the Divânji Sâheb Vithal Râo and Ballantyne Sâheb, although they had sworn that they would come, remained away under the pretence that the impending siege of the fort of

Kandornâ was engrossing their attention. After the Divân Sâheb Raghûnathji had completed the nuptials of his son and performed the Máhárudra Yagna, he retired from the world, and engaged in the worship of his God, but Jamâdâr Omar Mokhâsam's enmity towards him did not abate.

DISMISSAL OF THE JAMÂDÂR OMAR.

The ingratitude of Jamâdâr Omar Mokâsam impelled him one day to rush with some Arab Jamâdârs into the Rang Mahâl, and to lay his hand on the waist of the Navâb Sâheb, but Jamâdârs Sâlim and Hasan, his faithful attendants, and excellent good fortune saved him, and thus Jamâdâr Omar's evil designs were frustrated, and he was expelled from the city with contumely and disgrace, and commenced to strengthen himself in the districts.

The Navâb Sâheb, when he saw the evil designs and foolish ambition of the Jamâdâr, began to fear for his life, and sought aid from the Divân Raghunâthji, both by promises and oaths, and accordingly the Divân Sâheb, whose heart was devoted to the Navâb's interests, betook himself to Ballantyne Sâheb without the knowledge of the Divân Vithal Râo, who was a firm friend of Jamâdâr Omar's. Now Sundarji Khatri, who was a resident of Kachh and a dyer by caste, had emerged from poverty by the aid of the holy Râmeśwar, and first became of note in the world by trading in horses with the English Government.

and had by degrees become the agent of Ballantyne Sâheb. And Ballantyne Sâheb had made his agent, as it were, a Shâh Bâlâ whom Hindus send in front of the bridal procession as it passes through a city, and send with him their sons and daughters in gorgeous array: nevertheless he derives no advantage from the office of Shâh Bâlâ nor from the borrowed clothes and jewels with which he is decked, except the name.

But this Sundarji assumed the title of Subah, and by false and lying representations had frightened or cajoled all the world, and thus collected much gold. Since he was a sincere friend of the Divân Sâheb, he made an ally of him in this matter, and accordingly the author of this book, and Mugatrâm and Amrullah, repaired to the camp to see Ballantyne Sâheb. At this time the Arâbs had been expelled from Nawânagar by order of the English Government, and then Ballantyne Sâheb, according to the agreement made, came to Junâgaḍh with his army, and Aston Sâheb, who was in command of the troops, entered the city with a body of soldiers and two guns, to expel Jamâdâr Omar. This Jamâdâr, whose prosperity was thus cut short, was thus expelled the city with concealed face and bare feet, and after a time the affairs of the Jamâdârs were settled through Ballantyne Sâheb, as follows.

Jamâdâr Omar was granted the villages of Timbḍi and Pipliâ, and one lakh and fifty thousand jâmis by fixed instalments. Hasan Abu Bakr received 40,000 Jâmis (koris), and Sâlim Hamid obtained the village of Sângâwârâ, and they wrote bills of release for the moneys due to them as salaries, and their vakils took their leave. After this the Divânship of Junâgaḍh was again given to the Divân Sâheb Raghunâthji, through the intervention of Ballantyne Sâheb, who informed the Navâb Sâheb that it was the order of the Sarkâr Company Bahâdur, that he should permanently fix the office of Divân in the family of the Divân Sâheb Amarji. In this year the English Government conquered the fort of Ánjâr, but after some time they restored it to the Râo Sâheb by way of form.

Dismissal of Divân Raghunâthji, imprisonment and slaughter of Atits.

Sundarji Khatri, who entertained ambitious designs, instilled into the Navâb's mind a desire for the recovery of the forts of Dhorâji, Upletâ, and Mâṅgrol, the remission of a debt of fifty lakhs jamis (koris) due to the Mutasaddis, and the restoration of the jâgir of Bâlâsinor ; in this manner he gained over the Navâb to his side and alienated his favour from the Divân Sâheb—

Whoever came built him a house,
But went again and left it to another ;
Who likewise acted in the same manner,
So that the habitation belonged to no one.

In Saṁvat 1874 Shekh Amrûllah, who was originally an indigo dyer, and who had been allowed by the deceased Divân Sâheb Amarji to establish himself in the town, and who had by his trade in rich Ahmedâbâdi cloths and all kinds of stuffs, gradually wormed himself into the Court of the Navâb Sâheb, and into the favour of the Masâhebah Râj Kunwar, succeeded at last in attaining the rank of companion (*Musâheb*) to the Navâb Sâheb, and with Mugatrâm Bakhshi was despatched through Sûndarji to Ballantyne Sâheb with a nazarana of twenty-five thousand rupees in order to obtain his permission to put some old Mutasaddis out of the way who were stumbling blocks to the new Divân, and in order that the full and untrammelled authority of Divân might devolve on Sûndarji, and Ballantyne Sâheb, who was anxious to advance the interest of Sûndarji by every means in his power, immediately consented, and on the arrival of Amrûllah and Mugatrâm, the Navâb Sâheb threw Mehta Amarji Bin Rudrâji Jhâlâ and Mulchand Hematrám Nágar into prison, on which the Sanyásis of Śrî Trinetra Mahâdeva and the wine-sellers and Sayyids of Junâgaḍh who were their securities, issued forth from the city and commenced to sit in "dhornâ."* The Navâb Sâheb sent out Shekh Amrûllah, Miân Abd-ul-Qâdr, and Jhinâ Mehta,

* This strong expression is wanting in the translation from the Gujarati.

with Mugatrâm Bakhshi, to satisfy their demands, but as they would not listen, he sent Shahâmat Khân Bâbi, Jamâl Khân Baluchi, and others, with armed men to the number of a hundred, to kill them. The Sayyids considered life sweet and honour bitter, accepted terms saying "we seek safety from God," but they shed the blood of the Sanyâsis and wine-sellers except one of them, a strict performer of penance, who was dragged to the Ûparkot and slain there.

In fine, since Ballantyne Sâheb was an accomplice in this evil action, he instituted no inquiries regarding it, although he came often to Junâgaḍh to make new arrangements; once he even invested Prabhûdâs Nâgar of Bânsârâ with the dress of Divân on his promise to pay one-half of the debt due to the mutasaddis in eight years, by twenty instalments; in the same way he caused the pay of the sipâhis to be liquidated, but Prabhudâs was likewise unable to keep the office longer than a week or two.

In Saṁvat 1875 (A.D. 1819), on the evening of the 9th Jesht Vâd, such an earthquake took place that high edifices fell down, the surface of the earth burst, and water gushed forth from it, many persons were buried under ruins; and the next day the earth again trembled, and it appears to have been an earthquake felt over the whole world.

The Navâb Sâheb entrusted for the second

t

time Ratansi and Hansraj bin Jethâ Khatri with the collection of the jamabandi in the whole country of Kâthiâwâr, which had fallen into arrears for ten years, in return for their aid in expelling Jamâdâr Omar, though the Divân Raghunâthji had effected this at the cost only of a lakh and a half of rupees.

Sûndarji also, in his desire to obtain the office of Divân, caused an agreement to be made whereby a lakh of jâmis for vakil's expenses were settled as an annual payment to the English Government, and as security ten villages of Jetpûr and 63,000 jâmis ready money were respectively written over and paid, and the provisions in the bond regarding interest were expunged.

The Divânship of Sûndarji.

Sûndarji Shavji a Khatri had several times come with Ballantyne Sâheb to Junâgadh, and in Samvat 1876 he obtained the farm of all the parganahs from the Navâb Sâheb for a period of ten years, on condition of paying an annual sum of nine lakhs of jâmis, besides defraying the *ghanim vero*, and Ballantyne Sâheb stood security for him as to the Divâni, and although the said Sûndarji had formerly sworn that he would protect the Divân Sâheb Raghunâthji, he on this occasion entirely omitted to do so, and even contributed to his being dismissed. Sûndarji left his nephew Hansrâj at Junâgadh itself to conduct affairs, and administered the state under the protection of Ballantyne Sâheb. In this year the latter also issued a proclamation that the Sarkâr Company Bahâdur, after fighting with him, had extinguished the Government of Śrîmant Bâji Râo the Peshwâ, which had lasted during one hundred and twenty years at Pûṇâ, and had on several occasions vanquished the imperial troops (of the Emperor of Delhi).

DEATH OF THE DIVÂN SÂHEB RAGHUNÂTHJI.

In Saṁvat 1875, on Âsso Sûd 10th, the Divân Sâheb Raghunâthji, successor to the Divân Amarji, departed to Kailâsa, at the age of 56 years, and many persons who had enjoyed of his bounty for a long time were much distressed. He was a worshipper of Śankara, liberal, brave, upright, veracious, skilled in business, protector of the raiyats, in military affairs, in the mulukgiri expeditions, and in manœuvering the army he cannot be said to have been inferior to the late Amarji. The world bewails his loss, and at Benares several Sanyâsis subsist comfortably at his expense. He built the temple of Srî Bûdhâbâwâ, mentioned in the account of Mângrol, as well as the bathing kûnd called Sarasvatî kûnd, and a dharamsâlâ at Pâtan, and he caused *Gayatri purshachaus* to be performed, and the pilgrims who resort to Benares enjoy the allowance of food he has made for them.

WEDDING OF KESARBÂI.

In Saṁvat 1876 Kesarbâi, daughter of the Râo of Kachh and sister of Rao Sâheb Bhârâ, the Râja of Kachh-Bhuj, was married by the Navâb Sâheb Bahâdur Khân, Bahâdur Bâbi, on which occasion the gates of liberality were opened to the inhabitants of the world and presents were made to dancers, singers, courtesans, story-tellers, Bhâts, Chârans, Faqirs, Sayyids and Sheiks of the surrounding districts. Everybody obtained more than he expected, and many presents consisted of ready money, goods, horses, camels, and rings for feet and hands, made of gold and jewels. Eatables were also distributed, with opium, (drinks) of various kinds and medical confections. Betelnuts, cardamoms, cloves, and spices were distributed in such quantities that the poor folk sold them in the bazâr. From Kachh, furniture was brought with a female elephant, horses, camels, chariots, cows, sheep, male and female slaves, clothing articles of gold embossed with jewels, some of cast and some of hammered gold, and the articles of furniture amounted in value to five lâkhs jâmi koris.

After Ballantyne Sâheb, Barnwell Sâheb, with Chotâlâl, a Gujarâti Nâgar, who was his divân, came as Political Agent in Kâṭhiâwâr, and as he happened to be near Jetpûr, he came to the marriage-feast at Junâgaḍh on the invitation of the Navâb Sâheb, on which occasion Hansrâj (nephew of Sûndarji Khatri), made himself very useful by his activity. The above lady lived only four years after her marriage.

Interviews with the General Sâheb (Governor Elphinstone).

In Saṁvat 1876 (A.D. 1820) the marriage of the daughter of Dalpatrâm was celebrated, as well as the *vastu* (opening) ceremonies, which were performed in the temple of Sarasvatî, at the gate of Hatakêśwar Mahâdev and the four temples built around it. Since, however, I was vexed with the Navâb Sâheb, and as Hansrâj was my enemy, and as Ballantyne Sâheb connived at his conduct and did not reprove him, I went there with my full train to Goghâ. Therefore the author departed with his followers to meet Governor Elphinstone Sâheb, who had recently arrived there. The Governor Sâheb was so polite as to advance forty steps from his private tent to meet me, and on taking leave he accompanied me one hundred steps. Seven chairs were placed for my companions and vakils, and on three occasions he conversed privately with me in a separate apartment in the Persian language for three hours with great kindness and condescension. What words shall I use to express my thanks to so noble and exalted a personage, who was moreover wholly independent in the conduct of affairs, and the like of whom I never saw nor heard of. This world changeth and passeth away. He departed and left a good name behind him. When I went away he assured me of the friendly disposition of the English Sarkar, and told me to be under no apprehensions of injury from any of the rulers of this country, and presented me with costly dresses of honour. After my return to Junâgaḍh, I completed the marriage ceremonies of Kasibâ (the daughter of Dalpatrâm) together with the repast, she being weighed with gold and silver in the handsomest manner. This took place on Maha wad 7th, September 1877.

Capture and Release of Grant Sâheb.

When the Grasia prevailed, Bâwâ Wâlâ, a Kâthi, captured Grant Sâheb on the Koḍinâr road, and carried him off into the hills, whether he would or no, as his guest, and for several days took him about the forest and jungle. On that occasion (Major) Barnwell Sâheb, who was coming this way, wrote a letter from Ahmadâbâd to the author without any previous acquaintance, and merely on the strength of my friendship towards the Sarkâr Company Bahâdur, requesting me to effect the release of Grant Sâheb. I immediately despatched one or two men to the outlaws, and they brought me a letter from Grant Sâheb from that place, but as I possessed no acquaintance with the English language, I had recourse to Bhavânidâs, the Munshi of Ballantyne Sâheb, who informed his master of the matter. The

Sâheb, afraid lest I should effect his release and thus gain renown, sent Hansrâj with numerous troops, both horse and foot, and obtained the release of Grant Sâheb from captivity in exchange for the parganah of Visâwadar, and in course of time Bâvawâlâ, son of Râning, himself was killed by some of his enemies and Visâwadar reverted to its lawful owners.

Expulsion of Mr. Anderson from Dwarka, and Punishment of the Waghers by the English.

Handy Sâheb (Anderson) and Muhammad Átá Mûllah were the Thânahdârs of the Company at Dwarka and Beyt, but the Wâghers and Sangrâm Râja of Beyt rebelled and ignominiously expelled them from the fort. In vain did Muhammad Átâ Mûllah shake his beard, the cow-worshipping Wâghers gave them no time to put their shoes on, plain daylight became as dark to them as a midnight of the rainy season, and without reflecting on the disgrace, both Handy Sâheb and Muhammad Átâ Mûllah came and paid their respects to Ballantyne Sâheb at Junâgaḍh. Shortly afterwards the English army went and so chastised the Wâghers, that many of them were precipitated into the bottomless pit of annihilation. Râjâ Sangrâm was captured and safely brought to Surat, and was afterwards sent back to his country again with a small pension and bound over to keep the peace; and they slew Mûlû

Mânik and many other Wâghers in the Gomti river, and the survivors were treated mercifully and granted their former jâgirs, and this mahâl was bestowed anew on the Gàekwâr.

CHASTISEMENT OF THE KHUMÂN KÂTHIS BY THE BRITISH.

Jogidas and Hâdo Khûmân and others had for a long time been in outlawry in the country of Râwal Wakhtsingh, who called the English army to his aid. It was under the command of Stanhope Sâheb, and although its movements were rapid, no stop could be put to the depredations of the rebels, who were at last subdued by the skill of Barnwell Sàheb. He being a man of experience, able to impart wisdom to Loqmân, he took into custody some Kàthis of Jetpûr, who were relations and securities of those outlaws, and Chelâ Khâchar of Jasdân and Harsûr Wâlâ of Bagasrâ, and Dânta Kotilâ the zamindar of Dedân, and imprisoned them and attached their estates. He also took possession of the fort of Jetpûr and compelled them to produce and surrender the Khûmâns, whom in Samvat 1882 he handed over to Râwal Wajesingh (of Bhâonagar), and then he restored Jetpûr, Bagasrâ and Jasdan to their former lords.

Barnwell Sâheb, one of whose innate qualities was to bestow favours, procured for the author in Samvat 1878, the farm of the tâlukâs of Râjkot and Sardár, to be held for seven years (for a fixed rent), and in Saṁvat 1880 he procured for me the farm of Dhorâji and Upleta, and Mehtâ Amarlâl and Raghunâthji Vasâvaḍa were appointed managers on my behalf.

In Saṁvat 1879 Sûndarji Khatri, who had just returned from a pilgrimage to Haṛdwâr, died at the port of Mândvi in his own house. His nephews Hansrâj and Ratanśi, who managed the affairs of Junâgaḍh and of Bhûj, in the pride of their prosperity, cared very little for the Navâb Sâheb or the Jâm Sâheb, they sat on an equality with them in the darbâr, and tyrannically robbed the helpless raiyats of much gold, and despised the Nâgars now when their patron (Ballantyne Sâheb) was removed from Kâthiâwâr and obtained an appointment at Sâdrâ as Political Agent, and as the Navâb was not successful in regaining the jâgir of Bâlâsinor, of which Sûndarji had held him out hopes, and on which account Sûndarji had taken from him much cash, articles of value and beautiful horses; in consequence of this a great enmity sprang up between them and Leeson Sâheb, and Anderson Sâheb giving Hansrâj an agreement from the Navâb to pay his demands by instalments, expelled him from the town. On hearing this, his brother Ratanśi came from Bhûj and spent much money, but could not make peace between them. And if the English had not been their securities, they would have fared ill. Immediately after his expulsion from Junâgaḍh, Hansrâj obtained from the Jâm Sâheb the farm of the Nawânagar estate for a period of ten years, in consideration for an annual payment of seventeen lâkhs and thirty thousand jâmi koris, and he received much assistance from Barnwell Sâheb. Hansrâj and Devshi claimed from the Jâm twenty-eight lakhs of jâmi koris on account of the nazarâna of eight lakhs and fifty thousand rupees which they had agreed to pay the English Government on account of Joḍia and Balambhâ.

In Saṁvat 1885, when Blane Sâheb was appointed Political Agent, who could not distinguish between truth and falsehood, and who was of a very harsh and self-willed disposition, Hansraj lost much both by the farm and his other accounts. In short, he was disgraced, and since he had been occupied in farming and managing districts, his private trade had passed to other hands. The crow, in trying to walk like the partridge, forgets his own mode of progression. Mr. Blane now rooted out all the Khatris and withdrew the security and promises of the Company Bahâdur both from them and others in the Kâthiâwâr zillah, who had been relying in safety on the English Government.

Afterwards, since the change of Barnwell Sâheb, the officials of the English Government who have come to this zillah (whether Europeans or Hindus) are indeed our friends, but not the friends of justice.

Expect not fidelity from bulbuls,
They every moment other roses court.

Death of Kesarabâi, and murder of Ahmad Khân Faqir.

Kesarabâi, the sister of the Râo Sâheb Bhárá and spouse of the Navâb Sâheb Bahâdur Khân, departed about this time to the regions of Paradise.

Aḥmad Faqir, a discíple of Mohkim-ud-din Panjâbi, happened by the decree of God to ingratiate himself so much with the Navâb Sâheb that he began soon to address him as his spiritual director and his *aiblah*, politely bowing to him all the while in every conversation; by degrees however Makdhum Miân Chishti Ismail Khân, Sayyid Karwâ, and Fateh Khân entered into a conspiracy to ruin him. They brought Dêvaśi bin Sundarji, who possessed the nature of a devil, with Sundarji Sangvi, who excelled Kalelah and Demnah in acuteness, and Sayyid Karwâ from Râjkoṭ to Junâgaḍh, and induced them to murder Ahmad Khân (because he had been concerned in the dismissal of Seṭh Sundarji from the Karbariship of Junâgaḍh). The murder of Ahmad Khân was perpetrated on the 4th Muharram A.H. 1240 (Samvat 1880), and as a punishment for it, Chelah Esmâyl Khân and Kadava were one year afterwards expelled from the town; Makhdûm Chisith was, after a captivity of one year, compelled to pay a fine of sixty thousand jami (koris), and after giving securities, was allowed to depart to Nagar; but Fateh Khân suffered capital punishment.

Events of Samvat 1880.

The General Sâheb met the Navâb Sâheb (in Saṁvat 1880) at Kâtharota, and as the author was farming the revenues of Dhorâji and Upletâ, he also obtained the felicity of an interview on the 14th of Mâhavad.

After the murder of Ahmad Khân, his son Yusuf Khân received two villages as an inâm from the Navâb Sâheb, and went to his watan, but Devaśi Seṭh returned unsuccessfully to Râjkot; but Miân Hasan bin Nathu Miân, who was also one of the disciples of Mohkim-ud-din, attained the dignity of spiritual director to the Navâb, and gained over Sundarji Sangvi to his side, and administered the affairs of State on his own account. Meanwhile Miân Kamar-ud-din, the successor of Barâ Sâheb, who had been the spiritual guide [*pir*] of the Bâbi dynasty, fell into neglect; and the Navâb Sâheb became very fond of listening to songs and music, of dancing, drinking, eating forbidden things, associating with rosy-cheeked women, and attending combats of buffaloes and rams; often changed his servants, and allowed Hasan Miyân and his vakils to administer the affairs of State sitting in some shop in the bazâr. Lastly, Lakshmidâs Seṭh, Khushâl Chamanrai, and Bhûpat Râi Deśâi, and Govardhan Seṭh and the sipáhis who were followers of Ahmad Khân, were kept for two months in prison.

Mehta Govindji bin Amarji bin Rûdraji Jhâlâ, a Nâgar, was formerly the Mutasaddi of Mângrol and Kesod. Ahmad Khân, considering him a fit puppet, caused him to be appointed Divân in Saṁvat 1881, but he administered affairs dishonourably, and thought solely of amassing money.

Highway robbers from their haunts about Mount Girnâr, infested the parganahs of Hâlâr and Dhorâji, the inhabitants of which they plundered. They also ravaged the place of the Atits of Śrî T r i n e t r a M a h â d ê v a, which from ancient times is the ornament and honour of this country, and under the direction of Ahmad Khân, Hamir the Sindhi robber got hold of many lakhs worth of plunder from the monastery. Kaliângar, the helpless máhant of this monastery, being reduced to great distress by these depredations, preferred his complaints to Captain Barnwell, but the sowârs of the Navâb Sâheb, with several Atits who had a dispute about their hereditary property, pursued him and brought back Kaliângar, having captured him near Dhorâji.

These complaints Barnwell Sâheb sent me from Dhorâji. I at once sent a hundred men to their aid, and rescuing Kaliângar from Jamnâwar, where he was kept a prisoner, I sent him to Râjkot.

Barnwell Sâheb, being apprised of these disturbances, despatched Captain Wilson Sâheb with a regiment to overawe Junâgaḍh, in the vicinity whereof it remained encamped for two or three months, and at last the Navâb Sâheb went himself in person to Wanthali, agreed to restore the property taken by the robbers (from the temple) and to pay a fine of six lakhs and eighty-five thousand jami koris.

At that time the news arrived that English troops from Madras and Calcutta were invading the Kâmrup country, known as Barmâ, and situated between Calcutta and China, where the inhabitants profess the Buddhist religion. At the first battle, the army took possession of Rangun, but on account of the great mountains, brambles, sorcery, epidemic diseases, and the consequent difficulty of carrying on war, they returned after having conquered a portion of that country.

Ranjit Singh the Sikh first conquered Multân and afterwards Kashmir and Âtak by the strength of the sword; he had also occupied Kâbul and Peshâwar, but was unable to keep them.

Some freebooters of the Miyânâ people of Sindh invaded Kachh under their commander Fateh Ali, who on hearing that the English Sarkár intended to march troops against him, despatched his vakils to Bombay and sued for peace.

In Saṁvat 1881 so great a famine raged, that beasts went in search of grass to the meadows of the king of death, and many human beings died from want of bread and emaciation. In this year also the excellent and high-minded youth Śambhuprasâd, who was the shining lamp of us three brothers, withered away from the fierce wind of death on 5th of Jêshṭh sudh; but man is unable to contend with fate.

In the year 1882 Govindji Jhâlâ (whom Ahmad Khân had always been in the habit of addressing insultingly and replying to reproachfully, and who had, moreover, fallen into disgrace and oblivion like an owl), now after the murder of Ahmad Khân, and through the recommendation of Barnwell and Blane Sâhebs, as well as by the good pleasure of the Navâb Sâheb, obtained for the second time a contract for the farm of the revenues of Junâgaḍh for ten years under the guarantee of the Company Bahâdur. Some time afterwards, however, the Navâb Sâheb was displeased because the raiyats were oppressed by Govindji Jhâlâ, and at the advice of Hasan Miân Darvesh, he despatched Latif Miyân Bûkhâri and Sayyid-walan Miyân from Koḍinâr as his vakils to Bombay, for the purpose of complaining and making the Sarkâr acquainted with all the doings of Govindji Jhâlâ, and the author was likewise sent for to the Navâb Sâheb's presence.

At the time of the marriage of Lakshmiśankar, the light of my eyes and son of Śambhuprasâd, the Navâb Sâheb Bahâdur Khân conferred an everlasting honour on me by making his appearance in the assembly, and Langford Sâheb, although he had but recently arrived, was nevertheless, by his innate generosity, impelled to be present. Langford Sâheb was very painstaking, and so valiant that his mere arrival was sufficient to put a stop to robberies, and his praiseworthy behaviour is deserving of the thanks of all the people, whose unfortunate fate it was that he departed soon; but I heard that on account of the jealousy of some English Sâheb he did not prosper in the service of the Company Bahâdur.

In course of time Hasan Miyân again became reconciled to Jhâlâ Govindji, and he again made peace between him and the Navâb Sâheb.

After the death of the wife of Barnwell Sâheb he was much grieved and departed to the Cape, whence he proceeded in Saṁvat 1885 to England by the permission of Governor Malcolm, whilst Blane Sâheb, who had been a subordinate of his, took his place after he had departed, and substituted for the patience and good manners of Barnwell Sâheb, his own silly talk and ill-humour. At last, however, he had an attack of erysipelas, for the purpose of curing which—nay, rather to cure the heart-ache of the poor raiyats of Sorath—he departed to Surat, and thence to Europe.

In Saṁvat 1886, when Blane Sâheb became

ruler over the country, he did not allow the justiee of the English Sarkâr to take its course, so that the people were distressed and sent their complaints to Bombay, but on account of Newnham Sâheb's friendship for Blane Sâheb no one would listen to them, and on account of the departure of Governor Elphinstone Sâheb Bahâdur—may his prosperity endure for ever—also a great calamity befell those who sought redress for their grievances. Thus, for instance, the vakil of the author, although he had a personal interview with the Governor Malcolm Sâheb and wrote several petitions, yet never received any reply. However, what has happened has happened, and now I have but a short time to live.

On the occasion of the marriage of the Jâm Sâheb Raṇmalji to the daughter of Râval Wajesingh, râjâ of Bhâvnagar, the author sent a troop of fifty sowârs and a chariot with Lakshmiśankar and Śankarprasâd, who were during two months and a half treated in the kindest manner by the Jâm Sâheb—may God increase his prosperity! Their return cheered my saddened heart. Now, oh Ranchorji, give up telling these idle tales. The world is nothing but a dream or passing thought. They who have died have left nothing behind them but a name. I also must die and leave all, and nothing but a good name endures for ever. Be satisfied, then, be satisfied with contemplating the perfections of that God who is everlasting, immoveable, and immortal.

End of the History of Junâgaḍh.

The following additional circumstances I add to this book.

In Saṁvat 1885 Lâdunâth Jogi, whom the Râjâ Mânsinghji of Mârwâr considered his spiritual preceptor, came to adore Gorakhnâth, accompanied by a band of three or four thousand horsemen and footmen and tents and cannon. He went to Gorakhmaḍi with 200 chosen camel sowars, and performed the requisite circumambulations of the shrine, and bringing Piârnâth, the abbot of that place, with him to Junâgaḍh, he presented him with an elephant and then he returned to his own country; but when he reached the zillah of Becharâji on his way thither, he died.

In Saṁvat 1890 the Navâb Sâheb sent for Sadâshiv Râo, son of the Dakhani Divân, from Ahmadâbâd by means of Nânâ Miyan, and went to meet him on his arrival as far as the Sardâr Bâgh and handed over to him the ministry. He also seated Sadâshiv Râo beside him on his own elephant, and in this year (Saṁvat 1890) Râṇâ Vikmâtji came with his mother to perform the pilgrimage to Girnâr, and had an interview with the Navâb Sâheb and presented a horse as nazarânah. The Navâb Sâheb also visited him at his house, which was that of Raghunâth Râi. And it so befell that the Navâb Sâheb died suddenly, from a carbuncle which appeared on his rump, on Wednesday, Vaisâkh vad 1st, Saṁ. 1896, corresponding to the 24th of Rabi-ul-Â'wal, A.H.

1256. He was an excellent man, and his reign lasted for 29 years and 22 days, and his age at his death was 44 years and 10 months and 22 days.

Note on p. 222.

The following is Captain Grant's own narrative of his captivity :—

" In 1813 I was appointed by the Bombay Government, at the request of Captain Carnac, Resident of Baroda, to the command of the naval force then established by His Highness the Gaikvâḍ for the suppression of the Indian and Arabian pirates that infested the coasts of Kâṭhiâvâḍ and Kachh. We captured and destroyed several ; and in 1820 they were so much reduced that the Gaikvâḍ abolished his naval establishment, not considering it necessary to keep it up any longer. I then received orders to proceed inland from my station at Velan Bandar, or Diu Head, to Amrêlî, to deliver over charge of my vessels to the Gaikvâḍ's Sarsubha, or Diwân, in Kâṭhiâvâḍ. On my way I was attacked by a bâharwati, or outlaw Kâṭhî, named Bâwâwallâ, with thirty-five horsemen. My horsekeeper was killed ; my munshi severely wounded. I could not myself make any resistance, having only a riding whip.

" On first coming up, Bâwâwallâ said that he wanted to consult me about his affairs, and on this pretext got me to dismount. My people being rendered helpless, I was forced to remount my horse and gallop off with the gang, who took me into a large jungle, called the Gîr, where I was kept prisoner on the top of a mountain for two months and seventeen days. During the whole of this time two armed men with swords drawn kept guard over me. I laid among the rocks drenched with rain night and day, with the exception of two nights, when the gang forced me to accompany them, and we stopped in a friendly village. In this expedition I was occasionally allowed to ride, but always surrounded by a strong band, that made all attempt to escape impossible. In one village, where the people favoured Bâwâwallâ, the women took my part and upbraided him and his men for my cruel treatment. Towards unfriendly villages the custom of the gang was to ride up to the gates and chop off the heads of little boys at play, and then go off rejoicing and laughing at their cursed exploits. When they returned to the encampment after a day's murdering foray, the young Kâṭhîs used to boast how many men they had killed; and one day I heard the old fellows questioning them rather particularly whether or not they were sure they had killed their victims. 'Yes,' they said; 'they had seen their spears through them, and were certain they were dead.' 'Ah!' remarked an old Kâthî, 'a human being is worse to kill than any other animal; never be sure they are dead till you see the body on one side of the road and the head on the other.'

"At times the Chief Bâwâwallâ, in a state of stupor from opium, would come and sit by my side, and holding his dagger over me, ask how many stabs it would take to kill me. I said I thought one would do, and I hoped he would put me out of misery. 'I suppose you think,' he would answer, 'that I won't kill you; I have killed as many human beings as ever fisherman killed fish, and I should think nothing of putting an end to you; but I shall keep you awhile yet, till I see if your Government will get me back my property; if so, I will let you off.'

"When not out plundering, the gang slept most of the day. At night the halter of each horse was tied to its master's arm. When the animals heard voices they tugged, and the men were up in an instant. Their meals consisted of bâjri cakes with chillis, and milk when it could be got. I used to have the same. Once or twice my servant was allowed to come to me, and brought the rare treat of some curry and a bottle of claret from Captain Ballantine. The wine Bâwâwallâ seized on at once, thinking it was *dâru*, or spirits, but on tasting the liquor he changed his mind, and spitting it out declared it was poison, sent, no doubt, on purpose to kill him. By way of test, I was ordered to drink it, which I did with great pleasure, and finding me none the worse, he gave up his idea of poison.

"Among his people there were two young men who showed some feeling for me. One of these was shot on a pillaging raid shortly before my release They used to try and cheer me up by telling me I should be set free. Occasionally, when opportunity offered, they would inform me how many people they had killed, and the method they pursued when rich travellers refused the sum demanded. This was to tie the poor wretches by their legs to a beam across a well, with their heads touching the water, and then to saw away at the rope until the tortured victims agreed to their demands, then the Kâṭhîs would haul them up, get from them a *hundi* or bill on some agent, and keep them prisoners till this was paid.

"Sometimes they told me of their master's intention to murder me, which was not pleasant. He and his men had many disputes about me, just as his hopes or fears of the consequence of my imprisonment prevailed.

"I can never forget one stormy night: they were all sitting round a great fire; I lay behind them. Lions and wild beasts roared around us, but did not prevent me overhearing a debate upon the subject of what should be done with me. The men complained that they had been two months in the jungle on my account; their families were in the villages, very badly off for food, and that they would stay no longer. Their chief replied: 'Let us kill him, and flee to some other part of the country.' To this they objected, saying that the English would send troops and take their families prisoners and ill use them. So in the end it was agreed to keep me for the present.

"My release was effected at last through our Political Agent, Captain Ballantine, who prevailed on the Navâb of Junâgaḍh to use his influence to get another Kâṭhî who had forcibly taken Bâwâwallâ's *parganah* or district to restore it to him, and Bâwâwallâ thus having gained his object, set me free.

"My sufferings during confinement were almost beyond endurance, and I used to pray in the evening that I might never see another morning. I had my boots on my feet for the first month, not being able to get them off from the constant wet until I was reduced by sickness. Severe fever, with ague and inflammation of the liver, came on, and, with exposure to the open air, drove me delirious, so that when let go I was found wandering in the fields at night covered with vermin from head to foot. I shall never forget the heavenly sensation of the hot bath and clean clothes I got in the tent of the Navâb of Junâgaḍh's Divan, the officer who accomplished my release. The fever and ague, then contracted, continued on me for five years, and the ill effects still remain, my head being at times greatly troubled with giddiness, and I have severe fits of ague; my memory also is much affected, but I can never forget the foregoing incidents, though it is now upwards of fifty years since they occurred.*

"G. GRANT.

"Barholm House, Creetown, N.B., *April* 1871."

---

* From General Sir G. LeGrand Jacob's ***Western India, before and during the Mutinies***, pp. 108ff.

CONCERNING THE HISTORY OF NAGAR.

H â l â r is a separate country. Although it is not included among the tributaries of the Sorath Sarkâr, nevertheless the imperial functionaries came from Junâgaḍh to Nagar to levy the tribute and the Bâdshâhi *vero*. The tâlûkâs of D h r o l and R a j k o ṭ and the villages of the G o n d a l estate, pay khiraj, since the time of Sher Khân, who had the title of Bahâdur Khân, and the Divân Sâheb Amarji, and I will relate to those who care to listen to such histories some account of those places.

CONCERNING THE JÂM.

In past times the Khalifah of Bâghdâd, Hajjâj by name, led an army against Sindh in a religious war. In this campaign Dharasena, the Brâhman chief of the province of Ṭhaṭhâ, was slain in battle, and the Muhammadan religion was established by force and violence throughout the country of Sindh. They who did not wish to adopt the new religion and yet were not sufficiently strong to oppose it, agreed to submit, and after the rule of the Sûmrâs, Anirâo Samâ became, in St. 1340 (A.D. 1283-84), the ruler of Sindh. Of these, the Jádejâ Rajputs, who originally are of the Jâdav stock, entering the country of Kachh, conquered Bhuj by force of arms, and residing there, ruled the country and erected numerous forts in all directions, and one thousand, four hundred, and forty villages are within their rule. Jâm Lâkhan brought the whole of Kachh under his rule ; but since I am the historian of H â l â r, I will begin with Jâm R â v a l, the founder of Nagar.

Jâm L â k h â crossed the Raṇ from Bhadreśyar, which was his capital, with a powerful army. The râjâ of S o r a ṭ h came to oppose him, but the Jâm defeated him and drove him back. At this time Sultân Bâhâdur Shâh summoned the Jâm to his presence, and placing him in command of his own army, sent him to conquer Pâwâgaḍh, which he did, and as a reward for it, was presented with the parganas of Kûnaḍ, Ámbaran, with 12 villages in each, and Morbi. The Jâm Lâkha offered for this a *nazar* of some Kachhi horses and one hundred Ashrafis, and marching back to his country was treacherously slain near a place called Ambaran, by the zamindar thereof, whose name was T a m â c h i D e d â, and who committed the deed like a robber by entering his tent in the middle of the night.

His son Jâm R â v a l, to avenge his death, slew Tamâchi and then killed Parmâl Châvadâ, and took Dhrol, and Haradhol, after slaying also Nâg Jethvâ, took possession of N â g n a h, near N a v â n a g a r. Then he devoted himself during sixteen years to the cultivation and settlement of his country. He also conquered the town of B a k o t â.

Jâm R â v a l bîn Lâkhâ bîn Haradhol slew his uncle Hamir, and himself ascended the throne.

On account of this wicked deed his subjects, amirs, and relatives hated him, and Râo Khengâr, the son of Hamîr, desirous to avenge the murder of his father, called to his aid Sultân Mahmud Gujarâti, which compelled Jâm Râval, when the Muhammadan army was approaching, to seek the protection of Áśâpûri Mâtâ. He was thinking of making an offering of his own head to the Mâtâ, whose shrine is as glorious as heaven, when he heard the voice of an invisible angel exclaim—

"To thee do I the land of Hâlâr give,
From thee the land of Kachh I take."

Encouraged by this message, he collected his friends and followers, who amounted to nearly a hundred thousand and were of various Râjput tribes, such as Jâḍejâ, Ládak, Dhudhan, Dheman, Chârân, Dal, and Wagher, with whom he crossed the Salt-Raṇ and encamped before Morbi, on this side of the Raṇ, which had been given to his family on account of the conquest of Pâwâgadh and the surrender of Sûltân Muzaffar by Râo Bhârâ, and advancing thence he halted in the parganahs of Âmbran, Bâlambhâ, and Jodiâ.

The whole of the province was in the hands of different râjâs. The Jêṭhwâs ruled as far as Nâgnah, distant about a kos from Nagar; the Dêdâs and Châvaḍa Râjputs prevailed as far as the Machhu River; and the rule of the Vâdhel Râjpûts, as zamindârs, extended to the village of Khambhâliya; and as far as Kâlâwaḍ was possessed by Kâṭhîs under Jûnâgaḍh ; and all plundered in every direction for several years.

As all the zamindars united to oppose him, Jâm Râval marched against them, and drew up his van, centre, rear, and right and left wings in an excellent manner, and selecting a favourable moment to engage, he said to his comrades, "I will this day place my head under a crown or under a sword." Then after strenuous efforts and the display of great bravery and activity, he gained the day, driving back the Kâṭhis to the river Bhâdar, and the Jeṭhwâs to the salt creek of Bhokirâ, and the Dedâs and Châvadâs to the river Machhû, and he forced the Vâdhels to cross the Okhâ Raṇ, and thus obtained the country without any shareholder or partner.

Verse.

"The land is a tablecloth which belongs to
whom God willeth,
And at this table both friend and enemy may
partake."

Founding of the City of Navânagar.

The city of Navânagar was founded on Wednesday, the 8th of the light half of Śrâvan, in Saṁvat 1596, on the banks of the Rangamati and Nâgamati rivers, at a distance of two kos from the ocean, during the reign of the Emperor Humâiyûn of Delhi and of Sultân Mahmûd bin Muhammad Shâh, of Gûjarât.

At that time Sultan Ahmad laid siege to Junâgaḍh; and Râo Mâṇḍlik, being occupied with his own troubles, was not able to attend to anything else. In course of time the city began to prosper, and all kinds of artisans crowded to it. At present it is celebrated for its various textile fabrics, such as turbans, head-dresses, dhotis, and petticoats, which are exported to different countries by merchants. Here also silk stuffs, like those made at Âhmadâbâd and Surat, called *mashru*, *atlas*, and *pânchpatâ*, are produced. Here also painters, dyers, workers in shells, engravers, embroiderers, and tailors produce exquisite articles. This place abounds with kitchen and flower gardens; and in the latter also plants are reared from which essential oils and perfumes, *e.g. attar* and water of roses, *champeli* and *moghara*, are prepared and in great quantities exported to distant countries. In the bazâr all kinds of produce, green and dry, living and dead, is exposed for sale.

Here are Brâhmans who read the *Vedas*, and are distinguished by science, virtue, and kindness; they are preachers, readers of the *Purâṇas*, perform religious ceremonies, and the Agnihotri sacrifice. Among the other inhabitants the Bohoras, Khattris, and Bhátias engage in their respective occupations, whilst the Seṭás, Maliks, Râjput Jhâlas, and Sodhâ Vatandars constitute a most respectable portion of the community.

The chief ornaments of this place are the temples of Nâganâth, Bhiḍabhanjan, Jagannâtha,

Hat-keśvar, Jámnâtha, Ranchoḍrâi, and Kal-lyânji, the monastery of the Gokali Gosáins, and the temples of the Jains and tombs of many Bohoras. The talâo called Jâmsâr, to the west of the city, is always overflowing with sweet water. Four kos from the city on the seashore is the temple of Roji Mâtâ, which is both strong and famous.

The inhabitants all dress well, have a pleasing complexion, are intelligent, and the beauty of the women is so seductive, that even his lordship the Qâzi and the Sheikh-al-Mashâikh agitate their beards and sing the following Ghazal aloud :—

The dead why worship ? Purity is here ;
Why doubt ? come to the Ka'bah, God is here ;
The Kâbah, but of stone and loam you see,
Now come, adore an idol : here it is,—
I searched the world's book-case from leaf to leaf,
I saw your mark, and said this is my hope.
The Kâbah and the Zem-zem was a trope,
Its truth a pure heart is, such is my hope.
When God did give to man a shape, his own,
He said :—How pure his heart, our place is here,
In this garden I am each blossom's friend,
Here hope to find the scent of amity,
To this threshold bow your head, O Áhmad,
Because each king a beggar here becomes.

According to the saying "the people follow the religion of their kings," the adherents of Islâm generally shave their beards, abandon the worship of tombs, throw about colour at the Holi, and use the Râm-Râm salutation. Lastly, the city of Nagar is the ornament of the whole State, and is under the special protection of Śankar, who is the giver of all good gifts. Hardholji, brother of Jâm Râval, who slew Dhamal Châvaḍa, colonised the town of Ḍhrol.

Jâm Râval bin Lâkhâ bin Hardhol.

This Jâm was well known for his liberality, and reigned twenty-one years. His eldest son, Jayâji, lost his life by falling from a horse in the plain, near Roji Mâtâ's temple. Jayâji's son Lâkhâ, who was still a minor, received the parganah of Khilos in girâs, and his uncle Vibhâji became râjâ.

Jâm Vibhâji bin Jâm Râval.

This prince began to reign on the 11th Kartik sud, Saṁvat 1618 (A.D. 1561), and died seven years and three months afterwards.

Jâm Satrasâl bin Vibhâji.

Jâm Satrasâl bin Vibhâji ascended the masnad of his father in Saṁvat 1625, on the 14th of Mahâ vad, and was allowed to coin money by Sulṭân Muẓaffar, whose name it bore; but he ordered it to be called Mâhmudi, after his father. The permission was obtained in the following way:—On a certain occasion the Jâm presented a rupee to the Sulṭân with a kori as nazarânah, and said:—"In the same way as the dignity of râjâs is augmented by giving their daughters to His Majesty the Sulṭân, so I wed my 'Kûnwarì' to this rupee in the hope that her honour will increase." The Sulṭân was pleased with this sally, issued the permission for coining this money, and ordered it to be called *kûnwarî* in the Hindu language, and by the mispronunciation of the vulgar, it is now called *korî*. It is said that Jâm Satâji lived and ruled with independence, pomp, and splendour. During his time, Daulat Khân, son of Âmin Khân, the Mûtasaddi of Junâgaḍh, revolted from the Pâdshâh Akbar of Delhi, who despatched an army to coerce him, which arrived at the fort of Junâgaḍh, and when Daulat Khân was hard pressed he begged aid of Jâm Satarsâl. The Jâm Sâheb, whose fortune was in the ascendant, and who was desirous of an opportunity like this, sent his Kûnwar Bhârâji and Bhâiji Dal and Jasâ Vazir and Loma Khûmân the Kâṭhi, with 12,000 brave Râjpût horsemen to his aid. When the army of the Jâm had camped at Majevaḍi, about four kos from Jûnâgaḍh, Daulat Khân became alarmed, and began to think that it was not wise to trust to those who were desirous of gaining land, lest—God forbid—they should enter the city, and he should afterwards be unable to make them leave it. He therefore made apologies to his ally, whom he informed that he intended to negotiate for peace with the imperial army, and requested him to return to his own country. This news was most unpalatable to Kûnwar Bhârâji, who at once attacked the Delhi army on his own account, defeated it, and took a large booty, consisting of 52 elephants, 3,530 horses, 70 palanquins, many tents, cannon, and all kinds of arms. The next day he marched against Daulat Khân, who had broken his word, and who was so unable to offer resistance that he sued for peace through the Sayyids and Bhâts, and obtained it on giving up the parganahs of Chûr, Jodhpûr, and Bhod, containing 12 villages each. In this way he averted further misfortunes from himself. At this time Sulṭân Muzaffar Gûjarâti was fleeing from the Emperor Akbar's army and arrived in the country of Soraṭh, with a view of obtaining aid from Jâm Satâji, Daulat Khân, and Râjâ Khengâr, who was the zamindâr of Soraṭh; and raised an army from them of 30,000 cavalry and 20,000 infantry, and created confusion in the district near Ahmadâbâd. On this occasion the Khân Azam Gokaltâsh was appointed in place of the Khân Khânân as the Subahdâr of Ahmadâbâd. He marched to encounter Muzaffar, and encamping at Viramgâm, he despatched Nauranz Khân with Sayyid Kâsim and troops to Morbi, whence they sent letters to the Jâm to the effect that he should expel Sulṭân Muzaffar from his country. The Jâm however had the honour of his army too much at heart to comply, but, on the contrary, began to harass the imperial army by cutting off its supplies, and by killing stragglers, and carrying off horses and elephants whenever he could, so that at last one ser of corn was sold for a rupee in the camp.

Now, however, the Khân Âzam, with his own special forces, joined the main body. On account of the rain, mud, and the inequality of the ground, the imperial army was deprived of the chance of fighting a pitched battle, accordingly it was determined to march on Nagar, because the Jâm kept all his stores there, and in trying to defend them would be compelled to offer battle. Accordingly the army was put in motion, and when it had arrived in the qasbâ of Dhrol, the Jâm made his appearance with the auxiliary forces of Râo Bhârâji of Kachh, and several skirmishes were fought, in each of which the Jâm was victorious. Lomâ Khûmân the Kâṭhi had on a former occasion, in the campaign of Jûnâgaḍh, kept an elephant for himself, taken from the booty of the imperial army, and had on this account been much annoyed by Jasâ Vazir, and thus bore a grudge towards the Jâm, as was also the case with Daulat Khân of Junâgaḍh, whom the Jâm had now called to his aid, and who likewise fancied that he had suffered some wrong,—

If a man's evil day has arrived,
He will do what ought not to be done.

A fellow-feeling made these two individuals friends; accordingly they communicated with the Khân Âzam Gokaltâsh, and made an arrangement to bring the army of the Jâm into trouble by deserting it at the moment of onset. The enemy was greatly pleased with the news, and when the fight began, both Lomâ and Daulat Khân loosed the reins of their horses and fled. This sight so discouraged the Jâm, that he likewise alighted from his elephant, mounted a fleet horse, and fled for his life. Jasâ Vazir, however, succeeded with great trouble in maintaining his position till evening; he also guarded the household and the ladies of the Jâm, whom he placed in ships and despatched by sea, to escape being captured, and afterwards all returned to Nagar.

Preparations for the wedding feast of Kûnwar Ajâji were being made at Nagar, and therefore he had remained in the town. Being now vexed at his father's flight, he quickly mounted and joined the army in the field. On the second day, when the brilliant diadem of heaven shone from the firmament, the two armies encountered each other. The right wing of the imperial army was led by Sayyid Kâsim, Naurang, and Gûjar Khân; and the left by Muhammad Rafî, who was a celebrated general, with several imperial Amirs and Zamindars. Mirza Marhûm, son of Navâb Azim Humâyun, commanded the centre, and before him Mirza Anwar and the Navàb himself took their post. The van of the army of the Jâm was commanded by Jasâ Vazir, Kûnvar Ajâji, and Mehrâmanji Dungarâni. A cannonade from both armies opened the combat, and the imperial warriors as well as the Râjputs fought so well that the angels of heaven applauded their bravery. Muhammad Rafî assailed the army of the Jâm with his battalions, whilst Gûjar Khân and Mirza Anwar, the Navâb of high dignity, attacked

Kûnvar Ajâji, Jasâ Vazir, and a company of 1,500 Atits, who were going on pilgrimage to Hinglâj Dêvî, and who had on their way joined the army of the Jâm; and these fifteen hundred perished, together with Kûnvar Ajâji and Jasâ Vazir, whilst of the imperial army Muhammad Rafî, Sayyid Sharf-ud-dîn, Sayyid Kabir, Sayyid Ali Khân, and others, amounting to two hundred men, were slain and 500 wounded; and of the Jâm's army 700 horses were disabled and all the treasure plundered. This battle was fought on the 8th Áśo sud, Saṁvat 1648, or the 6th Rajab A.H. 1001. After this unexpected victory, the imperial army also conquered Junâgaḍh, Patandev, Dwârkâ, and the island of Śankhodwârâ. The imperial army now took up the pursuit of Sulṭân Muzaffar, who had fled to the country of Kachh to Vasta-Bandar when the imperial army had crossed the Raṇ Râo Bhârâ then surrendered Muzaffar to the imperial servants in exchange for the parganah of Morbi, but Sulṭân Mûzaffar committed suicide by cutting his throat, and thus died.

The reign of Jâm Satrasâl *alias* Satâji lasted 47 years, 3 months, and 18 days. He gave Gondal to his younger (third) son, Vibhâji, which was lying waste, and Râjkoṭ in lieu of Kâlâwar; and Vibhâji's descendants are still called Vibhânis.

JÂM JASÂJI, SECOND SON OF JÂM SATÂJI.

Jâm Jasâji was for some time kept under surveillance in the capital of Dehli, because, after the death of Kûnvar Ajâji, Jâm Satrasâl remained in Nagar in a subordinate position, and an imperial deputy administered the government of Nagar in concert with him. Jâm Jasâji, therefore, in the hope of winning the imperial favour and removing the annoyance of the deputy, went to Delhi, and by the protection and kindness of the Emperor's wife, Jahânârâ Begam, and the good offices of Raghunâthji Nâgar, the Bakhshi, was installed on the masnad of Navânagar on the 1st Phâlgun sud, in Saṁvat 1673, and in the year 1675, when Nûr-u'd-din Jahângir Pâdshâh visited Dohad, which is on the frontier of Gujarât, Jâm Jasâji obtained the honour of an audience. On this occasion he offered fifty Kachhi horses and 100 gold mohars to the emperor, from whom he received in return two elephants, two horses, and four rings set with diamonds. During his reign the Śrâvaks repaired a temple in the bazâr.

It happened that during a rainy night the Jâm was playing chess with his Jhâli Râṇî, who was the daughter of Râjâ Chandrasingh, and displeased her in the game by taking a knight, whereon the râṇî said :—" What manliness is there in taking a lifeless horse from the hands of a woman? Let him who boasts of his valour take a horse from my father!" This speech so vexed the Jâm that he immediately sent a large and well equipped army against the râjâ. The troops of the Jâm and of the Râjâ of Halawaḍ fought for six months with each other without any decisive result. Seeing he could effect nothing, the Jâm became helpless, and accordingly he despatched Śankardâs Nâgar, the Thânadâr of Rânâvâv, a brave soldier, to the seat of war, with the promise of a great reward if he could bring this affair to a happy end. Śankardâs went to Halawaḍ, and pretending to come on an errand of condolence to the râjâ, whose son had died, wrapped himself in a sheet, and made his entrance into Halawaḍ with 400 sowars during the evening repast of the chokidârs—a time when they are off their guard. He entered the apartment of the râjâ when he happened to be asleep, and putting a dagger to his breast, awoke him. The râjâ was in fear of his life; his mother, who was present, interceded with Śankardâs, but the latter carried him to the Jâm. When the râjâ arrived, the Jâm smiled and said:—"You are welcome." He replied "Śankardâs the Nâgar, who is a Brâhman, has outwitted me, and indeed it is no disgrace if we Râjputs are outwitted by Brâhmans." It was the intention of the Jâm Sâheb to keep the râjâ prisoner, but Śankardâs, who had made a promise to his mother to bring him back, begged that he might be excused. Hereon the Jâm issued orders to kill Śankardâs, the son of Dâmodar, The latter, however, by his quickness and the force of his sword, succeeded with his followers in carrying the râjâ safely back to Halawaḍ, but was himself slain, with all his followers; and the truth of the proverb that the company of princes is like that of lions, was again confirmed. Jâm J a s â j i spent much time in travelling. His reign lasted nominally for eight years, when his Jhâli Râṇi gave him poison, and thus deprived him of both his crown and his life.

Jâm Lâkha bin Ajâji.

He began to reign on the 30th Mahâvad, in Saṁvat 1681; he reigned 21 years, 1 month, and 10 days. In his time Sulṭân Nûr-u'd-din Jahângir ruled at Delhi.

Jâm Raṇmalji bin Lâkhâ.

His reign commenced on the 10th of Chaitra sud in Saṁvat 1702. He was born on the 9th Śrâvan sud at dawn. The subjoined figure represents his horoscope*:—

* No explanation is given of this horoscope in the Persian MS., but persons unacquainted with astrology may be informed that the twelve areas of this diagram are assigned to Mercury, the Sun, Venus, Saturn, the Moon, Mars, Râhu, Jupiter, Ketu, respectively, which was the combination of planets at the prince's birth.

His adopted son S a t â j i was born of a daughter of the Râṭhoḍ house of Jodhpur, and was expelled from the country after the demise of Raṇmalji, his father. He then went to the Court of Delhi and obtained the parganah of Kaḍi, in Gujarât, in jâgir, and I will now relate an account of what his father did.

One day Jâm R a ṇ m a l j i was hunting in the jungle and happened to perceive a Sanyâsi, reclining under a tree with a young and beautiful woman with arched eyebrows, whose charms captivated him; overcome by desire, he went and seated himself by her. When the Sanyâsi, overtaken by fate, had gone to bathe, the Jâm asked her who she was, and the lady spoke as follows:—"I am the wife of a Brâhman, and this godless Sanyâsi has inveigled me here by deceit; if you approve of me, I am at your service." "The Jâm ordered the Sanyâsi to be killed, and carried the woman away to his palace, but from his inordinate intercourse with her, he contracted a painful disease; and the pain becoming excessive he emasculated himself, but when he was healed, he married a Râṭhoḍ lady, who became his Râṇi. When she found her husband impotent, she bought a fine infant from her own tribe, pretending that she had given birth to him; she also sent for her brother from Jodhpur, and enjoyed full authority over her husband. Some time afterwards, however, Jâm Raṇmalji, fearing her machinations, assembled his nobles and ministers of State, and addressed them thus: "I have been impotent for a long time, and this is not my son, and it is fitting that my younger brother Raisingh should succeed to the throne after me." Jâm Raṇmalji lost his life some time afterwards with Sângoji Hardhol, fighting against the force of the imperial army, whereupon Raisingh expelled by force the adopted son the Râṇi had bought, with all the Râṭhoḍs, including also Govardhan Bhandâri and others, from Nagar. Raṇmalji's reign lasted 15 years, 3 months, and 18 days.

JÂM RÂISINGH BIN LÂKHÂJI.

By the agreement of the nobles and chief men, he was installed on the throne on the 13th Asâḍ vad, Saṁvat 1717. At that time Sultân Qutbû'd-dîn arrived from Ahmadâbâd with a powerful army. The Jâm hastened to meet him, and fighting a sanguinary battle on the plain of Shekpât, he lost his life. Hereon the imperial army occupied the city, and named it Islâmnagar. A mosque was built in the bazâr, and from that time the Bâdshâhi *vero* began to be levied. Kûnwar Satâji (Prince Tamàchi) and several other survivors of the battle left Nagar, which had no strong fort, and by sheltering themselves in the cactus jungle escaped to Okhâ. Jâm Raisingh reigned 2 years and 25 days.

JÂM TAMÂCHI TAGADH BIN RÂISINGH.

On the 8th of Śrâvan vad, Saṁvat 1719, Tamâchi succeeded to the throne and distressed the

Bâdshâhi Thânadârs and the râyats by the depredations he committed around Nagar, in such a manner that he obtained the cognomen T a g a d h (Reiver). Gradually, however, after the expiration of fully nine years, he was pardoned his offences through the kind offices of Mahârâja Jasvantsingh of Jodhpur, and Vizir Asad Ali Khân, Sûbahdâr of Gujarât, on whom, when he was yet a minor official, the Jâm had on some occasion or other bestowed his own horse; and in Saṁvat 1728 Nagar was restored to him, and he regained his throne, and the Qâzis and Muftis who had remained in the mosques were sent to hell. His reign lasted 27 years, 1 month, and 17 days. In those days Shâh Jahân Bâdshâh ruled at Dehli.

JÂM LÂKHÂJI BIN TAMÂCHI.

He obtained the masnad on the 10th Áso sud, Saṁvat 1746, and sat on it 19 years and 1 month.

JÂM RÂISINGH BIN LÂKHÂ.

His reign began on the 10th Kârtik, in Saṁvat 1765, but he was put to death by his brother Hardhol, the son of Hemâbâî Vâghelia Rajpûtanî, who held the parganah Hariânâ in *girâs*. He took possession of the throne, but fled for fear of the Mahârâja Jasvantsingh. The reign of both amounted to one year and two months.

JÂM TAMÂCHI BIN RÂISINGH.

He succeeded to the throne on the 11th of Bhâdrava sud, Saṁvat 1767. When he was yet very young, one of the slave girls of Jâm T a m â c h i, who was his nurse, entertained fears that

Hardhol might endanger his life, and putting him into a box, conveyed him to his maternal aunt, Bâi Ratnâji, at the Court of Bhûj, and begged her to protect him. His aunt spent large sums of money to promote his interests, and also wrote to her brother Râj Pratâpsingh to give his daughter in marriage to Mûbâriz-ûl-Mûlk, known also as Sarbûland-khân, the Sûbahdâr of Gujarât, and the daughter of one of his cousins to Salâbat Muhammad Khân Bâbi, who was at the head of the army, and they, being thus gained over, expelled Hardhol from Nagar and installed Tamâchi on the masnad.

In consequence of his good services, the parganah of Hariânâ was given to the Râj of Halawad. The villages of Charakhḍi, Trâkûrâ, and Daiyâ were given as dowry with the sister of Jhâlâ Nâranji, who was married to Salâbat Khân. In course of time, however, the sons of the latter, *i.e.*, Sherzamân Khân and Diler Khân, sold all three villages to Kûmbhâji of Gondal; and lastly, for the aid afforded by Râo Sâhêb Desalji of Bhûj, the fort of Bâlambhâ and several other mahals were mortgaged to him in Saṁvat 1775, and in 1792 the Râo Sâheb rebuilt the fort. Mûbâriz-ûl-Mûlk levied three lâkhs of rupees the first year, and on coming the second year, after some dispute, through the intervention of Salâbat Khân, he obtained one lâkh as tribute.

Afterwards Mahârâja Ajitsingh, who became the Subah of Ahmadâbâd, arrived with an army at

Nagar, planted a battery of artillery on a mound near the lake, and a sanguinary battle ensued, in which a great number on both sides drank the water of death. The Mahârâja returned unsuccessful, but the brother of the Jâm—Kâkâji by name—slew Jâm Tamâchi with the sword and sent him to Paradise. The reign of Tamâchi lasted thirty-two years and one month.

Jâm Lâkhâji bin Tamâchi.

He came to the throne on the 11th Âso sud, Saṁvat 1799, and died of small-pox, but some say by poison. He reigned 24 years, 9 months, and 10 days.

During his reign Nânji and Mehrâman Khavâs arrived from Halawaḍ, with Bâî Depâbâî whom Jâm Lâkhâji had married; and since Mehrâman was an able man, by the assistance of Mehtâ Bhânji and Jagjivan Ojhâ, he assumed the administration of the State. This monopoly displeased the other courtiers, who accordingly slew Nânji, the brother of Mehrâman Khavâs, in the Râjmahâl. Mehrâman Khavâs being a valiant man, taking no account of the chokidârs and guards, hastened to the spot; but finding the doors locked and obtaining no entrance, he effected one by causing some men to stand on each other's shoulders, and using them as a ladder to scale the wall. Having in this manner entered the palace with a band of companions, he fought with the guards from morning till evening, slew several persons, and captured the person of Depâbâî. Afterwards the chokidârs and the townspeople, who were alarmed at the tumult which was going on, submitted to the sway of Mehrâman Khavâs, and from that day his authority became paramount.

Jâm Jasâji bin Lâkhâji.

He was a minor when placed on the throne on the 11th of Kártik sud, in Saṁvat 1824. The Khavâses, Mehrâman and Bhavân, kept him under surveillance, surrounded him with men of their own tribe, and their own creatures and relations as attendants and servants both in the zanânâ and the palace. Whilst Mehrâman ruled alone Shâh Álam reigned at Delhi.

Râo Sâheb Godji of Kachh crossed the Raṇ with a large army and much artillery in order to realize what had formerly been promised him. Mehrâman Khavâs therefore erected batteries against the fort of Bâlambhâ, which was in the possession of the Râo; and ere Râo Godji had crossed the Raṇ, his thânahdârs were expelled with much ignominy, in Saṁvat 1824.

The origin of this enmity was as follows :—

Great fear had been entertained lest Hardholji should kill Jâm Tamâchi. Accordingly a female slave of Jâm Tamâchi, who was then an infant, put him into a box and conveyed him over to his maternal aunt, Bâî Ratnâbâî, at Bhûj, and asked her for aid. This lady spent a great deal of money to promote his interests, and through her efforts her brother Pratâpsingh, who was Râjâ of

Halawad, wrote to Mûbâriz-ûl-Mulk and gained him over, and through his aid brought Jâm Tamâchi from Bhûj and seated him on the throne, as has been recorded above in its proper place. In consequence of these expenses and services, Bâlambhâ was mortgaged to the Râo Sâheb G o d j i, who rebuilt the fort and received the revenues of the mortgaged mahâls. But now the fort fell into the hands of the Jâm, and the Râo was obliged to depart without being able to effect anything, and the munition of the fort and six field guns and the treasure remained in the hands of the Jâm.

K â k â j i, brother of the Jâm, was a man of violent temper, who had killed the râja of M o r b i and two or three amirs and a hundred common men and women with his own hand, and his hand and sword were alike always bloody. He, seeing an opportunity, slew Jâm T a m â c h i, and, rebelling, seized on the fort of Modpur, and thence ravaged the country. Mehrâman therefore closely besieged that place, and it fell out that as he was seated at the window of that fortress, a musket ball struck him on the neck so that he died.

Bâî Sâhib Depâbâî, who had formerly conducted all the affairs of the country, was much harassed by the arrogance of Mehrâman Khavâs, and departed on the pretence of a pilgrimage to Śri N â t h j i, but since she had been predestined to perish on a dunghill, she returned in obedience to her fate again to Nagar, and the wicked Mehrâman Khavâs sent an escort of

Sipâhîs and musicians to meet and to receive her, but when she arrived at the city, on the pretence that the day was unlucky he caused her to alight for the night at the house of Chatturbhuj, instead of entering the city, and dismissed her attendants. When the chariot stopped in the street, the Bâî Sâheb wished to alight, and placed one foot on the ground, and whilst the other was yet on the chariot, a sipâhî named Chând Ghori, of hellish disposition, who was a disloyal wretch, struck her a terrible dagger thrust from behind the screen which the slave girls were holding out in order that she might alight, which passed right through her body. Thus this noble lady, wont to repose on soft velvet cushions, and to consider even rose-leaves almost as thorns, miserably perished in an unfrequented lane, where her body lay for two hours after her attendants had fled. At last, at the intercession of Jagjivan Ojhâ and Mehtâ Bhânji, they burned her on a pile of aloes and sandalwood.

In Saṁvat 1832 Mehrâman Khavâs, being desirous of checking the dacoities of the people of Positra, resolved on conquering that strong fort and the country of Okha, and invited the Divân Sâheb Amarji to aid him. During the siege of the fort, they dug a mine under one of the bastions and blew it up. The Divân Sâheb, who had, with many others, taken up a position under the rampart, observed, when the smoke and dust caused by the explosion allowed of a free view, that a large breach had been opened, and that the garrison was manfully making a sally from a small door. Hereon muskets became useless and a hand-to-hand fight with the sword ensued, in which the garrison were defeated.

On this occasion Kâlû Mer, who had ere this treacherously come to Junâgaḍh and killed two Nâgar children and become liable to punishment, but had been suffered to depart under the protection of the Jamadâr Amran Arab and A'alam Khân Baluch, was now slain. The troops followed up the fugitives, and entering the fort at their heels, obtained possession of all the goods these freebooters had robbed from the ships of Arabia, Sindh, and the Dakhan, and of which there was great abundance This news was communicated by the Divân Sâheb to Mehrâman Khavâs, who was greatly rejoiced thereat, and feigned to be highly thankful and obliged to the Divân, but being of a treacherous disposition and fearing that the bravery of the Divân might become dangerous to himself, he intended to poison him, and invited him for that purpose to a repast:—

"Remedies are good before events."

When the army had returned and encamped at Khambhâliâ, the repast was to have taken place, but the Divân Sâheb refused the invitation on the pretence that he had just received the news of the death of Khushâl Râi Nâgar, the Duftari of the Nawâb Sâheb at Junâgaḍh.

In Saṁvat 1839 Mehrâman Khavâs made a league with Râṇa Sultâṇji and Kûmbhaji in order to ruin the Divân Sâheb Amarji, but was defeated in a battle fought at Pânchpipla. After that he called the army of the Gaikwâḍ to his aid, and conquered the fort of Devrâ, but was unable to keep it, and after repairing its defences, which had been broken down, he returned. In Saṁvat 1844 he built the fort of Navânagar of white stone, with five gates and eight posterns and twenty-three towers.

In Saṁvat 1850 Jâḍejâ Dâji of Gondal, Modaji of Dhrôl, Mehrâmanji of Râjkoṭ, and Ranmalji of Khirasrâ, lighted the flame of rebellion by laying waste the province of Hâlâr; and to punish these men, Mehrâman Khavâs marched an army into the parganahs of Râjkoṭ and Sardhâr. It so happened that the Divân Sâheb Raghunâthji, elder brother of the author, was at that time with me and my brother in Nagar with a large force.

The reason of the Divân's arrival at Nagar was as follows:—When the Divân Sâheb Raghunâthji had been imprisoned by the Navâb Sâheb Hâmid Khân, the fort of Chorwâḍ belonged to the author, whilst the fort of Sutrâpârâ was in possession of his younger brother Dalpatrâm, and we were liberated by the strength of our own hands. As Mehrâman Khavâs had a feud with the surrounding râjâs, he was in search of an experienced man, and thought our arrival would be a great assistance to him, and he therefore sent Mehta Adâbhâi, kamâviśdâr of the parganah of Kandornâ, with a hundred sowars, a drum, and a flag to Chorwaḍ to recall the Divân. The Divân Sâheb, considering this a good omen, disregarded the pressing invitations to stay of Sheikh Badru'd-dîn, the Zamindâr of Mañgrol, as well as of the Navâb Sâheb Hâmid Khân, and the Zamindâr of Gondal, and proceeded to Nagar, where he was received with much civility and politeness by Mehrâman Khawâs, who obtained for him, from the Jâm's government, the parganah of Pardhari and some villages in Kâṭhiâvâḍ in jâgir, together with the privilege of commanding the van of the army and certain other Sibandi commands. He received a seat opposite to, and on a level with, the Jâm Sâheb's seat in darbâr. Besides the Divâni Pâgah he had several Arab banners under him, namely, those of Jamâdâr Sheikh Zubaidi, Sâlih Abd'ulla, Muhammad Abûbakr, Hâmid Mohsin, and Hâmid Nâsir, as well as other companies of Sindhis, such as those of the Jamâdâr O'mar Durâ, of Râṇa Rukan, amounting in all to nearly eight hundred men. Mehrâman Khawâs regarded the Divân Sâheb as one of his own Âmîrs. At this period Farid Khân, Ali Khân, Khânbhai Seth, Bhagwânji Śodha, Gajasingh Jhâlâ, and Keshavji and Vasanji, the maternal uncle of the author Mehta Aḍâbhâ Nâgar, Keshar Thakar Lohâna, all of whom were jâgirdârs, joined the army with the Zamindârs of Hâlâr.

Gajsingh Jhâlâ from Halwad, Vakhtâji Desâi of Patḍi, and Bhupatsingh from Bhankoḍâ arrived with auxiliary troops, and in one week the whole parganah of Sardhâr [Hâlâr] was laid waste, and from several villages large sums of money were raised. At that time Vakhatsinghji Râval of Bhâvnagar, who with a large army had been warring against the Kâṭhis and had succeeded in wresting Chital from the auxiliaries of the Navâb Sâheb Hâmid Khân, came and encamped at Jasdan, and intended to conquer also the fort of Jetpûr. On this occasion, however, a meeting between him and Mehrâman Khawâs was arranged by the Divân Sâheb Raghûnâthji, and both armies approaching each other like two seas, remained stationary for twenty days. Vakhatsingh being related to Gondal, was, however, unwilling on that account to join Mehrâman in attacking that State; while Mehrâman on his part was unwilling that Vakhatsingh should continue his warfare against the plundering Kâṭhis. Hence they separated without coming to any mutual agreement.

On that very day Morârji bin Dûlabhji, the cousin of the Divân Sâheb, who had been deputy in place of his father at Jûnâgaḍh, and was also mûtasaddi for the parganahs of Mâṅgrol, Koḍinâr, Unâ, and Delwâḍâ, having been liberated from his imprisonment by the Navâb, arrived with a troop of cavalry and a band of Arabs, Jamâdâr A'wad Ali and Nûru'd-dîn, and Jiya and O'mar, and other Sindhis. Râval Vakhatsingh bestowed on him a fitting jâgir, and took him into his service. Owing to the evil of the times, Mehta Vasanji Mânkaḍ, maternal uncle of the Divân Sâheb, died this year at the camp of Magarvâḍâ.

Jâḍejâ Dâji, of Gondal, and Raṇmâlji, of Khirasrâ, and other Jâḍejâs invited Fateh Muhammad, the Kâmdâr of Râo Râydhan, to aid them in the plunder of Hâlâr, which was well cultivated and full of wealth. Now, as the Râo of Bhûj had an old grudge against Nagar, Fateh Muhammad, who was assisted by good fortune and possessed a good share of bravery, was waiting for an emergency of this kind, considering that it would be to the advantage of his fame; and accordingly he persuaded the Râo Sâheb that this would be a good opportunity to avenge the ancient injuries inflicted by Jâm Râval, and crossed the Raṇ with a mighty army and a large quantity of artillery, and entered the province of Hâlâr. When Bhawân Khawâs, the younger brother of Mehrâman Khawâs, heard of this event, he hastened with an army to meet the foe, and encamped at the village of Khâkhrâbelâ. Fateh Muhammad Notiyâr, passing him by a flank movement, encamped his army in the plain of Pardhari. In the morning, after the sun, the Sûlṭân of the firmament, had dispersed the army of the stars, Bhawân proposed to retreat, but Purshotam Vâniâ came to the aid of his inexperience, and encouraged him by saying that no apprehensions were to be entertained of Kachhi troops, sinee in the games of the children of this country a boy is often heard to say: "Let me be alone on one side, and on the other all the Kachhis." Bhawân, the empty-headed, being thus puffed up by the bravado of Purshotam, like a leather bag full of wind, turned the army towards the enemy, and induced the Divân Sâheb Raghûnâthji and his two brothers to take the command of the vanguard.

When we three brothers joined the camp with our cavalry, Fateh Muhammad, although at the head of an army numerous as locusts and ants, on hearing our drums and seeing our banners, coiled himself up within his limits like a sleeping snake, and untwining himself like a half-burnt rope, as it were an elephant which has burst his chains, or a lion which has broken his bonds, and advanced his cannon and rockets and camel-swivels and muskets, and behind them followed 15,000 Kachhi infantry with Sindhis, Arabs, and Afghâns, 20,000 Râjpût and Sindhi cavalry, and 400 mail-clad men like elephants. As these successively advanced to attack us, the Gondal, Râjkot, and Ranmâlji's forces stood ready to engage on the right flank.

The cowardly Bhawân Khawâs, having never made war, was in a fright, and was like one who pulls off his shoes before he has reached the water; he lost his presence of mind, and courage fled from his heart, and sought for some pretext to escape from this difficulty. He then said: "Let Râjâ Gajsingh of Halwad, who is related to both sides, begin negociations of peace; to-day there is a truce, and Jhilriâ, which is at a distance of four kos to the west of this, will be our next camp." The troops on receiving this news were glad to get out of their dangerous position, and on the pretence that their leader had so ordered, they borrowed speed from the wind and lightning, and quickly departed from that place. The army had not retreated farther than half a kos, when the author overtook Bhawân Khawâs by order of the Divân Sâheb Raghûnâthji, on whose part he delivered to Bhawân the following message: "The enemy has now arrogantly advanced. If we now retire and show our backs, it will be a disgrace to the government of Nawânagar, and will be imperilling our lives for nothing." Accordingly Bhawân, with all the grandees of the State of Nagar, unwillingly determined that the army should retrace its steps, and said: "Tell the Divân Sâheb Raghûnâthji to form the right wing with his cavalry, whilst I take part in the battle on the left, with the whole army and artillery." The author hastened back quickly to my brother, the Divân Sâheb Raghûnâthji, and informed him of this, and he immediately marshalled his forces on the bank of the river in one line of infantry and one of cavalry, ready for battle, like a rampart of iron. The fight commenced with an attack by the enemy, who rushed upon us with seven thousand infantry, shouting "Ali! Ali!"

They attacked us boisterously like the waves of the stormy ocean, and the roaring of the artillery and the hissing of the rockets caused the earth to quake. The Divân Sâheb also attacked them like a lion with two hundred infantry and one hundred cavalry, shouting :— "Har Mâhâdev !" After firing one discharge of musketry at the enemy at close quarters, they closed and fought with swords, spears, knives, and daggers; then the antagonists came by degrees to fists and cuffs, striking each other on the cheeks and breasts with their hands. After many had been slain on both sides, all parties got fatigued, and the enemy retreated, whilst the Divân Sâheb departed victoriously amidst the sounds of joyful music to his post, leaving two hundred Kachhis killed or wounded on the battle-field. When Fateh Muhammad perceived his troops in this condition, he became greatly enraged, and advancing from his position poured his men on the troops of Bhawân Khawâs like a rain-cloud, breaking his array and dispersing his troops as a mountain torrent washes away pebbles. Bhawân Khawâs, with six sowârs, escaped thence by hard riding, and took refuge on the mound of Khâriwak. His carabineers became food for the sword, and the Gondal force plundered the Nawânagar camp, thus left destitute of guards and protectors, until nothing remained but the tents and cannon of the Divân Sâheb, which were in his own charge, whilst the army of Nagar had nothing except the canopy of heaven for a covering and the torch of the moon for a light.

After Fateh Muhammad had defeated Bhawân Khawâs, he erected batteries against the Divân Sâheb. Artillery began to roar on both sides, and musketry also did its work ; Raj Gajsingh had withdrawn to one side, in the hope that as he was a relation of the Râo, Fateh Muhammad would not attack him, but was disappointed ; and the enemy, who were desirous to engage, attacked and charged them. But the brave men of his force withstood their charge and remained as firm as Mount Elburz, and did not give ground, and the Kachh troops, courage failing them, returned unsuccessfully to their own camp. Bhawân Khawâs, with a few trusted Khawâs adherents and others, reached Jâliâ weeping with only the clothes on their backs, whilst the Divân Sâheb remained on the battlefield, shrouded and buried the dead, and having loaded the wounded on camels, arrived in Nagar on the evening of the second day. But Fateh Muhammad, of victorious fortune, went on burning and plundering the surrounding villages as far as Khambhâliâ, and then, after levying ransoms from them, marched back.

Jâm Jasâji makes a friend of the Râo Sâheb Bhânji.

The Jâm Sâheb was so much distressed by the overbearing demeanour of Mehrâman Khawâs and the ambition of his sons, that he consulted the rich and the poor on the means of overthrowing his power; but Mehrâman Khawâs cut off the nose or the ears of every one who was discovered to have listened to the Jâm Sâheb, and some were lightened of their heads; and in this way several foolish persons were ruined, imprisoned, and put to death, and the plot spread so far that Bâi Achhûbâ, the Jâm Sâheb's wife, who was also much displeased with the state of affairs, held out to Shekh Muhammad Zubaidi, the commander of the Divâne Sâheb's Risâlâh, a bribe of one lâkh of jâmis, but he excused himself by asserting that he was unwilling to do anything without the command of his master. Accordingly, at his suggestion, one night the Jâm Sâheb dressed himself as a female and entered the Divân Sâheb's house, and taking the author aside, said: "This Mehrâman is a thorn in my liver, or a pebble in my eye; if you will expel him by any means whatever, I will give you the parganah of Jodhpûr in perpetuity, as well as one-half of all the moveable and immoveable property of Mehrâman Khawâs, which amounts in value to nearly one krôr." When I communicated this proposal to my brother, he gave a plain answer as follows: "I will not, for greed of this world's goods, bring disgrace upon the family of the Divân Sâheb Amarji, and cannot commit a treacherous act towards Mehrâman, through whose influence I have come to Nagar, but I shall, as far as possible, endeavour to restore peace between both sides." When the Jâm Sâheb despaired of being able to effect anything with the Divân Sâheb or the inhabitants of the town, he secretly despatched messages to the Jâḍejâ confederates and to the Râo Sâheb Bhânji, inviting them to plunder the district of Hâlâr with the villages which were in the hands of Mehrâman Khawâs, and granting them permission to do so. Accordingly they immediately commenced to hover about those places like vultures over a carcass, according to the saying:—

"How fortunate is it to attain two objects by one act:
One should run with alacrity at the smallest signal of a friend."

Account of the laying waste of Gondal by the aid of Âbâ Shelûkar.

Âbâ Shelûkar, who was the Sûbah of Âhmadâbâd, arrived with a powerful army on the frontiers of Hâlâr, levying tribute in Saṁvat 1850, and he brought with him the cavalry of Malhâr Râo from Kaḍi, which was under the command of Hanumant Râo, and the army of Navâb Ghâziu'd-dîn from Sami-Mûnjpûr, on condition of defraying the monthly pay of their troops.

Mehrâman Khawâs, by agreeing to pay what they demanded, obtained a promise from them that they would ravage the parganah of Gondal.

As at that time one of the beloved children of the author was being married, and he was necessarily unable to be present, Pasu [Thakur] Lohânâ, the Mutasaddi of the town of Kâlâwaḍ, who on account of the attachment between his mother and Mehrâman, considered himself as a son of Mehrâman Khawâs, was appointed to act as deputy by Mehrâman during my absence, but being a man of no weight or standing he did not conduct matters well.

Âbâ Shelûkar sent his Nâîb Amratlâl Nâgar to Nagar to request the presence of the Divân Sâheb, as without him no business could be satisfactorily conducted; but the latter despatched the author, to receive whom Âbâ Shelûkar ordered troops to march out, which escorted him with many demonstrations of honour to the camp, where he received for a whole month an honourable reception, and spent his time very pleasantly, seeing at night dancing girls perform and hearing songs and music, while the days were passed in the amusements of chess and card playing. After the expiration of a month after ravaging the parganah of Gondal and making it a grazing ground for wild beasts he returned.

It is related that Nânâ Farnâvis, of Puṇâ, was enamoured with the wife of Âbâ Shelûkar, but as he was unable to obtain access to her alone and thus enjoy this rose without a thorn, he appointed Âbâ Shelûkar to the Subâhdâri of Âhmadâbâd and farmed to him the revenues of that province for an annual sum of twelve and a half lâkhs of rupees for the space of five years, and thus removed the snake from the treasure.

Âbâ Shelûkar was himself a voluptuary, and had intercourse with many Moghal, Afghân, and Hindû females. They have said, "He who stops the road of others, some one will stop his road." And it so happened to him that a cow entered his grain-yard. But, somehow or other, he became acquainted with the actions and conduct of his wife, whom hitherto he had imagined to be chaste, and, therefore, pretending that he wished to visit Dwârkâ, he brought his wife with him to Gûjarât. I have myself beheld her on several occasions, and did not consider her to be very handsome; but as the verse says—

"You should see Laila with the eyes of Majnûn."

In this way Nânâ Farnâvis lost both the lady and the money.

Verse:—

"Sikandar even was unable to drink a draught of the water of life,
For such things cannot be effected either by power or gold."

Meeting of the Navâb Sâheb Hâmid Khân with Mehrâman Khawâs at Kâlâwaḍ.

When the Navâb Sâheb Hâmid Khân returned from the army, he had an interview with Mehrâman

Khawâs at the Qasbah of Kâlâwaḍ, on which occasion the Navâb Sâheb took hold of the hand of the Divân Sâheb Raghûnâthji and that of the author, and placing them in those of Mehrâman, said :—" These are deposits of mine, treat them honourably and kindly, and consider them for a short time as your guests."*

CONCERNING THE WÂGHERS OF OKHÂ.

In Saṁvat 1851 Mehrâman marched an army to Okhâ, in order to punish the Wâghers, and rased some of their villages to the ground.

The author having obtained leave, went on pilgrimage to Becharâji. On his way he encamped at Dhândhalpûr, where he became the guest of Godaḍ Khavaḍ. At this time a band of sowârs in the service of the Zamindârs of Limbḍi, Wadhwân, Dhrângadhrâ, and Chûdâ, carried off some of his cattle, but were pursued by the author, who recovered the cattle, after some fighting, at the village of Sejakpûr, but lost three men and horses. Again in the plain near Bajânâ he met a band of accursed ones of Jatwârâ, under their chief, a Vârâhi Jat, Nura by name, but after a little musketry fire we dispersed them, and afterwards all visited mother Becharâji. Bhâosingh Desâi, Zamindâr of the town of Pâtḍi, and his son

* This interview has already been alluded to before. Here, however, the translator from the Gûjarâthi writes that the Navâb said to Mehrâman that: "He had better treat them with the honour due to their rank."

Vakhatsingh and his brother Râsâji came to meet us with great civility.

FLIGHT OF THE JÂM SÂHEB JASÂJI.

In Saṁvat 1853, Śivrâm Kameḍân arrived with an army on behalf of the Śrimant Peshwâ and Gâekwâḍ Sarkârs, to collect tribute in Kâṭhiâwâḍ, and encamped at Pardhari. Mehrâman Khawâs despatched me with some followers to make arrangements about paying the jamâbandi, and Śivrâm himself came out about three miles riding on an elephant to meet us, and I stayed with him for a month and a half, and he treated me honourably. He seemed to me to be a man of great courage and ability.

Suddenly news arrived (in the camp) that the Jâm Sâheb with his brother Satâji had escaped by quick riding under cover of the night, and had encamped near the Kâlâwaḍ Gate. This happened as follows:—It had always been the intention of the Jâm Sâheb to overturn the power of Mehrâman Khawâs, therefore by promises of pay and service he allured the Arab Jamâdârs to his own side, and plotted with them; and they, to remove all suspicion, encamped at the village of Morkandâ and agreed to remain there waiting in ambush, till they heard the firing of a gun, on hearing which signal they were all to assemble at the Kâlâwaḍ Gate. Jamâdâr Sâlih, of evil fortune, who was on guard at the Kâlâwaḍ Gate, was admitted by them as an accomplice in this difficult undertaking. Accordingly at midnight on a dark night, considering the rain and clouds as an aid to his design, the Jâm arrived at the gate and commenced a musketry fire in the direction of Mehru's mansion. Mehru, awaking from the sleep of carelessness, saw the aspect of affairs changed. He immediately sent for the Divân Sâheb Raghûnâthji, and commenced to surround and cannonade the gate and its defenders.

The Arabs, who were listening for the sound of firing as a fasting man for the sound of Allah Akbar, at once ran to arms ; but owing to the good fortune of Mehru and the bad luck of the Jâm, such violent rain fell that night that the two rivers were in full flood. The hopes of the Arabs were thus blasted, that is to say, they could not cross over, and owing to the non-arrival of their aid, the Jâm and his adherents began to lose courage from the constant cannonade. Sâlih and most of his men being wounded, waved a flag of surrender. Mehrâman, at the advice of his chief ministers, showed them quarter on condition that the Jâm Sâheb should come to his (Mehru's) house, and live there at his ease like a parrot in a cage. And after obtaining in this matter the guarantee of the Divân Sâheb Raghûnâthji, of Mâhâdev Ojhâ whose family is distinguished by a reputation for high birth and learning in the zillâ of Hâlâr, of Muhammad Bârug and Nâsir Bârug, the Arabs, and of Mâlik Farid Khân Śetha, the Jâm Sâheb came down, and when his palankin arrived at the house of Mehrâman, which is on the main road, he was forcibly taken in and kept under strict surveillance, whilst Satâji, his brother, managed by swift running to escape to his own house. The securities could not, for fear of Mehrâman, forbid him thus carrying off the Jâm Sâheb, and the latter kept him in *durance vile* for two months without allowing him a change of clean clothes, or a barber to shave him, or the services of a washerman. The Divân Sâheb, who could no longer bear this state of matters, despatched the author to Mehrâman in order to effect the release of the Jâm Sâheb. Mehrâman, however, spoke so harshly and abusively that we both laid our hands on our daggers, but at last he suffered the Jâm Sâheb to depart to his palace. From that day, however, Mehrâman harboured great spite against the Divàn Sàheb, and endeavoured to get him removed. In the same year also his brother Bhawân Khawâs died an unnatural death from a razor wound. He was Mehru's younger brother.

ARRIVAL OF FATEH MUHAMMAD.

In Saṁvat 1853 Fateh Muhammad Notiyâr again crossed the Raṇ with the desire of ravaging Hâlâr. Mehrâman Khawâs elevated his standards against him, and entertained in his service the Afghân cavalry of Jamâdâr Sher Jang Khân and Alif Khân Sâhibdâd Khân, and Karimdâd Khân and Anwar Khân, who had been discharged by Malhâr Râo, the Zamindâr of Kaḍi, and promised the Navâb Sâheb Hâmid Khân two lákhs and fifteen thousand jâmis for his aid, and thus collected a very large force, and encamped at the village of Dhensarâ, of the Morbi Parganah, near the shore of the Raṇ.

Fateh Muhammad, from his inborn valour, encamped his force at the distance of a cannon shot. Mehrâman Khawâs drew up his men in battle array in two lines with the forces of the Navâb Sâheb of Mukhtiâr Khân Bâbi, the Jâgirdâr of Bântwâ, and Shekh Mûrtazâ with his troops from Mâṅgrol, and Jamâl Khân Balûch, Harisingh Pûrbiâ, and the Sindhis, and Pratâpsingh and Kesrisingh, grâsiâs of Bâlâgâm. Fateh Muhammad, giving up all idea of fighting, offered to treat for peace through Gajsingh, and made peace on condition that both sides should agree to whatever should be settled during the next months by the Divân Sâheb Raghûnâthji on behalf of Nagar and Kaliân Hirji on behalf of Jûnâgaḍh, and Karsanji Jhâlâ on behalf of Râj Gajsingh, the Shâ Shâvji on behalf of the Râo Sâheb, and thus by a treacherous peace he evaded all evil.

Râo Sâheb Râidhanji comes to Nagar and returns disappointed.

In Saṁvat 1854, Râo Sâheb Râidhanji arrived with (his Kâmdâr) Fateh Muhammad and an army more numerous than ants and locusts, accompanied by fire-raining artillery, and encamped in the plain of Navânagar, near the temple of Śri Nâganâtha Mâhâdeva.

Mehrâman Khawâs, being on bad terms, not only with his master the Jâm, but also with the ryots and qasbâtis, had no other friends except the Divân Sâheb, and did not consider Alif Khân, Zûlfikar Khân, and other Arab Jamâdârs friendly to him. Accordingly he built up the fort gates with bricks and placed two or three heavy guns in position, and stood ready to oppose them, but some who were within the town, such as Mâlik Farid Khân, Ali Khân, Daulat Khân, and other qasbâtis, colluded with Fateh Muhammad, and informed him that as the wall of the fort on the side of the talâv was not strong, that he ought to make his attack on that side, and that as soon as he had placed his scaling ladders against it they would make an attack from the inside, and thus fighting on both sides, they hoped to repulse the Afghâns, who were not furnished with firearms, and Fateh Muhammad accordingly did so. It happened, however, that Mehrâman Khawâs came at sunrise to inspect the batteries just as an angel alights from heaven. Accordingly, when the sovereign of the firmament ascended with his rays into the azure vault, and the Kachhi troops had placed ladders against the fort wall, some of them were slain and others thrown down. An assault was also made on the Khambhâliâ Gate, and many attacked the Divân Sâheb Raghûnâthji, whose position was at the Nâganâtha Gate. The thunder of the artillery and the confusion shook the earth, and in the tumult among the townspeople, during which the author happened to be on the mound near the talâv, his horse was killed under him by a musket-ball, and hastened to the posture of non-existence. In fine, by the protection of Nâganâtha, who is the tutelary deity of this country, Mehrâman Khawâs gained the victory, and Fateh Muhammad, several of whose men were slain or wounded, retired and laid siege to Khambhâliâ, where he met with the same honours he had earned in Nagar.

In Saṁvat 1855, Âmin Sâheb [son of Jemâdâr Hâmid] arrived from Barodâ to collect tribute in Kâṭhiâwâḍ. When he was encamped at Wânkâner the author was despatched by Mehrâman Khawâs for the purpose of settling with him the sum to be paid by Nagar, and was courteously met by Jamâdâr Nêhâl Khân and Jamâdâr Bachâ, by Mâdhar Râi Nâgar, and by Raghûnâth Modi, and it was settled that tribute should be levied at the rates of Śivrâm Kamidân, from whose time treble tribute was imposed on Kâṭhiâwâḍ. This amount Mehrâman afterwards extorted by force from the Nâgars of Nagar.

Attack of the Town of Bhânwad.

Mehrâman Khawâs sent the author in Saṁvat 1855 with a powerful army and two guns to subdue the fort of Bhânwaḍ, because the Râjpûts of the districts of Hâlâr and Bardâ and

Dalâsâ, the auxiliaries of the disappointed and conquered Fateh Muhammad, caused great confusion by their depredations. The siege was carried on during four months, and no pains were spared by Mûsâ Jân Farangi, who was afterwards executed by Abâ Shelûkar at Âhmadâbâd, and by the Afghân, Arab, and Sindhi troops, but the fort could not be conquered on account of the evil destiny of Mehrâman, the cowardice of Keshavji Kâmdhâr, and the bullet wound the author had received in his right arm.

Meanwhile Fateh Muhammad had, with the intention of raising this siege, arrived from Kachh and encamped in the vicinity of Nagar, and Mehrâman Khawâs, considering this a good opportunity, sent the Divânji Sâheb Raghûnâthji with Keshavji and an army by sea to aid Shâ Shâvji, who was fighting with the Râo Sâheb at Mândvi, but Shâvji, mistrusting the people of Nagar, declined their assistance and made peace.

At that time Śivrâm Kâmedân was collecting peshkash in the zillah of Panchâl, and Mehrâman sent the Divân Sâheb Raghûnâthji to make arrangements for the proper payment of the sum to be paid for his aid, and he accordingly departed to bring him to their assistance. The Divânji Sâheb arranged this matter with Śivrâm at the camp of Bhâdlâ and returned with him to Nagar. Meanwhile, ill-disposed persons instilled doubts into the heart of Mehrâman by telling him that the intentions of the Divân Sâheb were unknown, and that he might, by taking the side of the Jâm Sâheb, bring trouble on all parties. This fear impelled Mehrâman Khawâs to arrange an interview at Dhûmâo with Fateh Muhammad, and there concluded peace with him. When the army of Śivrâm approached, Mehrâman receded from his agreement and informed him by letter that as the business regarding which he had invited his aid was fortunately terminated, he need not take the trouble of coming; accordingly he returned.

Since the Divân Sâheb had concluded the negociation himself, he was unable to make any excuse to Śivrâm. He therefore took upon himself to convoke the pâtels of the neighbouring districts, and levying from them the money (to pay the army), gave it to Śivrâm Kamedân. Mehrâman Khawâs became still more displeased with the Divân Sâheb than before. Accordingly the latter went away from Nagar, and took up his abode at Dhrol, whence he carried on a secret correspondence with the Jâm Sâheb.

In Saṁvat 1856 Mehrâman Khawâs took leave of this world after a short illness, but as his children were by a Musalmân woman, they could not inherit his property, which was given to the sons of Bhawân Khawâs, *i. e.*, Sangrâm and Prâgji. They could not, however, remain in Nagar without molestation; accordingly they betook themselves to their jâgir, which consisted of the three forts of Joḍiâ, Bâlambhâ, and Âmran, with thirty-six villages. They took with them all the cash, but were unable to take with them thousands of kalsis of jowâri which they had buried underground; accordingly they lost this.

After these men had departed to these places, the Divân Sâheb was often politely invited to join them, but he always declined to do so. He gave this information also to the author who returned to Nagar after having accomplished half the journey to Jûnâgaḍh, and after reaching the fort of Devrâ, as has been already related in the account of Porbandar recorded in the description of it. The author's younger brother Dalpatrâm was sent to Harisingh the Râjâ [Thakor] of Limbdi, between whose father Harbhâmji and the Divân Amarji great friendship existed. Here he remained eight months, until the Jâm Sâheb invited the Divân Sâheb in a most complimentary and kind way to his court, and gave him the parganah of Rânpûr in jâgir and enrolled him among the nobles of his State.

The Jâm Sâheb collects Aspverâ (Horse-Tax) from Kâthiâvâḍ and other Districts.

When the Jâm Sâheb had satisfied his mind by the expulsion of Mehrâman's family, he marched with a large army to collect *aspverâ* (horse-tax) both from the mahâls where it was usually levied and also from other mahâls where this levy had not previously been made. In Saṁvat 1857 he demolished the fort of Jasdan. Now the Navâb Sâheb Hâmid Khân had despatched Jamiât

Khân Shirwâni and the Jamâdâr Umar to Nagar a month previously, to invite the Divân Sâheb Raghûnâthji to Jûnâgaḍh, and requested him to come speedily. Accordingly he went to that place [but through the evil advice of Karsandâs Wâniâ and Âzambeg Chelâ he was dismissed] and returned again, but the Navâb paid his expenses, and restored him his four hereditary villages. On his return, when the Divân Sâheb reached the town of Dhorâji, the Jâm Sâheb sent for him to join his army. He therefore advanced quickly and joined the Jâm at the camp of Kûndni, and he levied from each village of Jhâlâwâḍ as large a contribution as they could afford to pay, and he also sent a force to the Goghâbârah Parganah, which had never before been subject to his exactions and extorted what he could. On his return he displayed his victorious standards as far almost as the Girnâr Mountain. He collected a small tribute also from the villages of the Kâṭhis subject to Junâgaḍh, and he left a ṭhâṇâ in Jasdan, but it was unable to stay there. He now returned joyful and successful.

The Capture of the Fort of Kandornâ.

Now, since the Jâm Sâheb was much elated by the greatness of his army and the abundance of his treasure, he persuaded Mûrâd Khân and Fakir Muhammad Makrâni, who were displeased with the Râṇâ, to hand over to him the fort of

Kandornâ, a dependency of Porbandar, in consideration of a payment to them of a lâkh of jâmis and being granted their former service, but in Saṁvat 1864 Colonel Sâheb Alexander Walker conquered it from him [in two hours], and handed it over to the Râṇâ Sûltânji's minister. The eye of the age never saw and the ear of the time never heard a man more true to his word or of such lofty courage and such beneficent views.

The English and Gâekwâḍ Governments send Armies to Nagar.

In Saṁvat 1868 (A. D. 1812) an Arab without cause slew one of the English Sâhebs and took refuge in the fort of Moḍpûr, and the Jâm Sâheb, although strongly pressed and commanded, would not, as is customary with Râjâs—jealous of their honour—surrender the man who had fled to him for protection. The English Government had therefore a strong reason for acting against him.

Accordingly English troops arrived like waves of the stormy ocean, with Captain Carnac Sâheb and Gangâdhar Shâstri and Fatehsingh Gâekwâḍ Senâ-Khâs-khel Shamsher Bahâdûr and Mir Sâhib Kamâlu'd-din Hûsain, Mir Sarfaraz Âli Amin Sâheb and the Divân Vithalrao, and laid siege to Nagar.

The first day when the artillery began to play, several horses and sipâhis were killed, and on the second day the English guns entirely silenced those of the fort: their roar spread mortal fear among the townspeople; the Râjpût troops lost courage, but nevertheless the Divân Sâheb Raghûnâthji and Jamâdâr Fakir Muhammad fought one day with one of the English regiments. As neither party gave way, the conflict only ceased with night.

The lion-hearted Jâm Sâheb perceived that his Râjpûts could not hold their ground, and accordingly made overtures for peace, and reproached his Râjpûts saying: "On the first day when the Divânji Sâheb Raghûnâthji desired to negociate for peace you said that he had not a brave heart, and that as we are Râjpûts we shall listen to overtures of peace only after we have drunk the blood of our foes. All that was mere empty boasting." The Râjpûts and Gosain Govardhanji and the Mâhâjans, after consultation, made proposals to the Jâm, agreeing to conclude peace. Accordingly by the order of the Jâm Sâheb peace was afterwards concluded with the English through the Divân Sâheb Raghûnâthji, on condition of the Jâm's paying to them a lâkh of jâmis [koris] annually for a period of ten years towards the costs of the war, and it was also settled that he should pay thirteen lâkhs of jâmi koris, which were claimed by the Kachh Darbâr. The army then returned.

A Kachh Army crosses over to Hálâr.

In Saṁvat 1869, Fateh Muhammad crossed the Raṇ and came over with a numerous army to Hâlâr. On hearing this news, the Jâm

Sâheb called the Divân Sâheb Raghûnâthji from Kûtiânâ to his aid, in order to oppose the enemy. Agreeably to my brother's order, I, the author, set out at the head of 300 horse and foot and one cannon, and by marching continuously reached Nagar and encamped near the fort. The Jâm Sâheb Jasâji condescended to come to the author's tent and kindly praising him, said aloud in the presence of the whole company:—

"O Ranchodji,
Of Rûstam I have heard, but you, I see,
Can, hearing, be ever like seeing?

In this age, in which we meet with nothing but treachery, there is no man faithful except the Divân Raghûnâthji among my dependants, or who would jeopardize his life in my service. As I found no one worthy to undertake this difficult negotiation, I have invited him to take it on himself. To-day the army of Fateh Muhammad, which possesses thirteen cannons and other warlike engines, and in strength exceeds 20,000 men, will encamp in, and begin to devastate one of my crown parganahs. You should therefore set out at once and attack them with your cavalry near Hariânâ, where they will not have the shelter of a fort." Accordingly, the author pronounced the victory-giving name of Śankar, and mounted his charger, and encamped the same evening at Hariânâ. Meanwhile Fateh Muhammad erected his standards at the distance of a kos. The Jâm Sâheb, however, had the foresight to send me, within the space of two days, a reinforcement of one thousand infantry and four hundred cavalry with two cannons.

Some men at the court, however, were envious, and conceived themselves dishonoured by our recall; and Gokal Khawâs, Gajsingh Jhâlâ, and others brought neither arrows, guns, bullets, provisions, nor eatables, and a discontented soldiery, so that for two days the army was but half fed, and some men remained altogether hungry; nevertheless the author, trusting in God's help, and giving up all reliance on the aid of Gokal Khawâs and Gajasingh, went forth with a select company of one hundred Turkish (Rûmi) infantry and one hundred Masqâtis at dawn and attacked the camp of the enemy, who being, as it were, yet drowned in the sleep of carelessness, offered scarcely any resistance, and suffered our muskets to be fired into the tents; when lo! Sûndarji Khatri, Saudâgar, who on account of his selling horses to the English was connected with them, and who as a resident of Kachh had accompanied Fateh Muhammad, hung out a flag of truce! As soon as the firing had ceased, he alighted from his carriage and produced a letter from the Resident of Barodâ, Carnac Sâheb, which enjoined a cessation of hostilities. I considered it incumbent upon me to obey so exalted an order, and Sûndarji obtained from me a truce of three days as well as a promise of safety as to the life of Jamâdâr Fateh Muhammad, and he agreed to the restoration of everything plundered and compensation for everything burnt. As the safety of Fateh Muhammad was in jeopardy, he was determined to save his life by vulpine cunning, and thus obtained to aid him the influence of Sûndarji, who was the Dimnah of the period, and the order of the powerful English. Then he borrowed celerity from the lightning and fled in the moonlight, which is the foe of nocturnal thieves, without beat of drum. But the author followed (in spite of the prohibition of Sûndârji) at his heels at the distance of an arrow-shot, and captured all the carts and baggage which he left behind, until Fateh Muhammad recrossed the Raṇ after suffering a hundred disgraces.

The next day Colonel Cruchley Sâheb arrived at the request of Pingalshi Bhât* and Vithal Râo who came with the army of the Gâekwâḍ, and pursued him nearly to Kotâriâ. Here Fateh Muhammad was, for his honour's sake, obliged to fight, and after they had taken prisoners, some 30 horsemen with their horses, they returned.

The author, agreeably to the wish of the Divân Raghûnâthji, came and encamped in the parganah of Bâlambhâ, but as the Divân Sâheb Vithal Rao harboured a grudge against me, the Jâm Saheb

---

* The Persian MS. always uses the pun *Bâd furush* : wind-seller; wind-bag; boaster; to express the word *Bhât* and the translation from the Gujarâthi guided me to render it correctly; but here it has "Charan."

now made over the command of his army to Kâmdhâr Jasrâj and Gokal Khawâs, and sent for me to court under the pretence of wishing the pleasure of my company. The Divân Sâheb Vithal Rao now returned to his country, and two months afterwards, viz., in the month of Muharram, Jasrâj and Gokal returned unsuccessfully to Nagar.

As it is the law of this perishing world that we must all abandon it with sorrow, so the Jâm Sâheb Jasâji departed from it by a natural death on the 5th of Śrâvan in Saṁvat 1870 (A.D. 1814), after a reign of forty-six years, nine months, and nine days. His younger brother, by name Satâji, who had before this been offended with him and fled to the Khawâses, and after that had taken refuge with the Gâekwâḍ Government at Amreli, was by the advice of the same, in concert with the English, installed after the lapse of one year, in the parganah of Rânpur, which had been the Jâgir of the Divân Sâheb Raghûnâthji, and now he returned to the city and sat on the throne.

Jâm Satâji bin Lâkhâji.

Jâm Satâji was always sick, and also had no children, and had a weak, feeble body. Achhubâ Râṇi, the widow of Jâm Jasâji, with much foresight, adopted a son named Raṇmâlji from Jâḍejâ Jasâji, the Zamindâr of Bhânwaḍ, and gradually paid two lâkhs of rupees on this account to the two Governments [the Gâekwâḍ and the English], and it was agreed that he should succeed to the gâdi after the death of Jâm Satâji, who was in a dying state.

Satâji made a will, testified to by the nobles of his State, that the Kâmdhâr Jagjivan Devji, who had inherited this position since several generations, should be confirmed in the post; but Motirâm Bûch, the Nâgar, who aspired to it, with the consent of Achhubâ Râṇi, threw obstacles in his way by exciting the Arab Jamâdârs of Masqât, who were in the forts of Pardhari and Kandornâ. to rebellion, through Wâniâ Andarji, a vakil of Jâm Satâji. These men committed great depredations and much confusion ensued, but Jagjivan, on the strength of his previous connections with the Divân Sâheb Vithal Râo, Nâyib of the Gâekwâḍ Government, requested him to expel the Arabs from the abovementioned two forts, and promised to pay his expenses. Accordingly Vithal Râo began by introducing several Arab regiments into Nagar under the command of Bodar Khatri and others, whilst Sûndarji Khatri, the Nâyib of Ballantine Sâheb, on the other hand, as well as the new Sibandis who had always been desirous of obtaining employment, all contributed to drain the treasury of the Jâm Sâheb, and succeeded, on account of the misunderstanding between Jagjivan and Motirâm, in emptying it. In fine, the Divânji Sâheb Vithal Râo and Ballantine Sâheb and Sûndarji Khatri, on the agreement that their expenses should be paid, joined the Jâm with about one thousand men.

In Saṁvat 1872 they commenced, under the command of Hendly Sâheb, to besiege and batter the fort of Kandornâ. Both Jagjivan and Motirâm unmercifully squandered the money which did not belong to them, and after a protracted siege the Divân Sâheb Vithal Râo and Govind Râi mounted to chastise the accursed Masqâtis, who foolishly, miscalculating their strength, issued forth and commenced a musketry fire, and were ignorant that "the monkey who plays with the lion will defile the ground with his own blood." When a large number of the accursed ones were drawn up in order of battle, the victorious army of the English and Vithal Râo attacked them like a sudden misfortune, and dashed them beneath the iron hoofs of the horsemen, and by the thrusts of their buckler-piercing swords sent them to hell. They who escaped from the sword begged for quarter, and surrendered the forts to the servants of the Jâm Sâheb. After concluding this affair, the army marched to Pardhari and expelled the Masqâti Arabs from thence. They, however, took refuge in the fort of Jodiâ, with Sangrâm Khawâs. The Jâm Sâheb who had long been seeking a cause of offence against Sangrâm Khawâs, made the shelter of these rebels his excuse, and the English and Gâekwaḍ armies reached the place in the middle of the rainy season. Sûndarji, whose fortune was in the ascendant, and whose patron was Ballantine

Sâheb, consulted with the Râṇi Achhubâ, and collected an army to wrest the tâlûkâs from the Khawâses, and agreed to pay 8½ lâkhs of rupees for the aid of the English army, which sum was to be payable by eight instalments. When the army arrived near the fort of Joḍiâ, Sangrâm Khawâs and the garrison were alarmed at the shining muskets and waving banners, and lost heart. Sangrâm, pale and trembling, came quickly to the Commander of the army, and asked for quarter, and surrendered the fort with all its artillery and ammunition, and all his property, but his family departed under British protection to Morbi. Afterwards, however, by bribing the English officers of Barodâ and making friends with Sûndarji Khatri and the Divân Sâheb Vithal Râo, Sangrâm obtained the parganah of Âmbran in jâgir from the Jâm Sâheb, who was compelled to give it, whether he liked or not. Sûndarji Khatri, who was the agent and Nâyib of the English, obtained the farm of the parganah of Joḍiâ-Bâlambhâ for one lâkh and fifteen thousand jâmis, whereas its revenue exceeds two and a half lâkhs, for a term of eight years. This favour he obtained through the intervention of Motirâm, who was jealous of Jagjivan Devji, who was a connection of the author's, and who obtained for himself the towns of Râwal and Âsodar, the revenue whereof amounts to sixty thousand jâmis. When the English army returned, Sûndarji and Ballantine Sâheb, on the pretence of inquiring into the bad government of the Navânagar State, returned and made a false accusation against Jagjivan Devji, between whom and Motirâm there was much enmity, and hence Jagjivan was much annoyed and fell sick.

In Saṁvat 1875 I wished to go on a pilgrimage to the Narmadâ, and after going to Joḍiâ, to have an interview with Ballantine Sâheb, I spent several days at Nagar to make preparations for the journey. On this occasion the Bai Sâheb Achhubâ Râṇî kindly gave me employment in her pâgah, and borrowed from me seventy-five thousand rupees on the security of the Kandornâ Parganah. But in Saṁvat 1880 Barnwell Sâheb becoming himself responsible for the payment of this sum, handed over that parganah to Hansrâj Śeth; but when Barnwell Sâheb left this country with a sad heart on account of the loss of his wife, whom he loved dearer than life, Wilson Sâheb, who remained but a short time in power, was inimical to me, because I aided the Navâb in all matters and opposed the management of the Khatris and the Jhâlâs, who were protected by him. He therefore wrote what he pleased in the records, and then left. After him Blane Sâheb, who had cotton in his ears towards the voice of justice, rejected my claim for my money, which amounted to nearly eight lâkhs of jâmis, and caused me great loss. And he, not regarding the pledge of the English Government, abased whomsoever Barnwell Sâheb had exalted. In

Saṁvat 1876, on the *ekâdasi-day* (eleventh of the light half) of the month of Phâlgûn, the Jâm Sâheb Satâji departed to the next world. The length of his reign was 5 years and 6 months and fifteen days, and he was succeeded by Jâm Raṇmâlji, son of Jâḍejâ Jasâji, and the adopted son of the Jâm Sâheb Jasâji.

JÂM RANMÂLJI.

In Saṁvat 1880 Barnwell Sâheb, who was a man able to appreciate respectable persons favourably disposed towards the Government of the Company Bahâdûr, and who much resembled Alexander Walker in this matter, in order to keep under subjection the Jâm Sâheb Raṇmâlji, who was an impetuous young man, impatient of any kind of restraint, conferred the farm of the whole country of Nagar for a period of ten years for an annual sum of seventeen lâkhs and thirty thousand jâmis upon Hansrâj Seth, nephew of Sûndarji Khatri, who had already a claim of twenty-six lâkhs of jâmis against this State; but afterwards, on account of the disagreement of both parties, and on account of the disapproval of Wilson Sâheb and Blane Sâheb, the contract was annulled by the Jâm Sâheb without considering the seal of the English guarantee, but following the advice of counsellors like minded with himself, thus he dissolved the farm and dismissed Hansrâj.

After the departure of Wilson Sâheb, who was not worthy to govern, and knew not black from white, Blane Sâheb carried on matters con trary to the usages of previous rulers [? Political Agents]—

Whoever came a habitation built,
But went again and left it to another,
Who also entertained crude designs,
So that the habitation no one used!

In Saṁvat 1883 (A.D. 1827) the people of this country again fell into misery; the Nâgars and Sipâhis are without *watan*, the living have no bread, and the dead no shroud.

In Saṁvat 1885, on the 5th of the light half of the month of Mâha, the wedding of the Jâm Sâheb Raṇmâlji with the daughter of Râwal Wajesingh, the Râjâ of Bhâvnagar, was celebrated with great pomp. Gold was given freely, colour was scattered, and largesses bestowed. At the invitation of the Jâm Sâheb, the author sent to the wedding his children Lakhmiśankar, Śankarparsád, Maniśankar, and Reváśankar, with 50 sowârs, and they were highly delighted.

Oh Ranchoḍji, whence did you come, and whither have you arrived? Where did you live and whither have you emerged?

If you write the history of each country at such length, it will be necessary to write another book. Enough! Enough! for life is short and this history very long.

In short, this State of Nagar contains three ports and fourteen inhabited mahâls, governed independently and prosperously. The etiquette in use is that formerly in vogue among Moghuls of the courts of Dehli and Âḥmadâbâd. The mahâls are: Khambhâliâ, Lâlpûr, Rânpûr, Bhânwaḍ, Moḍpûr, Jodhpûr, Kandornâ, Kâlâwaḍ, Pardhari, Joḍiâ, Bâlambhâ, Âmran, Hariânâ, and Kâthiâwâḍ; and the ports are Nagar, Joḍiâ, and Salâyâ, and pearls are found in the sea at Sachânâ. The Kâthiâwâḍ mahâls are four, viz., Âtkot, Barwâlâ, Bhâdlâ, and Sânthli, and there is an iron mine in the Khambhâliâ Parganah. The mahâls of the brethren of the Jâm are as follows: Dalâsâ, Dhrol, Khirasrâ, Râjkot, Sardhâr, and Gondal. The whole revenue of the Jâm's country amounts to thirty-five lâkhs of jâmis, but in former times it was double this amount.

ACCOUNT OF OKHÂ.

Five thousand years ago Śri Kṛishṇa with all the Jâdavas, who consisted of fifty-six tribes, and whose number was incalculable, came to live here fleeing from the city of Mathurâ through fear of Kâl Yavan, Râjâ of Kandahâr, and founded the city of Dwârkâ in that island and dwelt there. After the lapse of several years, the Jâdavas came to Patan Deva to bathe at Prâchi and perform adoration to Somanâth; but in the drunkenness of wine, which is the mother of evil, the whole tribe fell to fighting amongst themselves, and most of them drank of the goblet of death, and Śri Kṛishṇa himself also, being pierced by the arrow of a hunter, departed to adorn the throne of Vaikûṇṭh. The Wâdhel Râjpûts, though originally belonging to this tribe, had been captured in former times, both men and women, by Sûltân Mahmûd Ghaznavi, and then again adopting the religion of the glorious Veda were re-admitted to the Hindu community. They and the Wâghers, who plunder both by land and sea, dwell here and inhabit this country. In Saṁvat 1370 Shams Khân built a mosque in the city, and in Saṁvat 1547 Sûltân Mahmûd Gûjarâti laid waste the country. In Saṁvat 1648, Khân Khânân led an army here in pursuit of Sûltân Muzaffar, but Sangrâm and Śawâ Wâdhel conveyed Muzaffar over to the country of Kachh. In Saṁvat 1526 Malik Toghân was the thâṇâdâr here on behalf of Sûltân Mahmûd, and at that time Râjâ Bhim was taken prisoner. In Saṁvat 1858 English ships arrived, which cannonaded the fort ot Beyt, and several brave men of the English troops landed and made an assault, but by the aid of Śri Dwârkânâth they were unsuccessful and retired. But they burned all the piratical craft of both Dwârkâ and Beyt, in which piracies were constantly committed. At that time the author happened to go on a pilgrimage to Śri Ranchoḍ Râi with a caravan of sixty wagons and one hundred sowârs. Mûlû Mânik and Vairsi Mânik came as far as Gûrgadh to meet him, and showed him many civilities; and at Dwârkâ the vakils of Bâwâ Sâdârâm, the manager of the temples of Trikamji and Lakhmiji, came to invite him, so the author went to Beyt in a ship, and there paid his vows to Śri Ranchoḍ Râi, Trikam Râi, Mâdhû Râi, Purshotam Râi, and Kaliâṇ Râi, and to Deokoji and Kûseśwar Mâhâdeva, and the costs of this pilgrimage amounted to sixty thousand jâmis.

In this country are situated Śankhar Nârâyaṇ, Âd Nârâyaṇ, and Chakra Nârâyaṇ, and Śankhar Talâv; and the temples of Kûseśwar and Kapileśwar and Gaṇapati, and the shrine of Hâji Kirmâni and others in this city are of much benefit both to the better classes and to the commonalty; what more shall I say?

The temple of Jagat, which was built by Râjâ Vajranâbh, is very lofty, and bathing in the Gomti is famous in every country. As my pen can go no further, my readers will no longer be fatigued.

In Saṁvat 1735 (A.D. 1679), on account of fear of the Mûsalmâns, the idols were conveyed to the island of Beyt. In Saṁvat 1781, Kâkâbhâi and Hâlâbhâi repaired many of the temples at Beyt.

In Saṁvat 1864 the English army, under the command of Colonel Alexander Walker, conquered Positra; and in the year 1875 the English Sarkâr established a ṭhâṇâ, but two years afterwards Hendly Sâheb and Muhammad Atâ, who were the Ṭhâṇâdârs, after a short struggle were expelled by the Wâghers. Now the abovementioned Hendly Sâheb was of a peaceful and gentle disposition, never injured an ant or killed a fly, nor did he spend a charge of powder or fire a single arrow, but withdrew himself from Okhâ safely without in the least caring for his honour.

In Saṁvat 1876 a powerful English army came and attacked Okhâ both by sea and land and stormed the fort of Dwârkâ. On this occasion many of the Okhâ Wâghers, such as Mûlû Mânik, Vairsi Mânik, and others, and most of the tribe of Mânik numbering in all nearly two hundred and fifty persons, perished in the waters of the Gomti, and an English garrison was placed there. However, according to the policy of the time, they handed this place over to the Gâekwâḍ, who at once posted Bâbâ Wasikar there as his deputy, with a garrison of two hundred Arabs and Makrânis.

There is scarcely any water in this country, and on account of the paucity of the inhabitants and abundance of prickly-pear, but little cultivation exists. The Wâghers used to support themselves by committing robberies both by sea and land, and there is nothing here except small shells and chakras (a shell also), and the earth called *Gopichandan*, and a pleasant green appearance, and certain small shells which these jungly folk burn before the dying. Their income is derived from the fees levied from the bands of pilgrims which come to worship Dwârkânâth, and these suffice for the ministrants at the shrine, the Râjâ, and the Wâghers. In this zillâ there are good camels and brave men.

The Râjâ of Kachh built Kachhigaḍh to repress

the plunderers of Okhâ, but God knows the truth.

What I have seen or heard from historians that I have consigned to writing as a memorial of this perishable life, and this book I have called وقايع سورتهہ—History of Sorath, and I wrote it for the perusal of my beloved and intelligent son Śankarprasâd.

THE END.